# After You've Said Good-Bye

# After You've Said

## Learning How To Stand Alone

# Trudy Helmlinger

BROOKS PUBLISHING COMPANY
Bakersfield, California

Copyright © 1982 by Trudy Helmlinger. All rights reserved. No part of this publication may be reproduced, stored in a retrieval system, or transmitted, in any form or by any means, electronic, mechanical, photocopying, recording, or otherwise, without the prior written permission of the publisher.

Library of Congress Cataloging in Publication Data

Helmlinger, Trudy,
After You've Said Good-Bye

Bibliography: p.
Includes index.
1. Separation (Psychology)
2. Bereavement —— Psychological aspects.
I. Title.
BF575.G7H45        1982            158'.2              82-9472
ISBN 0-932370-35-7
ISBN 0-932370-36-5    (pbk.)

**Second Edition**

10  9  8  7  6  5  4  3  2  1

ISBN  0-932370-35-7
ISBN  0-932370-36-5 pbk.

Printed in the United States of America

# HOW THIS BOOK CAN HELP YOU START LIVING AGAIN!

I wrote this book to help people grow through the grief process which naturally follows the loss of an intimate relationship. It is also designed to help rebuild self-esteem. In it are chapters on depression, anger and self-pity; special instructions for the one who was left behind and the one who initiated ending as well as lists of common pitfalls to avoid while going through a divorce—or, the death of *any* love affair.

The most effective way to use this book is to skim through it and pick out the chapters which best apply to you. Don't try to read it all in one sitting. Take the time to study it and practice what you learn. If you are depressed right now, you may at first have trouble concentrating. Don't worry about it. Go slowly and be patient with yourself. In time, this symptom will disappear.

No one has to tell you that saying good-bye is traumatic. But I would like to remind you that it is *not* the end of your happiness. You are going through a normal life crisis that *can* be the beginning of something new and exciting. The fact that you're reading this means that you're ready to give up some of your pain and start living again.

So, let's get on with it!

Trudy Helmlinger

## AUTHOR'S ACKNOWLEDGMENT

No one writes a book alone. Without the guidance, support and encouragement I received from others this book would not exist.

My patients and students have shown me that it is possible to survive and grow stronger through the crisis of saying good-bye.

My colleagues shared their expertise. My friends and family took care of "everyday business" while I labored over blank sheets of paper.

Pat Musgrave and Duane Newcomb encouraged me to write the first edition of AFTER YOU'VE SAID GOOD-BYE. My publisher, June Curran, orchestrated this revised edition and taught me to pay attention to detail. Ruth Weine added her editorial skills to make this more readable.

To each of them individually, my warm and special thanks!

# CONTENTS

How This Book Can Help You Start Living Again

## 1   ENDING DOES NOT EQUAL FAILURE    1

| | |
|---|---|
| Outgrowing a Neurotic Relationship Means Good-Bye | 2 |
| Conquering the Fear Of Living Alone May Mean Leaving | 6 |
| Finding the Guts To Risk Financial Security Opens the Door To Go | 6 |
| Discovering Your Prince Is Really a Frog | 8 |
| Unmarrieds Living Together | 9 |
| Buying Women's Lib May Mean Selling the Little Woman Role | 11 |
| Getting Out Of Limbo May Mean Leaving | 12 |
| Standing Up For What You Want May Mean Walking Out! | 13 |
| Summary | 14 |
| Experiments and Exercises | 15 |

## 2   EXPLODING THE TOGETHERNESS MYTH    16

| | |
|---|---|
| Two Against the World Is Neurotic | 17 |
| There Is More To a Person Than Being Half Of a Pair | 18 |

| | |
|---|---|
| A Happy Pair May Not Mean Two Happy Individuals | 19 |
| Romantic Love Burns Out Quickly | 20 |
| Being Together Can Be Lonelier Than Being Alone | 21 |
| Together and Sharing Are Not Synonymous | 23 |
| One Can't Make the Other Happy | 24 |
| Having Someone Does Not Mean You're Not Lovable | 24 |
| Summary | 25 |
| Experiments and Exercises | 26 |

## 3 FALLOUT FROM DISSOLUTION 29

| | |
|---|---|
| Loss Of Self-Esteem | 30 |
| Loss Of Identity and Living Structure | 32 |
| Loss Of Ambition; Indecision | 35 |
| Bitterness | 37 |
| Self-Pity | 38 |
| Physiological Changes | 40 |
| Changes In Sleep Patterns | 42 |
| Changes In Sexual Patterns | 42 |
| Financial Pressures | 44 |
| Loss Of Friends and Familiar Surroundings | 45 |
| Summary | 47 |
| Experiments and Exercises | 47 |

## 4 ALONE AND FREE: THIS IS THE TIME TO DECIDE TO LIVE 49

| | |
|---|---|
| Initial Reaction Is Often Relief | 50 |
| Second Phase: Overwhelming Depression | 52 |
| Your Normal Need To Withdraw | 53 |
| The Pull From the Past: a Protective Device | 55 |
| How To "Pick Yourself Up" | 58 |
| How To "Brush Yourself Off" | 59 |
| How To Start Living Again | 61 |
| The Other Side Of Scary Is Excitement! | 62 |
| Experiments and Exercises | 64 |

## 5   HOW TO BUILD YOUR OWN BACKBONE    67

Getting Yourself In Proper Perspective    67
How To Give Up Your Ex-Love's Total Perception
Of You    69
Developing Your Own Self-Perception    71
Get Feedback From Others    74
Match Inner- and Other-Directed Perceptions    75
How To Develop a Self-Improvement Priority List    77
How To Build On Strengths    78
How To Corral and Tame Frailties    80
How To Protect Your Vulnerable Spots    82
How To Develop Your Latent Talents    83
How To Use Anger To Get You Moving    84
Experiments and Exercises    85

## 6   GAINING STRENGTH OUTSIDE YOURSELF    91

How To Get Emotional Support From Old Friends,
Family, and Acquaintances    92
How To Get Ego-Building Feedback From New Friends    94
How To Make Yourself Look Better    95
How To Gain Positive Feedback At Work    96
Getting the Most Out Of Inspirational Literature    97
Gaining Strength From Others In a Similar Situation    98
Gaining Courage From Religion    100
How To Find Competent Professional Mental Health
Support    100
Experiments and Exercises    102

## 7   SEPARATION PITFALLS AND HOW TO AVOID THEM    104

Trying To Help Each Other Through the Crisis    104
Getting Back Together    106
Trying To Be Friends    107
Saving Old Love Letters, Mementos, etc.    109

|   |   |   |
|---|---|---|
| | Pulling In Memories To Fill the Emptiness | 109 |
| | Checking Up On Your Ex-Love | 111 |
| | Trying To Get Friends To Take Sides Or Pumping Them For Information | 111 |
| | Wishing It Hadn't Happened and Hoping It'll Change | 113 |
| | Beware Of Anniversary Dates | 114 |
| | Panicking With Free Time: Weekends and Such | 116 |
| | Falling In Love With the First Person You Meet | 118 |
| | Experiments and Exercises | 119 |
| | Summary | 120 |
| **8** | **FOR THE ONE WHO WAS LEFT BEHIND** | 121 |
| | How To Put a Limit On Self-Pity | 122 |
| | How To Fight Self-Pity and Self-Doubt | 123 |
| | How To Clear Your Eyes and Look At Whom You've Lost | 125 |
| | How To Determine What You've Lost | 127 |
| | Accepting Responsibility Improves Self Respect | 129 |
| | Self-Induced Traps and How To Avoid Them | 132 |
| | Ways Of Reaching Out To Others | 136 |
| | On the Thought Of Moving | 137 |
| | Summary | 138 |
| | Experiments and Exercises | 138 |
| **9** | **FOR THE ONE WHO FINALLY CALLED IT QUITS** | 140 |
| | Moving Is No Picnic, Either: Problems Encountered By Those Who Left | 141 |
| | Causal Factors Of Guilt | 143 |
| | Healthy Ways To Deal With Guilt | 145 |
| | How To Get Yourself In Proper Perspective | 148 |
| | How To Equalize Blame For Dissolution | 149 |
| | Common Self-Induced Traps | 151 |
| | Utilizing Strengths To Handle Obstacles Coming Up | 151 |
| | Experiments and Exercises | 153 |

## 10  HEALTHY WAYS TO MOURN — 155

- How To Give Yourself Permission To Grieve — 156
- Ways Of Allowing Yourself To Feel Pain — 158
- Getting the Perspective On Loss — 160
- Techniques That Help You Let Go Of Pain — 162
- How To Get a Little Help From Your Friends — 165
- How To Bury the Dead — 166
- Unhealthy Mourning Practices — 168
- How To Stop Grief From Overwhelming You — 172
- Summary — 174
- Experiments and Exercises — 174

## 11  DEPRESSION: THE ENERGY CRISIS — 176

- Origins Of Depression — 178
- How To Figure Out Why You're Depressed — 180
- How To Fight Depression — 182
- How To Find Ways To Win — 185
- The Art Of Feeling Better — 187
- Pitfalls That Reinforce Depression — 189
- Experiments and Exercises — 193

## 12  ALL ABOUT ANGER — 195

- Understanding Your Anger — 197
- Traps That Increase Anger — 199
- Admitting Anger: Your First Step Toward Breaking Away — 203
- How To Gain Control Over Your Anger — 204
- Dealing Directly With What Causes Your Anger — 208
- Using Your Anger Constructively — 211
- Learning To Let Go Of Part Of Your Anger By Replacing Losses — 214
- Experiments and Exercises — 214

## 13   HOW TO CONQUER YOUR SELF PITY    216

    People Prone To Self-Pity    217
    Traps That Reinforce Self-Pity    221
    Admit Your Self-Pity Without Judging Yourself    224
    Take Back the Power You Give To Others    225
    Give Up the "Doormat" Syndrome    226
    Other Ways To Give Up Self-Pity    229
    Get Involved In Interests Outside Of Yourself    230
    Experiments and Exercises    231

## 14   OVERCOMING YOUR LONELINESS    233

    On the Fear Of Being Alone    235
    Understanding Your Own Loneliness    237
    How To Combat Loneliness By Yourself    239
    Fighting Loneliness With Environmental Change    242
    Fighting Loneliness With the Aid Of Others    243
    Pitfalls To Avoid In Loneliness    245
    Experiments and Exercises    248
    Transition Exercise    249

## 15   STARTING ALL OVER AGAIN    251

    Viewing Yourself As a Single Adult    252
    New and Exciting Vacations    253
    Fun Ideas For Around Town    254
    Other Singles and Where To Find Them    256
    Dating Again    258
    Assessing New Loves    265
    Look Before You Leap Again    266
    Experiments and Exercises    267

## BIBLIOGRAPHY    269

# 1

# ENDING DOES NOT EQUAL FAILURE

The ambulance screeched to a halt in front of the emergency entrance of a large metropolitan hospital. Doors banged while the attendants scurried down the hallways with their stretcher aimed toward the emergency room.

In the next thirty minutes, white-coated doctors and nurses mechanically labored over the body of the patient strapped on the stretcher.

The patient, Mary L., an attractive twenty-five-year-old teacher, had tried to kill herself by overdosing. She is alive today *only* because a friend dropped by her apartment unexpectedly for a visit.

In spite of the fact that Mary seems to have everything to live for, she attempted suicide because her boyfriend had left her and she felt like a failure.

Mary's story is not unusual. Psychiatric hospitals and mental health clinics are filled with successful adults who nonetheless identify themselves as failures because of the breakup of an intimate relationship.

Each year millions of people end intimate relationships. According to the Bureau of Statistics, one out of every three marriages ends in divorce, with an average marital life expectancy of 7.8 years. And the duration for unmarried relationships isn't any longer. Intimate relationships can no longer be viewed as unions that last forever; realisitically, they simply don't.

Although not every single who was once part of a couple attempts suicide, few are able to shake off the awful feeling in the pits of their stomachs that they are failures.

It's natural for us to feel this: we've been programmed to believe that normal, well-adjusted adults marry and live together forever.

In our newspapers, we honor couples as *successful* who have been married for fifty years. When someone divorces or breaks up an intimate relationship, it is automatic to wonder what went *wrong* and who was to *blame*.

The idea that together is success and apart is failure is reinforced daily—in our churches, by families and friends, and through the mass media.

Is it any wonder then, that Mary or any of the rest of us who end a relationship decide we are failures? Actually, it's almost impossible to feel good about yourself when your relationship ends.

Yet, most mental health professionals will tell you that ending a relationship can be a sign of personal growth.

With that idea in mind, let us look at some of the healthier reasons to end a relationship and examine the idea that ending does not always equal failure.

## Outgrowing a Neurotic Relationship Means Good-Bye

The *parent-child relationship* is a very popular union in which one partner assumes the role of the *protective*, all-knowing, parent figure. The other member takes the role of the child who is coddled or needs guidance from the parent in order to function. The partner in the child role usually feels the need to be taken care of; the one in the parent role ordinarily feels superior to the other.

> Bill and Nancy have been married for eight years. They have two children and live in the suburbs of San Francisco. Bill is nine years older than Nancy. She was 18 when they met and was living at home with her parents. Bill was already out on his own with an established career.
>
> From their first meeting, Bill knew that Nancy needed the *extra* support and direction he gladly provided. Nancy, automatically, depended on Bill for his guidance. Their relationship helped each member feel more secure.
>
> Three months after they met they were married.

Maintaining this type of relationship is costly to both. The price Nancy pays for security is feeling inadequate, and believing that she needs to be treated like a child in order to survive. Bill pays a high price too. Constantly feeling responsible for another adult is emotionally draining. There is little time left for him to take care of his own needs; nor is he able to obtain the occasional reassurance and comforting that we all need in an adult intimate relationship.

In order for the *parent-child relationship* to endure, both members need to remain emotionally stagnant. Bill has to continue feeling that he is emotionally stronger then his wife. Meanwhile, Nancy must continue to believe that she is too incompetent to survive without constant parenting.

If one member outgrows the *parent-child relationship* and the other does not, this neurotic tie will be severed.

Gradually, Bill began feeling trapped, rather than flattered, by Nancy's insecurities. He missed being able to share his life with someone who felt competent as an adult. The women at work looked more and more attractive to him, and Bill wished that he could *make* Nancy more self-reliant. Whenever he talked with her about doing more on her own, Nancy got hysterical. Finally, after several months of trying in vain to change her, Bill walked out.

He had outgrown the neurotic need to have an insecure adult be overly dependent on him. But Nancy was not ready or willing to grow up and, perhaps, save the relationship. You can't call Bill a failure because he left the relationship. A natural part of developing self-esteem includes outgrowing the neurotic need to take care of another adult as you would a child. Bill couldn't have the mutually satisfying interdependency that is the basis of adult intimacy as long as Nancy had to be carried.

It is just as common in a *parent-child relationship* for the mate in the child position to outgrow the role and no longer need or desire a live-in parent.

After the children started school, Nancy began taking classes at the community college. Since everyone there treated her like an adult she began responding like one. Although this was emotionally healthier for Nancy, and could have been the impetus for a healthier marriage, it produced unresolvable problems. Bill felt *threatened* by Nancy's maturity. He was unable to accept her as an adequate adult and she was unwilling to give up her new growth; so Nancy moved out.

To decide that Nancy is a failure because she developed adult self-confidence is absurd. Failure to *feel* like an adult is neurotic—outgrowing childhood insecurities is emotionally healthy.

## Ending Does Not Equal Failure

The ending of a parent-child relationship is not failure; after all, none of us can or should promise that we will always remain the same. Even though ending any intimate relationship is painful, no one should be labeled a failure for the growth that precipitated the time to say good-bye.

Another common neurotic relationship is the *to-regain-my-youth* variety.

Dick is a 40-year-old college professor who struggled with his fears of growing old by attempting to look and act younger than his age. Motivated by his unresolved fears of aging, Dick changed his physical appearance (hairstyle and wardrobe) and began to date one of his students.

If you were ever in this kind of relationship, maybe you can remember feeling a little funny—but excited, too. Being sexually attractive to someone less than half your age can be very flattering. And, as long as our hero is still panicked about growing older, he will prefer a *to-regain-my-youth* relationship.

But growing up in this kind of relationship means saying good-bye.

Gradually, Dick became disenchanted with adolescent games. He began feeling foolish, and ironically, much older than forty because of the contrast between them. Growing older, he acknowledged, has different challenges than growing up and he wanted to enjoy them with someone more mature. Once Dick had developed emotionally he stopped dating his student.

Dick's relationship was understandably doomed from the beginning. The emphasis on youth in today's culture makes it inevitable that some of us will scramble away from growing older by running toward our adolescence again. So don't *add* insult to injury by condemning yourself as immature for leaving this kind of neurotic relationship.

## Conquering the Fear Of Living Alone May Mean Leaving

The fear of living alone can produce overwhelming anxiety in perfectly competent adults. In fact, many couples who probably *should* separate stay together because of these fears.

If you are one of the thousands who held on to a relationship long after there was any other reason, you remember how scary it was to even think of being without someone. Maybe you didn't love your mate and perhaps you even longed for a different kind of life, but you found it hard to plunge into the unknown alone.

I'm sure you asked yourself all kinds of questions. How will I survive without someone with me? Will I ever find anyone else? What will happen to me if I get sick—who will care if I live or die? What does it mean if I live alone—am I unlovable?

Everyone's afraid of being alone and of being unlovable. But, somehow, if you gathered enough strength to begin finding answers to some of these questions, you found that you actually did have the ability and guts to walk on your own without holding someone else's hand.

It wasn't easy. Even if the only thing left in the relationship was another body in the house, at least you felt connected to someone.

And now it would be unfair to call you a failure for being strong enough to walk out of a relationship that was dead and face the unknown alone. Cowards hover in the corner for protection; competent adults strike out on their own!

## Finding the Guts To Risk Financial Security Opens the Door To Go

It's a fact that two people living together can live more cheaply than two people living separately. Anyone who has lived alone can attest to it.

## Ending Does Not Equal Failure

Financial security, however, meets more than survival needs for most of us. Statements such as "The clothes make the man," and "Money can't buy happiness, but it buys very good substitutes" are widely repeated and often believed. As much as possible, we ignore the poor and admire the rich.

Is it any wonder then, that couples stay together for financial reasons long after the emotional reasons for their union are dead?

> Jim and Pat have been married for 30 years and during that time they have established a high standard of living. Even though they are no longer in love with each other, neither wants to give up the lifestyle and status that they have established. Pat, especially, feels vulnerable because she is over fifty and has never worked outside of her home.

It's easy to understand why you might stay in a relationship like that, even if it's been dead for years. Having to worry about bills or wondering if you'll have enough money to afford what you need or want can be demoralizing. Especially if you are *finally* in a position where money isn't one of your foremost worries. Naturally, it would take a lot of guts to risk financial insecurity again.

But if the economically dependent mate is able to gather the courage to risk managing a household at a lower (perhaps minimal) standard of living, the relationship will end—if that is the primary reason for staying together.

> Gradually, Pat began examining her motivation for remaining with Jim. They had long since ceased to be lovers or friends and it occurred to her that what she would miss most about leaving was giving up the comforts of her home. The idea of sacrificing financial security for an unknown future was frightening, but remaining in a loveless marriage was worse. Jim would probably pay spousal

support and she was sure that she could get a job doing *something*. Armed with the courage of her decision, she initiated the divorce.

Neither Jim nor Pat could be blamed for the dead relationship; it was inevitable. Modern-day stresses placed on a marriage often erode intimacy.

To *finally* leave a dead relationship takes courage. And, if you have recently crossed the same frontier, you know how hard it is to do. To walk away from financial security requires confidence. Don't undermine your morale by condemning yourself as a failure for leaving a loveless union.

## Discovering Your Prince Is Really a Frog

The adage "love is blind" can either be beautiful or tragic—depending on what the lovers see when they open their eyes. If your Cinderella turned into a scullery maid or your prince into a frog, you know how disheartening that can be. For a while you may be in shock. Then, you might decide to look for some magic, perhaps on a second honeymoon, to make it right again. In the end, though, your Cinderella will still belch at parties or your prince will still give you warts. Endings are always sad, but an ending doesn't mean failure.

If you have sworn to yourself or your prince that you will never find a love as great as yours, you may spend years trying to keep the fairy tale alive. But, when you finally gain enough insight and courage to admit you've been duped by your heart, you will take Cinderella back to her stepmother or the prince back to the pond.

The failure, if there is any in this kind of relationship, is not in the ending, but rather in its beginning. It's not your fault that the fairy tale is over; it never was real to begin with.

## Unmarrieds Living Together

The odds against an intimate relationship enduring without the bonds of matrimony can be overwhelming. Let's look at some of the facts:
  1. Most couples choose living together vs. marriage as an alternative. One or both of the partners assume that an intimate relationship will not last and, therefore, are unwilling to enter an "until death do us part" contract.

> David and Mary (the teacher who attempted suicide) fell in love while they were student teaching. Both talked about marriage, but Dave didn't believe in permanent commitments. They agreed to live together and see what happened.

Trying to build a long-lasting relationship by beginning with the doubt that anyone, including you and your love, will succeed is stacking the deck against yourself.
  2. A living-together situation or trial marriage implies that the couple is testing its strength and ability to last. The primary objective in testing is to discover the breaking point, which every relationship has. And, as you probably discovered, if you were in this kind of relationship, you, too, have your limits. Did you really need to test that to find it was true?
  3. Testing the endurance of an intimate relationship without an avowed emotional commitment to permanence can be disastrous.

> Conflicts never get completely resolved. Rather than compromise, both Mary and Dave fell into the habit of ending normal disagreements with angry, "I don't have to stay with you!" declarations.

Arguments like this hurt, especially if you started with the doubt that any intimate relationship lasts and added the fear that yours wasn't any different.

4. The additional social pressures from friends and family members who may condemn an intimate relationship outside the bonds of matrimony can be an added burden to the unmarried couple.

If we live in a new age with all our social values changing, why do our families still live in the Dark Ages? The answer is not as relevant as the result, which is an extra strain on you if you're living with someone outside the bonds of matrimony.

5. If a couple decides their relationship will last, or are convinced that they want to commit themselves to work toward that goal, they usually join the ranks of the married.

6. An intimate relationship held together by ambivalence and lack of commitment has difficulty surviving the bombardment of everyday stress and strains.

> Mary and Dave lived together for a year before they finally decided to call it quits. They had joined forces feeling that intimate relationships don't last—and, after a year, had convinced themselves that this was true for them, anyway. Neither had much of a personal stake in making it work; neither gave in very much to the other's needs or desires. In addition, Mary felt that living with Dave had alienated her from her family, and she didn't wish to pay that price for a life with Dave.

Although there are a number of positives in the theory of trial marriage, the reality of today's society (and of our own internalized value systems regarding commitment and responsibility), is that making it last is a highly risky wager at best. The intimates who live together are bucking overwhelming odds for permanence.

The ending of this type of intimate relationship should not be seen as a failure, but, rather, as something expected. You did not fail if you ended a relationship of this kind. It was set up at the beginning to be temporary.

## Buying Women's Lib May Mean Selling the Little Woman Role

Harry and Madge had been married for 25 years when they finally agreed on divorce. Both had grown up believing in traditional roles for husbands and wives and had patterned their lives on those beliefs. Gradually, however, Madge began to alter her ideas and seek satisfaction as a *separate* individual. The idea that her husband was her Lord and Master slowly eroded and in its place was the concept that both partners were important and valuable. As Madge changed her own value system regarding her role as a woman and wife, her marital relationship became strained beyond the point of constructive repair or mutual satisfaction.

Today, more than ever, the changing male/female roles are shattering the once seemingly peaceful marriages of people like Harry and Madge. As women like Madge revolt, rulers like Harry find that they no longer have their kingdoms and subjects to command. Although, in rare instances, couples are able to renegotiate their relationships, the more common solution is dissolution.

Little Women who become liberated are often very angry at their old Lords and Masters, and dethroned kings rarely step down with grace.

Certainly the ending of this kind of relationship cannot be seen as a failure of either party. Harry and Madge grew up in one culture and suddenly began living in another. As our society changes its expectations of the rights and responsibilities of sexual roles, many intimate relationships may explode because of cultural shock—not because of any failure of the partners involved.

It takes quite a person to adjust to a new role in our changing society. The *I'm a failure* syndrome is an extra weight you need not carry with you.

## Getting Out Of Limbo May Mean Leaving

It is hard to decide to do something big—like move to a new town, change occupations, or end an intimate relationship—even a dead one. In fact, the decision to end an intimate relationship can be so difficult that some people choose to stay in limbo.

If you were in a stormy relationship, do you remember how long it finally took you to get out? There was a point when you weren't very close any more, but you stayed anyway. Gradually you grew away from each other and, if you shared your thoughts and dreams, you noticed you weren't doing that any more. You were talking to someone else about your problems, and the conversations between you and your ex-love sounded like letters to your family, with whom you have nothing in common. Everything was superficial and you talked about the weather—or the neighbors. Sometimes you shouted about yourself in fights, but that was the only time you really showed how you felt. And that wasn't really all you felt—only what you were afraid of.

Funny how you've forgotten that. You've been so busy missing your lost love and feeling like a failure, that you've forgotten how empty and cold your relationship really was.

How long did it last after that? The idea of leaving scared you so much that you probably stayed a lot longer than you should have—for your own sanity.

But, finally, the relationship got painful enough, and leaving became less frightening to you. So, you gulped what little pride you could find and ended it. You should have done it sooner, but it took a lot of courage, especially when you were not absolutely sure that dissolution was the best of all possible choices and you secretly wondered if you deserved anything better. There are a lot of risks in sticking your neck out and saying: "This is what I'm going to do," and then doing it.

Why did your relationship die in the first place? Who knows? Maybe it was a relationship that was doomed from its beginning. Or, maybe, you grew out of it—or there was too much pressure placed on it from the rest of the world.

## Standing Up For What You Want May Mean Walking Out!

Some people stay in a relationship that is less than what they would really be happy with because of their negative expectations. The secret fears that many of us have about not being good enough convince us to settle for less.

> Doug and Janice have been married for 4 years. Their relationship has never been close but both agree that it *could* be worse. They lead totally separate lives and spend very little time together, even on weekends. Janice longs for more intimacy but concludes that her expectations are overly romantic; especially for a long-term marriage.

If you were in this kind of relationship you probably remember the loneliness you felt. The longer you stayed in it, the less you believed that you deserved something better, and the more undeserving you felt. But, if you began seeing your good points along with your frailties, you may finally have concluded that you deserved something better, resulting in the demise of the relationship.

> Another year passed and their relationship continued as before. Doug was gone most of the time, and Janice relied

on friends for companionship and emotional support. Then she began to notice that many of her friends had the kind of marriage that fit her ideal. As she compared herself to her female friends, she discovered that she was just as attractive, intelligent, and considerate as they were. Her faith in intimacy returned; and, as her self-confidence built, she decided *not* to settle for less than what she wanted in marriage.

The failure in this relationship is in its inception, not in its death. For Janice, or anyone, to sell herself short and settle for less than she really wants or deserves is absurd. The relationship had no future, and its death was necessary to enable Janice to enjoy life.

Making the decision that you do *not* have to settle for something less than what you want and that you *deserve* a caring, sharing, mutually accepting relationship with an intimate does not mean you've failed or that you're a failure. It does, instead, initiate a very significant change and a greater possibility for growth.

## Summary

At the beginning of this chapter, I shared the idea that although most people who end an intimate relationship feel they have failed, this is, in fact, contrary to much of our reality.

A relationship, we have seen, can be terminated for a number of healthy reasons. In fact, Margaret Mead suggests that we are no longer in a culture that is compatible with permanency in intimate relationships. It is her belief that the idea of "til death do us part" came from a society where life was not that long, nor were people exposed to so many different alternative mates throughout their lives.

According to Norman Scheresky and Marya Mannes, co-authors of *Uncoupling: The Art of Coming Apart*, there is a lot of information which shows that intimate relationships are lightly entered but hesitantly left. Intimate relationships fail, they say, because they are entered into when we are least likely to exercise sound judgment about priorities. Inflamed by passion, consumed by hope and giddy with love, we enter into an intimate relationship without even the questionable objectivity we display in choosing a new car.

It's difficult to let go of *any* relationship, so don't overburden yourself with the thought that you are a failure just because you are no longer part of a pair. Later, as you gain self-confidence, you will be able to understand more objectively why your relationship ended. In the meantime, remember that ending does *not* always mean you're a failure.

**Experiments And Exercises**

The following exercise is repeated at the end of the book so that you may compare your progress and emotional growth. Jot down the first words that come into your thoughts as you read the sentences.

1. If I were to use three words to describe myself, they would be _____, _____, and _____.

2. If I were to use three words to describe my ex-mate, they would be _____, _____, and _____.

3. When I look at my past, the word that comes to mind is _____.

4. When I look at my present, the word that comes to mind is _____.

5. When I look to the future, the word that comes to mind is _____.

6. My three greatest fears are _____, _____, and _____.

7. My three greatest strengths are _____, _____, and _____.

8. The quality I would like to develop in me is _____.

9. Right now I feel that I can look forward to _____.

# 2

# EXPLODING THE *TOGETHERNESS* MYTH

One of the reasons you may be feeling a lot of extra pain, now that you're single again, is that somewhere down the line you probably bought the *Togetherness Myth:* the one that says "You're nobody 'til somebody loves you" or "Together you can be happy, fulfilled, and maybe even conquer the world."

Sure, being together *can* feel better than being single, and, it is comforting to share your thoughts and feelings with someone you love. But, it does not necessarily follow that being together means happiness and inner peace. Or even comfort and mutual respect.

When you're in love, the Togetherness Myth is romantic, but romanticism is as fanciful and fictitious as its dictionary definition. And, when you're saying good-bye to an ex-love, it's time to give up the fiction and look at some of the facts.

Join with me now as we begin looking at some of the realities that explode the Togetherness Myth.

## Two Against the World Is Neurotic

The song *You and Me Against the World* romanticizes a neurotic relationship in which two people are bound together by their mutual distrust of the rest of us. In view of their attitude, the fact that they got together in the first place is a mystery. But, together they are—and ready to fight or avoid everyone else in the world.

Look at how the "game" is played and notice its neurotic foundation:

*Rule 1* To play *You and Me Against the World* (Y.M.A.W.), you must have a basic disbelief in your own value and an assumption that, given a chance, "people" will hurt or reject you.

To qualify as a potential Y.M.A.W. player, you must:

1. Never accept/believe compliments or praise.
2. Pay attention to the parts of you that aren't perfect (too skinny or fat, nose too big, chin too small, etc.).
3. Always feel you *should* do better. And always do everything for yourself because you can't depend on others.
4. Believe that no one could ever really care for you.
5. Have few friends. (One is *ideal*.)
6. Encourage others to gossip about acquaintances and use that to prove that no one should be trusted.
7. Have a motto: "Do Unto Others Before They Do Unto You."
8. Never tell anyone how you feel—remember the motto.
9. Always look at the "bad" in others and the world.

*Rule 2* Two potential Y.M.A.W. players must meet, "fall in love," and agree to mistrust all others for the duration of the game.

*Rule 3* Both players should spend all of their time (outside of work) with each other. It is preferable that they work at the same job—or live on a farm together.

*Rule 4* If the players decide to have friends, they should probably be one other couple who share in their mistrust of the world.

Naturally they must be mutual friends. Probably it's best if they're relatives.

*Rule 5* It's a good idea *not* to have children. (The players wouldn't want them to grow up in this kind of world.) If, however, they waver and decide to parent, the children must be taught not to trust anyone—except, maybe, the family.

There are other rules, of course. But these are the basic ones which most people who play the game abide by.

You can look around for yourself and probably see a hermit couple in your own community. It's even possible that you grew out of a relationship like this.

Healthy adults don't play this game. At least, not for very long. They know they need more than one relationship. Sure, an intimate relationship is of primary importance. But we all need friends and family too. If you're a healthy adult, you don't fight the world; you recognize that you're part of it. And you encourage most people to be your friends, not your enemies.

## There Is More To a Person Than Being Half Of a Pair

Objectively, you must agree that there is more to an individual than being half of a pair. Yet as silly as it sounds, we romanticize that neither value nor identity appear until one has become the other half of a pair. How often have you heard—or even said—"this is my other half" or "meet my better half" to reinforce that belief?

Most of us are guilty of thinking in this fashion—at least to some degree. I remember that even as a child I never thought of my favorite aunt without automatically listing her husband in my mind. I saw them as a *unit*. It wasn't just Aunt Mary *or* Uncle John, it was Aunt Mary *and* Uncle John. After he died there was much more to Aunt Mary than being Uncle John's widow. But, in order to live again and feel like a whole person, she had to find again those other parts of her identity—mother, business person, friend, relative, amateur golfer, and sexy single lady—and build on them.

And, just as Aunt Mary had to give up the myth that she was nobody without Uncle John, so all those who say good-bye to an old love must be able to see themselves as separate individuals. Not just as half of a pair.

Begin to think about who you really are. I am a woman, marriage counselor, part-time writer, amateur skier, lover, friend, daughter, aunt, and niece. All of these parts (and more) make up my identity.

They make "ME." And when one of them changes, I still continue to be a valuable person. In spite of the Togetherness Myth, I am somebody special—even outside of a love relationship. And so is everyone else.

If you are no longer part of a pair, it's time for you to give up your romanticism.

## A Happy Pair May Not Mean Two Happy Individuals

The Togetherness Myth tries to make you believe that a happy pair means two happy individuals. If you are happy with HIM or HER, then you'll be happy. I know that there are times when two happy individuals can make a happy pair—but the opposite just "ain't necessarily so!"

There are a number of happy pairs made up of insecure, unhappy individuals. The sado-masochistic units: he beats her, she knows he loves her because of it. The parent/child partnerships: she knows what's best for him and he obeys her. There are others, of course, but I think I've made my point.

Whenever I hear the statement, "You two are so lovely together, you must be very happy," I smile. What that observer doesn't know is that I am "happy together" only because I am also happy separately. As an individual, I *must* feel good about *me* to be able to feel good about anyone else—including *him*.

When someone says: "I *should* be happy—my marriage is good," that person needs help to break out of the Togetherness Myth nonsense and see himself or herself as an individual: as a separate person with individual needs, wants, and desires, as well as the ability to make himself or herself happy or unhappy.

Although all this sounds fatalistic, it was written, nevertheless, by a very romantic soul who still watches old movies on television where the hero and heroine meet and fall passionately in love. Then, surmounting all tragedies with their love, they go off into the sunset to cure the lepers in Africa. Neither one of them wants anything but the other. And, as they fade off into the sunset, the audience fantasizes that Africa will be a bit brighter because of their love. But—

## Romantic Love Burns Out Quickly

If the audience were around to watch the next scenes, they'd be very disillusioned to see that the fiery passions have been transformed into cold routine. He works all day in the leper colony. She's at home with the kids. He comes home tired. She's exhausted. By the time dinner is over, the dishes are washed, the kids are in bed, and the mosquito nets are pulled down, it's time to sleep.

There isn't much fire in their love anymore. In fact, there's nary a spark. The trouble is that most of us romantics will never know such mundane facts; the movie always ends at the embrace scene.

So, part of the Togetherness Myth is created on the silver screen—and in our dreams. We may see that our parents don't have a Cary Grant–Ingrid Bergman love affair, but we somehow build the fantasy that ours will be the way it is in the movies.

What a shocker when we discover for ourselves how quickly the passionate flames are doused if and when we stay with our Cary or Ingrid beyond the embrace scene. For many people, this reality can produce an added sense of guilt or failure; they have failed to achieve their fantasy goal of a lasting, fiery love.

Love is a feeling that is learned. We can be instantly infatuated with someone or sexually aroused. But love is a matter of learning to risk, to care for, to trust, and to mutually respect one another.

If you buy the movie version of love with the smoldering desires and dazed enchantment, remember that movies rarely show the lovers with a full-time job, bills that come due, a house that gets dirty, a yard that needs mowing, or kids who get sick. Two people need *more* than flame and fantasy for the foundation of a shared, real life together.

## Being Together Can Be Lonelier Than Being Alone

It is easy to blindly accept the idea that if you "have" someone, you will not be lonely. But the truth is that being "together" with someone has little to do with whether a person feels lonely.

> "I can't talk to my husband. He doesn't know how I feel. Or care—or even listen. I'm so lonely I could die. At night, when I reach over to touch him, I can feel his body, but I still feel alone. What would I ever do if he left me? I'm so lonely now, with him. I think I would die of loneliness by myself."

That statement is not unusual. I've heard it, with variations, repeated over and over again. Being together has not made people less lonely.

And, ironically, sometimes being alone can be less lonely than being together. I remember a comment made by one of my clients, Callie:

> "Sure, I'm lonely now. But I'm not as lonely as I was when I

was married. Then, there were all those people in the house, but I couldn't reach them. My husband. The kids. They seemed so close—yet so far away. I guess I just withdrew from everyone after a while. Now that I'm alone, I'm forced to reach out to people. And, although it's not easy, and sometimes I slip back, I'm actually *less* lonely now than I've been in years."

Callie was 46 years old when she made that statement, and for over half her life (25 years) she'd been married. A year after the marriage was over, she was well into the healing process.

Callie isn't the only one to describe this sensation of feeling less lonely without a mate than with one:

"I felt isolated."
"There was no one to turn to."
"I thought there was something *wrong* with me because I felt lonely."
"I wondered why other people seemed so close and we weren't."
"I planned most of my activities without my wife, because she never wanted to go anywhere."
"Thank God, I had my children!"
"I don't know what I would have done without a hobby."

The explanation for this phenomenon is quite simple. When there is someone else "with" you, you expect to share, to love and care about one another. It is natural to expect that you will not feel lonely. But when you live with someone and discover—as many people do—that these expectations are not met, you may feel even lonelier. The pain is deeper if loneliness triggers frustration at not being part of a close intimate relationship. So, if you've bought the Togetherness Myth, you may damn yourself for feeling lonely when you are not physically alone. But, the fact is, unless two people *work* at developing intimacy, being with

someone can be lonelier than being alone.
Often when individuals are alone, they *expect* to feel lonely. So, they learn to accept a certain amount of it and develop plans to combat the rest, like reaching out ot meet new people or learning to enjoy their own company at times.

## Together and Sharing Are Not Synonymous

Another part of the Togetherness Myth that can increase an intimate's frustration and loneliness in a relationship is believing that being together means sharing. According to this belief, when you are part of a pair, you have someone with whom to share all your good times, bad times, troubles, happiness, feelings, and experiences.

Only, sometimes, when you think you're going together, you discover that your partner has taken a different route. Troubles are shared with your friends or relatives or kept to yourself. Happy times begin to mean going bowling with the guys, having lunch with the women, drinking with your co-workers, or working on your hobby alone in the garage. For many intimates, sharing means they live in the same house together and share their anger at each other. Sometimes it doesn't even mean that. Thousands of married couples live separately during the week and only see each other on weekends.

It is in the movies, poetry, and songs that being together means sharing your life. It is part of the Togetherness Myth and is in the theme for the happily-ever-after group. In real life, being together means sharing only when you work hard to include your partner in your life. Genuine sharing and open communication does not come automatically or magically with being together, as the myth might imply. I know that doesn't make sharing quite as romantic and it pokes another hole in our balloon, but when we become realistic about how to develop a sharing relationship, it becomes much more possible to attain.

## One Can't *Make* the Other Happy

No matter how much you love someone, you cannot *make* him or her happy if the sorrow comes from within. Sure, you can cheer someone up temporarily, and be there to wipe away the tears, but you cannot stop someone else from always feeling hurt and crying—if it's against his or her nature.

The Togetherness Myth would have you believe that one person can *make* another happy if only there's enough love. But, the fact of the matter is that *you* are the only one that can make you feel happy and enjoy being alive. Someone else can help, but only with your *active* participation.

Lyrical phrases like, "When you're in love the whole world is beautiful," are inspiring. And the poems which tell of love that changes a pauper to a prince are romantic—but fictional. In reality, people believe what they want to believe and what fits their own self-image. No amount of love, being together, success, or money can *make* someone happy who has decided, for whatever reason, that he or she will never be happy.

I stress this because many intimates labor unsuccessfully under the delusion that they can make an unhappy love feel cheerful if only their love is strong enough, or if they are the "right" persons. And ex-intimates hurt themselves when they feel that they will never be happy again because they have lost the love that brought sunshine into their lives.

Someone can give you an invitation to feel happy (or sad). It is in your power to decide whether to accept that invitation.

## Having Someone Does Not Mean You're Lovable

People in love rarely question whether they're lovable. People out of love worry they're not and take as proof the fact they they are alone.

Everyone has a fear of being exposed as an unlovable person.

And, sometimes, when we lose an old love, we assume the reason for that loss is that we've been discovered; our fear has allegedly become a reality.

It's silly when you think about it, isn't it? That any of us should be so wrapped up in our fears of being unlovable that any rejection would be seen as "proof" we're no good.

In spite of the fact that most of us can look around and see many pairs that are built and held together for neurotic or social reasons, we still force ourselves to forget the facts and believe blindly in the fiction that being together *proves* you're lovable.

The point is that people get together for a whole raft of reasons. Some of these are, perhaps, just as sensible and "right" as others, such as, "It's time to get married and you're the kind of mate I want." Therefore, being a part of a pair is no more a measure of one's lovableness than it is proof of one's happiness or self-confidence.

## Summary

If you read over what's been said in this chapter and look at the examples from your own experience, you will quickly see the Togetherness Myth as a fantasy—not a fact. You want to believe that "love cures all"—or "together down the highway of life" will be magical. Sure, being together can be warm and wonderful and much better than being alone, but it can also be cold, routine, drab, and lonely. It takes hard work, not magical pixie dust, to develop intimacy. Remember the times in your own relationship when being together meant arguing, loneliness, and feelings of being used or misunderstood?

At the end of an intimate relationship you need to explode the Togetherness Myth for yourself and look back on it with more realism and less romanticism. It's natural to paint a rosy picture of the past for yourself if the present looks bleak. But believing in the Togetherness Myth when it wasn't true for you, can only help to keep you sad and perpetually frustrated.

## Experiments and Exercises

How would you rate your own belief in the "Togetherness Myth"?

---

see it                                                                                                      see it
as *Fact*                                                                                                      as *Fantasy*

Where would you rate youself *before* you met your ex-mate?

---

saw it                                                                                                      saw it
as *Fact*                                                                                           as *Fantasy*

If there is any difference, what do you think causes it?

Most people want to believe in the Togetherness Myth when they are alone and feeling "down." How does this fit with your own pattern? When do you want to believe that it's true? What does that tell you?

List the parts of you that have nothing to do with being part of a pair:

1.
2.
3.
4.
5.

This exercise is designed to help you explode the Togetherness Myth for yourself. Do it when you feel strong, not down, and when you have some uninterrupted time for yourself.

## Exploding The Togetherness Myth

Imagine yourself as a movie camera reviewing old scenes from your past. Reflect on a time in your relationship when you were together but *not* happy. What was going on? Could you share your feelings with your ex-love? What happened when you tried? Try to re-experience that scene (and your feelings) now. When you feel finished take some time to reflect.

Use this space to list what you've discovered from the above.

1.
2.
3.
4.
5.

List what you *could* in fact count on your ex-mate to provide for you.

1.
2.
3.
4.
5.

List what you wished he/she would, but did not, provide for you.

1.
2.
3.
4.
5.

After looking at your relationship realistically, how would you evaluate your belief in the Togetherness Myth now?

|  |  |
|---|---|
| see it as *Fact* | see it as *Fantasy* |

If you felt like half of a pair, what can you do to make yourself "whole"?

1.
2.
3.
4.
5.

# 3

# FALLOUT FROM DISSOLUTION

Intimate relationships don't always end with a bang; sometimes they just fizzle out. But, even when the relationship has been dead for years, you may *still* be hit by some of the fallout of dissolution when you finally admit that it's over.

A friend of mine was telling me:

"Here I am, six weeks after I've kicked Bob out of the house, feeling like one of the walking wounded! I don't eat. I have trouble sleeping, I'm worried and confused. I can't make even the simplest decisions anymore—like how to rearrange the furniture or what to eat tonight.

"It doesn't make any sense," she announced. "Our relationship was over a long time ago. Yet, when I'm alone, I find myself wondering what Bob's doing and dialing part of his telephone number before I hang up.

"What's with me? How can I miss someone I didn't even love anymore? Or was I wrong about that too? I just don't know anymore—it's hard to believe that I used to think I was strong!"

My friend's doubts and fears are natural. In fact, most people who go through a dissolution experience some sort of "buyer's remorse" for the first three to six months: a period of doubt and confusion about what they've bought in saying good-bye to a part of their past.

And, although every human being is different, there are some common side effects in ending an intimate relationship that most of us experience. I've labeled these feelings, patterns, and realities the "fallout from dissolution." They are as present in the ending of a love affair as fallout material from the explosion of a bomb (even when the love affair died through lack of interest).

Looking at this fallout will help you to understand that it is a natural part of the grief process and nothing to fear or avoid.

## Loss Of Self-Esteem

Whether you experience a minor nagging of self-doubt or a loud voice shouting, "I'm a loser!" it's almost impossible to avoid a blow to your self-esteem when a relationship is over. To some extent, this can be healthy if it motivates constructive self-exploration.

For example, it's important for my friend Helen to look back on her own behavior and attitudes in her relationship with Bob. Vehemently insisting that she has been victimized by Bob and that she, personally, had no part in the demise of their love, might keep her stuck in the same pattern (like the lady who just divorced her fourth alcoholic husband!) So, anything you can learn *now* about your part in the break-up will be most helpful to you—for the next time around. Your natural instinct to question yourself after it's over is a way of trying to grow emotionally so that your next relationship will be stronger. Therefore, do some self-examination. Look at your part in creating the distance. Maybe you chose the wrong partner at the beginning, or maybe you didn't grow with your partner but away from him or her.

## Fallout From Dissolution

Helen discovered, in looking back, that from the very beginning Bob had told her he was afraid to have permanent intimacy.

> "I remember when we first started dating, Bob told me he usually got bored with a love affair after a couple of years. It's funny, I heard him—but I didn't believe him. Know what I mean? But I think I did act unconsciously on the fear that he'd leave. I smothered him by asking him to meet my every need. I was jealous of his friends. The tighter I hung on, the more he wanted to be free. Next time I fall in love, I think I'll do it with at least one eye open. Learn to give my man more comforting and less smothering".

Whatever insight you achieve, learn from it and use it! Avoid beating yourself with feelings of self-doubt, inadequacy, and blame. They can become overwhelming and immobilize you in self-condemnation and depression. Before Helen could learn from the past, she found herself sinking more and more deeply into a depression. Piled with self-doubt and self-condemnation, she tore apart everything she did with self-criticism. She was so busy beating herself down, she had little energy left over to pull herself up.

> "I feel so empty and abandoned now. And when I look at next year—or the years after—it looks just as bleak. I deserve to be alone. Even though I kicked Bob out of the house, he had really left me before then. He's living with someone else now. You know, I was so afraid that he'd get tired of me and find someone else, I drove him away. If only I'd been different. But, it's too late now—I'm alone".

But Helen discovered, as many ex-intimates do, that she wasn't *that* awful nor did she remain alone forever. Once she was able to feel her sadness and evaluate her relationship with Bob more objectively, she began feeling better.

## Loss Of Identity and Living Structure

Loss of identity and living structure may not always be a feeling or fear. It can be a reality.

A father without his children loses the role of teacher, disciplinarian, friend, referee, and part-time football coach—at least on a day-to-day basis. He and his children must learn, if they are to adjust at all, how to substitute an "always there" relationship for "sometimes near."

> For the last six years, Ed and Marsha's marriage was glued together by their love for their sons, John, age 14, and 12-year-old Mike. Ed owned his own hardware store and could make a lot of "free" time to be with the boys. He was a scout leader, Little League manager, scorekeeper for the junior high football team, and president of the local P.T.A. As concerned parents, they decided a marriage held together just for "the kids" was unhealthy. And so, when they were divorced, Marsha and the boys moved near her family, two hundred miles away.
>
> Ed's visiting rights consisted of one weekend a month and every other holiday. His role as a full-time father and active member of the community disappeared. And, although he saw John and Mike on "visiting" days, his life felt pretty empty. He missed his role as teacher, coach, and concerned citizen for children's rights.
>
> Finally, after he had floundered for several months, a friend suggested he join Big Brothers. "A guy like you needs kids—and there are a lot of boys around who need a man."
>
> At first Ed said no. It wouldn't be like fathering his own sons. But then he decided to try it. He felt he had nothing to lose.

As a matter of fact, Ed found that by joining Big Brothers he gained a lot. He got back part of his identity as a leader and teacher of boys. It wasn't the same, but it was a whole lot better than nothing.

Then there are times when a "sometimes near" relationship is an improvement for both father and child. With less time and tension, both can put more effort into building their relationship.

Mark was 35 when he and Marie were divorced. They had been married for ten years and were the parents of three children: Mark, Jr., age 8; Danny, age 6; and 3-year-old Karen. Since the birth of their first child, Mark had spent most of his time and energy making money as an insurance agent to "give the kids the things they need to feel secure." When their marriage dissolved, Marie took the kids and Mark gave child support.

Then with the family absent, he discovered that there is more to child support than money. His children were no longer the hassle they were before. He didn't see them breaking toys or ripping the Levi's he'd spent so much money to buy.

What he did see was that, to feel safe, they needed his emotional support and understanding as much as or more than his money. And, he still wanted a relationship with them. So, with the tensions of the marriage gone and less time to take his children for granted, Mark put more effort into the hours he had with them. End result: Mark's relationship with his three offspring was better after the divorce than during his marriage.

There are other identities that are lost or changed in saying goodbye. A housewife with no husband is a housekeeper. A wife and mother changes to a working single mother. A lover without his mate becomes an ex-love. A friend and companion turns to an enemy. A partner becomes an acquaintance. The list goes on and on—

With each of these changes, there is an "identity crisis" followed by an adjustment: A period of time when you, as an ex-intimate will need to begin looking at yourself as an individual again, rather than as part of a pair; a time to decide, once again, "Who am I now, and what do I want to be or do?"

It's never very easy but for some it's more difficult than for others. A woman who saw her major role as Mrs. has trouble viewing herself as a Ms. And, the longer she was the "better" or "other" half of a pair, the harder it may be for her to feel "whole" on her own.

For example, Mrs. Jones, who was married for 25 years, will probably have a harder time adjusting to her new role as an ex-intimate than Mary Smith, who had a love affair with Cory Johnson for six weeks. But both Mrs. Jones and Mary Smith will have the same shift in perspective with regard to how they see themselves, including the pleasure of discovering they are, indeed, "whole" people.

If you're going through an identity crisis of your own right now, find some comfort in the fact that you've gone through others in your life (going from grade school to high school, adolescence to adulthood, your first job to the second one, etc.), and remember that with each change you were able to grow!

The other day I was talking about loss of identity and living structure with one of my co-workers. Six months earlier she had divorced her husband of seven years and moved from a charming old house in the country back to an apartment by herself in the city.

"It must have been awfully hard for you," I said, "to give up that home with its beautiful yard for a dinky apartment."

"Hard?" she smiled, "It was the best thing that ever happened to me. That house was so old—and big. I spent most of my spare time working on it.

"You know I used to feel like I *should* always be accomplishing something. With that house, I had plenty to reinforce my 'workhorse' image.

"I'd always been taught that you have fun *after* you've finished your work. And there was always plenty of work with that house—and little time for fun.

"When I moved into my apartment, I discovered I had lots of free time. Nothing needed to be repaired or repainted. At first it was hard to adjust, but, let me tell you, I love it! I'm finally learning after 30 years to take time and enjoy life, rather than work my way through it.

"I can't tell you what a change that's been for me," she bubbled. "I've become a lot less up-tight or critical of me and other people. I'm really a lot healthier and happier than I've ever been.

"When you write your book, Trudy, make sure you tell the readers not to be afraid of giving up some of their old self-images. It could be a blessing in disguise."

## Loss Of Ambition; Indecision

But even when the changes become a blessing in disguise, during the transition period it is natural to feel some loss of ambition and indecision.

Like my friend Helen, who had trouble "even making the simplest decisions on how to rearrange the furniture or what to eat tonight." And major decisions such as: Should I move? What do we do with the kids? Now that I'm free, what am I "free" to do?—these were real stumpers!

Major decisions *can* be stumpers for anyone—even people who are still in an intimate relationship and have someone to support them in such decisions. It's funny, most people don't notice until they're alone how often they depend on others to help them with choices.

But an ex-intimate may need to make some major changes with very little emotional support or "cheering on" from a fan club. No wonder it's natural in an ending to give up your ambition or decision-making power—for a while.

It's hard to know which comes first: indecision or loss of ambition. If you have trouble making decisions (and all of us do), it's easy to give up. On the other hand, if you give up after you've said good-bye, making decisions doesn't seem worthwhile or possible. Either way, it's a self-defeating cycle.

When you feel good about yourself and your past choices, it's easier to have ambition and quickly decide what to do next. But when you feel, as Helen did, "like one of the walking wounded," your desire to zip through and conquer the challenges of single life is temporarily lost.

Ex-intimates who find themselves in a quandary about what to do now may find it helpful to stop running around in circles or standing in a daze and *sit down*. With a pencil and paper in hand, write down questions that need to be answered and choices that have to be made now and sometime in the future. List "Current decisions I've decided to make" on one sheet of paper and "Decisions I would like to make later" on another.

Avoid asking vague, unanswerable questions like "what's the meaning of life?" or self-defeating ones like "has my life been worthwhile?" Your list may include anything from "where do I want to live?" to "what should I have for dinner?" Some decisions will be easier than others.

Include on your list some decisions that are relatively easy for you. By making these and owning your ability to do this, you will help build your self-confidence. When you list the choices you have for major decisions, such as where to live, try to give yourself at least three options. Then write down the pros and cons of each. Once you have listed all of the alternatives (with their good and bad points), pick the one you *lean* toward. Try to get out of the "bag" of waiting until you can make the *perfect* decision. Many of your choices right now may be between alternatives you don't exactly like anyway.

If you make a mistake, don't be too harsh on yourself. Take comfort in the fact that few decisions are absolutely irreversible. As my co-worker said,

> "Once I was forced to make decisions on my own, I discovered that I really was a worthwhile person. And I began looking at what I wanted to do because I actually felt I had options for the first time in my life. It's terrific to discover that I have freedom of choice rather than the burden of decisions."

## Bitterness

It's hard to decide what you really want to do if you're seething with bitterness. It takes a lot of energy to be bitter and disagreeable. You can lose a lot of friends in the process. Still, it is part of the fallout of dissolution and it's perfectly natural to feel bitter at times.

But please be careful about how much bitterness you hold on to. You can get stuck.

> Betty had been married for 16 years when her husband left her for another woman. Betty blamed *everyone* for the divorce, except herself. Her daughter was a hassle, her husband was a baby, and the "other woman" was a fool. She was glad when her daughter moved in with them. They deserved each other. Her only hope as far as they were concerned was that she'd live to see the day when they'd all be sorry.

In the meantime, she planned to get everything she could from her husband. "That Bastard will pay!"

She spent most of her free time (outside of the lawyer's office) trying to get her friends to take sides. But most of them avoided her. One referred her to therapy.

It's easy to understand that Betty's bitterness was masking her hurt. And that she needed to grieve for her loss and gain support and understanding to feel better. But it was very hard for Betty to ask for any comforting or to give it to herself. Her bitterness was self-consuming and was making it harder and harder for her to trust people.

In therapy, she learned how to let herself feel the hurt without being overwhelmed, to understand her own part in the demise of her marriage, and how to trust and have respect for people again—herself included.

So, when you find yourself getting bitter, go ahead and feel the sorrow beneath and learn that you can trust yourself and others for support. Don't become another Betty Bitterness. Even if you have a right to be bitter, you may want to ask yourself if it's worth it to be so disagreeable.

## Self-Pity

If you feel bitterness long enough, pretty soon you'll begin feeling sorry for yourself. Or is it the other way around? In any event, self-pity is just as much a part of the fallout as bitterness and, often, hits at about the same time.

> *Total stranger passing by:* What are you doing down there?
>
> *Little person in a hole:* I'm feeling sorry for myself.
>
> *Total stranger:* How come?
>
> *Little person:* Because I fell into this hole.

*Total stranger:* Oh? Well, can I throw you a rope to help you climb out?

*Little person:* No thanks. It probably wouldn't do any good anyway. Even if I did get out no one would care. And I'd probably just fall into another one anyway.

*Total stranger:* Well, okay. I'll be back later if you change your mind.

*Little person:* I knew he'd leave me.

Poor little person! Once he fell in the hole of self-pity, he refused to let someone help him climb out:

*Little person:* It's awfully dark down here. Too bad I'm stuck. I don't deserve it. I wonder what everyone else is doing? No one probably even misses me. I knew this would happen. I guess I'll go to sleep.

*Total stranger:* Hi! I'm back.

*Little person:* Big deal.

*Total stranger:* Don't you want to get out yet?

*Little person:* Well, maybe—it *is* empty and dark down here.

*Total stranger:* I can still throw you that rope if you'd like to climb out. But you'd better make up your mind quickly, I'm leaving soon.

*Little person:* (First to himself) If the stranger leaves, I may be stuck here forever. (And then, shouting out loud) Stranger! Throw me your rope—I want *out* of this hole!

Hurray, little person! It took some guts to grab the stranger's rope and pull yourself up again. There's nothing wrong with licking your wounds when you've been hurt, but it is very easy to get wrapped up in self-pity. Especially when you've said goodbye to an ex-love. Part of the healing process is to give yourself sympathy occasionally. Growing beyond that may take some time and conscious effort on your part.

## Physiological Changes

All parts of us—mind, body, and feelings—can be affected by the death of an intimate relationship because they are so closely linked.

Several years ago a friend of mine developed diabetes after the death of her father. Although she must have had a predisposition toward that disease, her grief was so strong that it affected the metabolism of her body. The doctor explained to her that diabetes triggered off by emotional trauma was rare, but not unknown. Few people develop diabetes over the loss of an intimate relationship, but many do experience temporary physical upsets.

According to Dr. Aaron T. Beck, author of *Depression: Causes and Treatment*, there are several common physiological changes that may occur when a person is depressed. Among these are:

1. Changes in appetite and subsequent weight loss or gain. Some people lose or gain as much as 50 pounds.

2. Loss in energy levels. If you are normally active, you may find you have little energy and tire easily. Feelings of being "run down" or "too weak to move" are common.

3. Excessive energy or hyperactivity may occur. If you are normally calm, you may suddenly develop great bounds of energy—to the extent that you may become restless and fidgety after short periods of time.

4. Difficulty in concentrating and shortening of attention

span. Reading a paragraph in a magazine and then remembering what it said can be an impossible feat for the first days or weeks.

5. Frequent headaches or a feeling of tightness in the head may occur. Many people complain of feeling "like there is a tight band around my head."

6. Upset stomach or nausea and vomiting. Although this is usually a temporary complaint, there are cases recorded in psychiatric literature where this symptom lasts for years.

7. Menstrual disturbances are often seen, with amenorrhea (absence or suppression) being the most common. Excessive cramping may also occur.

8. Changes in intestinal functioning may occur with subsequent constipation or diarrhea.

9. Resistance to viral and bacterial infections may go down. People who are normally healthy may find themselves in bed frequently with a common cold or the flu bug.

So, not only may you feel like one of the walking wounded during this crisis period, but your body may actually react as if you had been through a war.

Cures for these symptoms take time. It's important to remember that many of these physical upsets are natural and to be expected. The first few days and nights are comparable to a time of acute illness. Your reflexes may be slow and your attention span brief, as your mind darts from the past to the present to the frightening future. Gradually the fog will lift and the pressure will cease as you begin to see your way more clearly.

Treat your physical symptoms as they occur. Even though you may need to *force* yourself, continue to eat well-balanced meals. And avoid excessive use of alcoholic beverages. If the symptoms persist, go to your family physician for treatment.

## Changes In Sleep Patterns

When you lose a person close to you, you may need to sleep for a while to find the guts to start again, or you may spend your nights trying to figure out the past, plan for the future, and worry about your inability to sleep.

Human beings are the most flexible animals in the world. Within a short period of time, most ex-intimates discover they are either tired of sleeping their life away and get on with the business of living, or they get tired of stalking in the night and begin to sleep again.

Either way, it's important to remember that sleep patterns may change during the first few nights or weeks after you've said good-bye. Don't panic. In time you will return to normal.

## Changes In Sexual Patterns

The scale for "normal" sexual patterns of ex-intimates varies from complete celibacy to promiscuity. During the time of ending and while you're going through the grief process, almost anything is normal.

Adults who are normally active sexually may find that they have lost their drive or interest in sex. As one man confided to me, "Women don't arouse me any more. Sex got so bad during the last few months of our relationship, that I'm beginning to wonder if I'll ever be 'turned on' again." Gradually he did gain back his sexual drive and interest, but it did take time. First the wounds to his pride and self-image had to begin healing.

Loss of sexual drive and interest is most often seen in the partner who was left behind. The one who feels rejected is the most prone to depression and feelings of failure. And, from that viewpoint, it is natural to shy away from encounters (especially sexual) that will once again place you in a position where you may be hurt.

*Fallout From Dissolution* 43

Depression and loss of libido, according to Dr. Beck, may go hand in hand. Time spent going through the process of both grief and rebuilding self-confidence seems to be the only cure.

On the opposite end of the scale, many ex-intimates find that their sexual drive increases. Men and women who normally see themselves as "homebodies" may find they are haunting the bars at night looking for one-night stands. Although the sexual behavior is different, the core issues of feeling empty, alone, and inadequate are similar. A man or woman who becomes sexually promiscuous after the loss of an intimate relationship is, in his or her own way, dealing with the grief process.

Increased sexual activity can be an attempt to substitute sexual intercourse for feelings of intimacy. It can also be an angry statement (a way of getting even with members of the opposite sex). Or it serves as a way of proving to yourself that others still do find you sexually attractive. Whatever the underlying reasons, it is not unusual during the grief period for an ex-intimate to be more sexually active.

Although it might seem unusual, many ex-intimates continue to have sexual intercourse with each other long after they have parted. One man I met continued to go to bed solely with his ex-wife ten years after their divorce. This is highly unusual, but it is pretty common for ex-intimates to continue gaining sexual support and comfort from each other for several weeks or months after their relationship is over, thus making it much more difficult for either partner to bury the relationship and go on. However, it does seem to be part of the natural ending process for some ex-intimates, especially those who have been together a long time.

Masturbation is another sexual behavior that may again (or for the first time) become prominent during the grief period. Although there are no accurate statistics in this area, it is my guess that many ex-intimates do at times quite naturally seek gratification through their own bodies. I have talked with a number of ex-intimates who tell me that, when they lost their sexual partners, they began meeting their own needs through masturbation. Some shared that this was their only source of sexual gratification for awhile, others said that they did this in conjunction with seeking sexual comfort/sharing from others.

So, during the time of ending, and while you're going through the grief process, almost any change in sexual behavior is natural. You need not be overly concerned or worried about your changing sexual patterns; it is part of the fallout of dissolution.

The important issue with regard to sexual patterns is how you feel about yourself. If your behavior makes you feel guilty or even more like a failure, and the understanding that it can be a natural, normal process does not help, then try to alter it. In time, as your wounds heal, your sexual patterns, desire, and interest will probably return to status quo. Or, if you did not enjoy sex in your previous relationship, you may pleasantly discover, with your next love, that you do. One lady who was married for 35 years and is now divorced and remarried, has happily found that she is finally enjoying sex.

## Financial Pressures

> Bob loves Carol, but can't afford to marry her because of the alimony and child support he pays Alice, his first wife.
>
> What to do? Get a husband for Alice. That will get Bob off the hook.
>
> Bob finds Ted, a recent divorcé and introduces him to Alice. Ted and Alice fall in love. But Ted can't marry Alice because he's paying alimony and child support to his ex-wife, Gertrude.
>
> Obviously, in order for Bob and Carol, Ted and Alice to live happily ever after, they have to do something about Gertrude.

That would get Ted off the hook to marry Alice, which would free Bob to marry Carol.

Solution? Find a husband for Gertrude who could afford to take care of her financially.

Sound crazy? Not really. It's a variation of the comedy plot in the movie "The American Way of Divorce." It can also be a not-so-comic plot for many real-life divorcees. Money is tight, and the rising costs of living makes taking care of two separate households very difficult.

Today, many husbands and wives find they both have to work just to keep up with high prices. And, when they are divorced, some couples are really in financial trouble, especially if they have children. Lawyers charge money. Moving costs a lot. Living separately eats up cash.

It's hard to avoid the fallout of living poorer. In fact, you can probably count on extra financial pressures after you've said good-bye.

## Loss Of Friends and Familiar Surroundings

Another fallout that you can probably count on when you say good-bye to an ex-love is the loss of friends and familiar surroundings.

As my co-worker who moved from a country home into a city apartment told me:

> "I miss some of the friends we had together. On Sunday afternoons we'd gotten into the habit of doing something with two other couples. A barbecue or picnic, or maybe just lounging around. I really like them—but I haven't seen them very much since then. We don't have very much in common anymore. I can't tell whether they're awkward or I am, but the few times we've been together since then have been very strained."

The amount of this fallout varies with each ex-intimate. The ex-mate who stays in the same house or neighborhood obviously loses less of his or her familiar surroundings than the one who moves across town or to another area. Likewise, the ex-intimate who has friends *outside* of the relationship will have less change or lose fewer friends than the person who was totally dependent on the intimate relationship to provide outside friends.

The longer you have been in an intimate relationship, the greater chance that your friends are also your ex-mate's friends. The couple that was divorced after twenty-six years of marriage probably has more mutual friends than the couple who lived together for only six months. In any case, when it's over, your friends will be affected by the ending. And you may abruptly or gradually lose some of them.

According to Dr. Arthur Miller's article in *Divorce and After*, there are a number of different reactions that friends may have to a divorce, or, I might add, to the ending of a nonmarried relationship as well. Included in this list are:

Anxiety because of their own marriage
Shame
Preoccupation with the divorce
Desire for a sexual relationship with one of the divorced partners.
Pleasure at the divorced person's suffering
Feelings of superiority or surprise
Experience of emotional loss and grief
Conflict over allegiances
Disillusionment with friendship
Crisis over personal identity
Preoccupation and curiosity about the settlement

As a wounded ex-intimate, it may be hard to understand how some of your friends can desert you in your hour of need.

Just remember the ending of your relationship has kicked off painful or awkward feelings in your friends as well. And some of these are often handled by their saying good-bye. You may also discover, as did my co-worker, that you no longer live in the same world as your friends from the former life. So, as part of the fallout of dissolution, you may leave some of your old friends behind—just as you did when you left your parents' home.

## Summary

So there you have the ten most common instances of fallout from dissolution. You may not experience them all, but it's important to remember that most are self-limiting. Usually, they come and go with a great deal of frequency during the first few days or weeks. Then, gradually, they subside.

Everyone is different and the intensity and duration for most fallout varies with the length of the relationship, the ex-intimate's own feelings of insecurity before and during the relationship, and the number of roles or identities tied up in the relationship.

Whatever the length or intensity, it is important to let yourself experience the feelings and grow through them. They are part of the grief process. If you totally avoid or deny your feelings during the mourning phase, you may be stuck with them for the rest of your life.

### *Experiments and Exercises*

Below is a list of the fallout of dissolution. Everyone will experience some or all of these during the grief process. Identify the ones currently haunting you.

- ☐ Self-doubt, lowering of self-esteem
- ☐ Change or loss of specific role identities

- ☐ Change or loss of living structure (home)
- ☐ Loss of ambition
- ☐ Trouble making decisions
- ☐ Bitterness
- ☐ Self-pity
- ☐ Change in appetite/plus weight loss or gain
- ☐ Loss in energy level (feeling "tired")
- ☐ Excessive energy level (feeling fidgety)
- ☐ Short attention span
- ☐ Difficulty in concentrating
- ☐ Headaches
- ☐ Upset stomach, nausea
- ☐ Menstrual disturbance
- ☐ Diarrhea or constipation
- ☐ Lowered resistance to flu and cold "bugs"
- ☐ Change in sleeping patterns
- ☐ Change in sexual patterns
- ☐ Financial pressures
- ☐ Loss of friends
- ☐ Loss of familiar surroundings (home town)

Now list those you have identified:

- Which ones do you feel will improve with time?
- Which ones will need some effort and change on your part?
- Are there some which you have already resolved or learned to handle effectively? How did you do it?
- Pick one you feel would be the easiest to work through and plan how to attack it

As you read through the book, periodically return to this list and re-evaluate your progress. Change the fallouts you want to work on as you grow or replan your attack on those which need more work.

# 4

## ALONE AND FREE: THIS IS THE TIME TO DECIDE TO LIVE!

Who knows which one of you really made the decision to bury your love? The one who first shouted "I want out!" or the one who first turned away in bed? In any event, love between two people doesn't usually die a quick and violent death; rather, it is eaten away slowly by the lack of kindness, respect, and consideration in a retreat further away from each other.

By the time it's over (whether it's a matter of thirty years or just a few short months), you may be sharing very few of your thoughts and feelings with each other or yourself. So when you finally walk out or are asked to leave, it may not feel *real* but rather as if the scenes that you're viewing (the packing and moving out) are happening to someone else. Many people describe this phenomenon as a sensation of being an actor in a movie: playing a part but not feeling the role.

This *shock* effect is a self-preservation technique your body uses to help you through the exit scenes, so that you can function when underneath it all you may feel like folding. It lasts anywhere from a few hours to a week, depending on how much time you need to go through the mechanics of physically separating and relocating yourself. And, when you have done all that, then it may hit like a ton of bricks that you are ALONE.

What follows is fairly predictable (with slight variations) but still very agonizing.

Couples who end a relationship are individuals who want *more* from a mate than just living together. But when the first impact of good-bye hits you and living alone becomes your reality, it is easy to forget what you originally wanted.

Remember, now that you're up to your neck in alligators, that your *original* goal was to clean the swamp. And while you'll feel everything from, "Yippee I'm Free," to, "Golly I'm Scared," this is the time to decide to live!

## Initial Reaction Is Often Relief

There isn't just sadness in saying good-bye to an old love affair. There's freedom from fighting and fencing with someone and relief from feeling "on guard," especially if the relationship has been a particularly stressful one.

Relief is a normal reaction in the earlier stages of the grief process. A patient of mine who had been married to an alcoholic for fifteen years speaks of her freedom from worry and anger when she finally left her husband.

> "I'd forgotten what it was like to take a deep breath and relax. I was always so tense—never knowing when Jake would lose his next job, or come home soused. *Anything* was a reason for him to get drunk—he celebrated good times with Scotch and drowned the bad times with beer. I never knew whether to comfort like a mother or nag like a fishwife. I think I did both. Thank God, I'm finally out of that!"

## Alone And Free: This Is The Time To Decide To Live! 51

The sense of relief is a natural part of any ending even when the relationship hasn't been all bad or self-destructive. The decision has finally been made. The internal battles of "Should I go or should I stay?" are ended.

As Geri confided:

> "After a week of mechanically going through the routine of moving, the first thing I felt was relief. A kind of peace within. And a freedom. My ball and chain had been cut away and I was free to do what I wanted—when I wanted. I felt like dancing! There was no one to nag at my every mood or action any more. The fighting had stopped and the war inside me seemed settled. It was nice not to struggle with me—or with Steve."

The love between Geri and Steve had died a gradual and agonizing death. Their first year was beautiful, like love from a storybook. But then it began to sour. At the end of five years, there was no longer magic between them—just a cold war. Both had careers (she's a nurse and he's an insurance agent), and often the stresses at work were taken out on each other at home. Work all day, be pleasant to strangers, come home at night, and labor or just die from exhaustion. Spend the weekends on the house or recuperating from the week. They began to lose sight of their love and blame each other for their internal unhappiness. Steve yelled at Geri, she turned away in bed. He accused her of coldness, she stiffened even more. So, before the age of thirty, both Steve and Geri had decided to part. No wonder she felt relieved when the marriage was over. A war, even a cold one, is draining.

There is little reason to give you any advice through this stage. It's a phase to enjoy, and in time you will be able to happily develop an awareness that you are free. Free to make your own choices. All things (within reality, of course) are up to you. If you want to eat artichoke hearts for breakfast, lunch, and dinner—do it. Arrange all the furniture in the center of the room if you like. Cover your home with flowers. Watch TV or try your hand at painting. You can have your home as neat or as sloppy as you want. Nothing can hold you down—enjoy this stage and worry only about yourself. Feel free to make your own mistakes and your own successes. You will discover that you're a separate person with the right to live as you see fit—not as someone else would like you to.

## Second Phase: Overwhelming Depression

Just about the time you've settled in to feeling good, patting yourself on the back for saying good-bye, or telling yourself you don't feel as bad as you thought you would, it suddenly hits: My God, I'm alone! The house is empty and so am I.

You can hear your heart beating and feel the ache. Disconnected and hollow are the words most often used to describe the depression in this second phase. The sadness of not belonging or feeling obligated to someone close can lie heavy in your body. Moving is a chore and lying still impossible. The more you've invested in your old life, the larger the loss and the greater the pain.

This is the time that the impact of loss will hit you the hardest. What you thought of as your world will seem gone. In its place will be the emptiness you feel so keenly now.

As Geri related:

> "During those first few days, I cried myself to sleep, when I slept at all. Thank God I had a job to go to. I woke up tired, dragged to work, often looking like death warmed over. By the end of the day, I was ready to go home and drop. I was miserable with people or by myself."

> "I couldn't concentrate on anything. My mind kept flashing on Steve. I so desperately wanted him back, but knew

he was gone. I felt trapped. Everywhere I looked there was nothing. I'd lost all my friends and happiness. What I had left meant nothing. If only I could go back—back to the beginning and start over again, or make it up to him somehow. But I didn't have the energy to do anything—I just hurt."

Almost nothing you do will relieve the pain you feel so intensely the first few days or weeks. At least, not for very long. It's like a fever that has to run its course before it breaks. You will need to feel some of the pain in order to let it go.

Geri's statement that she'd lost everything and was helpless to regain it is a natural evaluation for an ex-intimate to make in this second phase. For that is how it seems: Your old love is gone, mutual friends seem to avoid you, and the image of yourself as part of a pair is erased. The sadness and loss may pierce so deeply that you feel like dying. All that seems left is your loneliness and pain.

*Please briefly state your problem:* "Going through a divorce, I'm depressed and feel like killing myself. I can't find a reason to live. I need help."

Although the words vary on the admission forms at the mental health clinic where I work, the theme remains the same. Someone's going through an ending and is immobilized by depression and loss. The most intense part of this depression usually lasts no more than a few days or weeks at the longest. After that, there may be periodic feelings of severe depression and loss but usually your natural survival instincts will keep you from ever feeling so desperate again.

## Your Normal Need To Withdraw

Part of the healing process, ironically, involves withdrawing from people, isolating yourself for awhile and, in general, giving up on life. It shouldn't last very long, and for many people it is just a matter of several hours or an occasional couple of days. But this is the time to lick your wounds after you've been hurt; examine your needs, goals, and wants; and find a reason to go back out into the world again.

> "I can't say how long it lasted or how often it came back. All I know is that during the first three months after my divorce, there were times when my only contact with people was when I was at work. Otherwise, I stayed in my apartment and did nothing. Just laid around and listened to music. I remember coming to the conclusion that I'd done everything I'd ever wanted to do and that anything now would be a repeat. I could get over Steve, probably. Maybe even find someone else to love—but then what? I examined my life and took note of all my successes and failures. My parents wanted me to be a nurse and so I did. Well, I'd done that and I'm very good at it. I've traveled around the country and seen almost everything I wanted to. I have all the material possessions I want. I've had a lot of good friends in my life—many of them are lost or forgotten now. But I could do everything all over again, if I wanted. So what's the reason to keep trying?
> 
> "Even the thought of giving up didn't bother me. I remember thinking that it was odd for me—such a goal-directed person—to quit trying. But that's what I did."

The process that Geri talks about is normal for many ex-intimates. If you've been hurt deeply by the loss of your mate and have decided that you don't want to keep going through your life making the same mistakes and having the same hang-ups, you need to take the time to stop. And, maybe, even give up on living for a while. At least the part of living that has you out in the world interacting with new people again.

## Alone And Free: This Is The Time To Decide To Live!

Like anything, of course, you can go too far on giving up or isolating yourself. But, within moderation, it is a healthy process. Geri ended up finding herself some reasons to live:

"I discovered first of all that I'm very goal-directed and that actually part of the reason for my unhappiness with Steve was that we really weren't going anywhere—just working to survive. I found that most of my goals had been handed to me by someone else—my parents, the nursing instructors, or Steve. What kept me feeling so lost during the divorce and also contributed to my unhappiness in our marriage was other people handing me expectations to meet. And my trying to meet them—while really resenting them. Now I have no one to rebel against, or feel obligated to please. That's healthy for me. I'm actually becoming a much less uptight person because of it. Now my reasons for living are much more simple: to continue being a separate person and enjoying others for their own specialness. It's hard to describe this feeling I have. It's like I don't have to play *games* with people any more to get their approval. I make my own goals and please myself."

Without the time of isolation and withdrawal from life, it would be difficult for you to reach such a deep understanding of yourself and to find, just as Geri did, your own personal reasons for living.

Such reflections can give you emotional strength, so do not be afraid of periodic isolation or of questioning your goals—but don't overdo it and remain stuck there.

## The Pull From the Past: a Protective Device

"It seemed to me that I became obsessed by the thought of Steve and my memories of him—especially at the beginning. Suddenly I loved him more than ever and thought about what we used to do together, where we went, what fun we had. Every tune on the radio reminded me of the past and all that I'd lost. I'd wake up in the middle of the night, dreaming about yesterday. It was like I couldn't keep my thoughts on today or tomorrow. Like some unseen force kept pulling me back."

This sensation of being pulled back to the memories of yesterday almost against your will is consistently brought up by ex-intimates.

"Last Christmas we went skiing, that was a lot of fun. I remember ___ ___."

"I still keep a bottle of Scotch around, Brad loves it."

"Whenever I date a new girl, I remember what it was like with Marge."

"I haven't changed anything in the house since George left."

"I remember the night we first heard that."

"Sometimes I go through our old photo albums and just reminisce."

"I still have our old house key on my chain."

"If I'm not busy my mind wanders back."

"I've even caught myself talking to Carol when I'm alone."

"I keep his picture in my wallet."

The healthy side of this natural phenomenon is that it protects you. It gives you a chance to go through the mourning process and piece by piece say good-bye to the past.

"I found I did not dwell very long on any one situation or event. It was like my mind was going through a sorting

### Alone And Free: This Is The Time To Decide To Live!

process—'the time we repainted the living room—forget it Geri, you've already said good-bye to that.' Some of the memories were harder to bury than others. A few I've still kept. But, it's nice to know I have control over that now—at first I didn't feel like I did."

Pleasant memories may also act as a reminder that you can have a loving relationship. Especially if your present situation casts some doubt.

"I had a fight with my new boyfriend the other night and I almost immediately began doubting whether I even had the ability to love. Then I remembered my relationship with Steve and felt better. In a strange way, it gave me comfort and strength to know from the past that I am capable of loving."

Unpleasant memories can be used to help an ex-intimate feel better about saying good-bye. Like the divorcee whose ex-husband is an alcoholic. "Any time I get lonely or scared I remember how much worse it could be with Jake."

Both pleasant and unpleasant memories are brought up by ex-intimates as a protective device against falling in love again too soon—before all the wounds have healed. This is a natural defense and a part of the healing process every ex-intimate needs.

"Sometimes I wonder if I need the memory of Steve and our past to keep my heart from falling for someone my head knows isn't right."

If you find yourself asking a similar question, the answer is probably "yes." You'll need time to get over an old love affair and learn from the mistakes that were made. Pulling in the past to make space in the present will give you that time.

But be careful you don't take too much time dwelling in your past. Even though a little bit of it can be healthy—too much daydreaming can be dangerous. Filling up your present with past memories can be like filling a stove full of smoke rather then fire. It's cloudy and full, but the room is still empty and cold. Reminiscing should be gradually replaced by new experiences from your present.

## How To "Pick Yourself Up"

Like most other ex-intimates, somewhere along the grieving process you'll fall flat on your face. Maybe more than once. You'll trip over discouragement and disappointment or slip on hurt feelings and whammo! You're down on your knees or flat on your back again. When that happens, especially the first time, you'll have to make a decision not to give up on living. It may take some time for you to come to that choice—an hour or a month. It doesn't always come easily. Sometimes you don't even notice at first that you've given up. But, sooner or later, it will hit you and the decision will come. So, whether you pull on the strings of your hopes for the future or push yourself up with the anger from falling, look inside your world for a reason not to give up.

As one woman related:

> "There was a point in time when I knew that I'd given up on living. I mechanically worked, came home to my dog, and avoided any other contact with life. After several days of this hollow existence, it hit me one night while I was walking that the oak tree near my apartment was gigantic. I hadn't noticed it in a long time and thought that was strange because I've always loved nature. It's hard to describe, but suddenly I knew how small and insignificant the loss of one person really was in my life. He was as big as I

wanted to make him—and so was that tree. There is so much more to living then being a robot, and without even noticing I had gypped myself out of several days in my life."

Whatever you discover in the world that's worth living for, begin gathering your strength. Take the time to brush yourself off, renew some faith in yourself, reaffirm your goals, and learn from the fall before you start over again.

## How To "Brush Yourself Off"

As an ex-intimate, you will be up and down emotionally like a yo-yo through the first few days or weeks after you've said good-bye. The process gets easier, and you will find that the yo-yo effect will level off after a while, but still it's important to take some time after you've picked yourself up from one of your falls to look at what happened, clear out the cobwebs, and replan your goals.

The first part of brushing yourself off is to look at what parts of you were injured by the fall:

1. What got damaged: my pride? self-confidence?
2. Do I look worse physically then before?
3. Was I betrayed by a friend—or slapped by a stranger?
4. Which wounds will take time to heal?
5. What will help me to feel better?

After you've answered the preceding questions, begin to look at what caused you to fall. Sometimes, especially in the beginning phases of the grief process, ex-intimates are extremely vulnerable and overly sensitive. If an old friend tells you he's busy or someone doesn't answer her phone, it's possible to *overreact* and decide you're alone in the world and no one cares. Take a look at your self-image and extreme sensitivity and do some reality testing in this area. Accept the fact that the whole world does not center around you (even if you feel as though the whole world has crumbled in on you) and that your friends or the strangers you meet sometimes react because of their own needs. A friend can really be busy but still care. The lady at the supermarket doesn't crowd in front of you because you're unimportant; she does it because she's in a hurry—and rude.

So look through the past twenty-four hours' events and see what caused you to trip. Then, try to understand it, putting your own wounded pride and lack of self-confidence in perspective.

By now you should know what areas of you have been injured and what caused you to fall. The next thing you can check is whether there is a way to avoid tripping over the same kind of problem again or diminishing the depth of your fall the next time you slip.

> "I was feeling lonely, so I called my old girlfriend—but she was busy. Then I felt even lonelier and stupid besides. Next time I'm lonely, I won't call her—I'll call someone else that I'm pretty sure will be available. Maybe I'll think of three or four people before I start calling."
>
> . . .
>
> "I was passed over for a promotion at work and when I talked to my boss, he said I didn't deserve it, anyway. I think he was right. I need to get more involved in business—I've been letting work slide."

Once you've discovered what started your fall, the "brushing yourself off" process may lead you to develop new goals and directions for living. Such as meeting new friends so that you have more than one person to call for a Saturday night date or a Wednesday card game. Or going back to school to sharpen up your employment skills. Or learning to be a little less sensitive and not overreacting to every little comment you hear.

## How To Start Living Again

After you've taken a deep breath, look around at the parts of the world you want to enjoy again or maybe for the first time. Like taking a big bite out of a fresh, crisp, red apple and letting the juice run down your chin, or allowing the warmth in a small child's eyes to touch you. It's rediscovering that the world is a pretty nice place after all, and glowing over your decision to participate in its life again.

Knowing that your attitude and mood affect your perception of everything, look at the parts of your world you will need to repair or replace, like your own self-esteem or self-confidence. In spite of all the rationalizations and reality testing in the world, it's hard to leave an intimate relationship without suffering a number of blows to your pride.

Building that confidence back up again—or maybe for the first time in your life—is a gradual process, but one that is worth the time and effort it takes. Now begin looking with a healthier attitude at what you have left in your world. You may have already spent several hours bemoaning your fate and staring blankly at what you don't have any more. But this time, look at it differently. Look at what you have left that you want to keep: your health, some of your old friends, children and family perhaps, a house or material goods, an occupation, fun hobbies, and special talents. At first it may be hard to find very much. Most of us have the habit of taking for granted the positives like good health, a sense of humor, friends that we love, etc.. But *now* it is important to look at all of your assets, so practice that skill.

Once your list has been made of the things that you'll keep, make up a column of new goals. Some will be short-range and some will take time, but write them all down. On the first draft of your list, let your imagination go wild. For example:

### New Goals

1. Join a belly dancing class
2. Start a boarding home for single millionaires
3. Write your favorite movie star and announce that you're available
4.
5.
6.
7.

### Make Sure You Include

8. Finding new love interests
9. Building up employment skills
10. Creating new friendships
11. Developing dormant and obvious talents

If you have trouble coming up with ideas, look through magazines and books or check with some friends. When your list is complete, go back through the ideas and decide how long each project will take, plus the steps necessary to accomplish your goal. If you decide, for example, that you would like to become a real estate agent, check out the professional requirements and skills needed to do that, including availability of training and employment in your area.

Finally, it's time to decide which goals you will choose. Be careful not to set your ambitions so high that you fail. Put yourself in situations where you'll meet someone. But, on the other hand, never underestimate yourself or the heights you can reach.

## The Other Side Of Scary Is Excitement!

As you went through your list of new goals, you may have noticed the ones that were scary were also exciting. The idea of quitting a safe, secure job to start a small business of your own can be exciting, but still very frightening. The two feelings are closely connected. Sometimes the fear is of failure or embarrassment: "I'd like to do that but what if I fail?" And, sometimes, the fear comes from stepping out of a normal secure routine, like moving away from your old home.

The degrees of excitement vary with the amount of risk and change in routine that's involved. A teen-age boy who moves away from his parents' house into an apartment down the street, but comes home for meals, will be less excited about his freedom than the one who moves completely on his own to a new town. The one that stays near home is in reality less on his own two feet and taking fewer risks than the one who is away from his family completely.

Part of the good-bye process is leaving security and routine and saying hello to change and the unknown. It is natural for anyone in a transitional phase, including an ex-intimate, to feel afraid and excited, at times simultaneously.

As Geri related:

> "When I finally decided to leave Steve, I began thinking about all the different things I could do—go back to college, save some money, and go traveling. I had all kinds of ideas. But during the first few months, I traded actually doing some of those things for being afraid to try anything new. When I finally did begin taking some classes and short weekend trips to new places by myself, I not only enjoyed myself, but began feeling excited again."

The process is slow, and at first, if you're feeling numb or depressed, doing something new—meeting new friends, moving into a new neighborhood, or changing back to single status again—may just scare you and leave you depressed. But after a while you will begin feeling the excitement that creeps in along with the fears.

If you don't allow yourself to feel the excitement of change, it may mean that you're overloaded with feelings of failure and insecurity. Some of these feelings are a natural fallout from saying good-bye to an old love and a lifestyle of being part of a pair. Others may come from a basic sense of insecurity that was there before or during the "marriage" as well.

Many of these fears will lessen with time and with doing some things to help you feel a little more secure and less disconnected, such as: establishing your own new home, gaining support from friends, and building up your deflated ego. As you begin feeling a little less shaky about being single again, you will find, just as Geri did, that there will be times when you actually enjoy and are even excited about your new single status.

There's no doubt about it, the journey from leaving an ex-love and being part of a pair to enjoying single status and starting anew can be a painful and agonizing trip. In order to successfully reach your destination, you will need to bury the parts of your identity which have died. There is sadness in saying good-bye to these familiar pieces in your old existence, but to become a growing individual, you must let go of some of the old dead lifestyles and develop new, more functional ones for today and tomorrow.

**Experiments and Exercises**

This exercise will help you get in touch with and nurture your sense of relief over good-bye. Choose a time when you will not be interrupted or distracted by noise. Wear something comfortable and choose a comfortable body position.

● Go back through your memory of the past few days as if you were a movie camera and re-experience a time when you felt an inner calmness or sense of relief. Remember the scene: what had just happened—where you were—who was present. Try to re-experience the relief you felt then. Some people find it helpful to verbally state and repeat: "I'm relieved that it's over" until they finally feel the words in their bodies. Deep breathing exercises often help you learn to flow with your relief—practice taking slow, rhythmic, deep breaths.

During the next two days notice those times when you feel relieved and allow yourself to flow with that feeling.

Set aside some time each day (30 minutes or so) for the next month to enjoy your relief and calmness. As you continue practicing, you will find it easier to develop awareness of this feeling in you and will be able to recall it upon command.

Emptiness can be controlled as easily as your sense of relief, but requires experiencing your loss. Instead of running from sadness, pick a time when you decide that you feel "good" enough to allow yourself to feel your loss. Then, close your eyes and give yourself permission to feel your emptiness. (Sometimes repeating "I feel empty inside" helps your awareness). Go slowly and experience your pain in small doses. Cry when you feel like crying. If you get scared, pull yourself out. Some people find it helpful to tell themselves: "It's going to be okay _____, you're just feeling your hurt right now." As you repeat this phrase—or something similar—you will begin closing off your awareness of the emptiness in you.

After this exercise, take some time to reflect and ask:

● What did I learn from this about my *own* control over feeling empty?

● What can I do to fill up some of my emptiness? Would calling a friend help? How about developing some new goals? Taking the responsibility to begin loving someone new?

Following is a partial list of "energy guzzlers" ex-intimates unwittingly use to stop their growth. Go through it and note the ones you currently practice.

> Living in the past
> Bemoaning your fate
> Cutting down your self-esteem
> Wishing it hadn't happened and hoping it'll change
> Waiting by the telephone for ex-love to call
> Checking up on ex-mate
> Trying to get friends to take sides
> Pumping friends for information about ex-mate
> Staying too busy to allow self-awareness
> Skipping meals
> Not getting enough sleep
> Frantically searching for a new love

Go back through the list and pay attention to those energy guzzlers you have already dropped.

Now pick one you practice which you feel should be the easiest to give up and make a concerted effort to stop doing it for a week. Then constructively evaluate your progress.

From time to time go back through this list and work on one or two of these guzzlers until you no longer waste your time on any of them.

Use this space to jot down examples of when you got your feelings hurt or felt disappointed *but* were successful in getting over your hurt. Note how you did it—techniques or an attitude that was successful for you. Refer to this "resource" when you feel hurt the next time.

# 5

# HOW TO BUILD YOUR OWN BACKBONE

Building up your self-confidence isn't as difficult as you may fear. It requires some effort at first, especially if you're in the habit of cutting yourself down or finding other people to do it for you. But, with some concentration and a little bit of faith on your part, you can begin rebuilding your own "backbone"—that part of your character that protects your heart and your feelings from too much abuse.

By the time most ex-intimates have finally said good-bye they are, at best, discouraged about their own worthiness and their value as friend and lover. So, don't be discouraged when you feel like giving up and decide that resigning is what you'll do for awhile. Floundering is also part of saying good-bye to the past and hello to the future. To get beyond the floundering stage, you'll need to develop and use your own backbone.

## Getting Yourself In Proper Perspective

When the reality that the partnership is over finally hits you, you may feel a loss of identity and self-esteem—especially if the relationship was long or a trust was broken. Ex-intimates often walk in a daze not knowing who they are and questioning every part of their being. "Who am I really?" "I hate myself—I'm awful." We have already talked about many of the reasons for this: individuals viewing themselves as part of a pair rather than as separate people; the belief that togetherness is winning and single again is losing; and the erosion of self-esteem caused by a lack of respect and kindness in the latter part of a "marriage."

To rebuild your self-confidence, begin looking at yourself *realistically* rather than so judgmentally. You can't begin feeling better if you decide that you are basically worthless and deserve to be left alone. So, one of the first tasks at hand in building your backbone is to look at who you are without immediately condemning what you see.

To help you view your behavior more objectively, add your own examples to the following table:

| Judgment | Reality |
|---|---|
| 1. I was too quiet. | 1. Sometimes I don't talk. |
| 2. I should have been more understanding. | 2. I withdraw when I get scared or shout when my feelings get hurt. |
| 3. I never do anything right. | 3. Right now I'm discouraged. |
| 4. All I do is sit and feel sorry for myself. | 4. Sometimes I feel sad. |
| 5. I demanded too much. | 5. |
| 6. I'll never love again. | 6. |
| 7. | 7. |
| 8. | 8. |

Now, take some time to reflect on the lists in the table. What can you learn from them? During the next 48 hours pay attention to how often you weaken your own backbone with self-criticism. Then, practice the art of self-acceptance.

It's natural to evaluate the reasons your relationship ended, but do this when you begin feeling better about yourself. That way you can do something about changing the parts of you that may need improvement for the next intimate relationship. The automatic tendency to look at your mistakes in your old relationship when you're feeling low can overwhelm you. Therefore, set aside changing the faults that you find for another day.

When you begin looking at who you are, avoid comparing yourself with others or with the you you'd like to be. To decide that you'd like to be better than you are or like someone else, when you're feeling rejected, serves no constructive purpose.

So, at the beginning when your self-confidence is low, stop reinforcing your self-condemnation. Then, you'll discover the increasing strength of your courage and pride, both of which you'll need for growth during the mourning phase.

## How To Give Up Your Ex-Love's Total Perception Of You

No one lives in a vacuum. We gain much of our image of who we are and how we fit into the world from those around us. The closer someone is, the more important that person's opinion becomes. It begins as children when our parents tell us by their words and actions what they think. If they tell us we're worthwhile, we believe it, and if they tell us we're bad and will always get into trouble, we see ourselves in that light.

For example, if your parents told you that you couldn't be trusted, you probably began to believe that. You may have looked for examples of times when you did something dishonest like cheating on a test for fear of failure as *proof* of your parents' opinion that you could not be trusted, rather than as an example of your own normal need for success.

But children are not born "good" or "bad"; they are molded into their parents' fears or views of what they'll be like. I suspect that most of us, as adults, already know how easy it is to believe our parents' perception of us and the world, and how difficult it is to make up our minds while seeing their opinions as the results of a similar process. As a matter of fact, many people never give up their parents' ideas and marry someone just like their mother or father.

In any event, it's obvious to most of us that we human beings often believe other people's opinion of us and sometimes accept it as our own. This is just as true for ex-intimates as it is for children with parents. By the time you finally say good-bye, you may believe a number of negative things about yourself which are not necessarily true. Giving up your ex-love's negative perception of you will be hard, but necessary, to build up your self-esteem and to see yourself as you really are.

Letting go of your ex-love's image of yourself requires several steps. First and foremost, you *must* learn to see your ex-mate as a human being with strengths *and* frailties—not as a god without faults. Once you have taken your ex-love out of the god category, begin looking at all of the things he or she said about you. Include the positive along with the negative and your table may look something like this:

| Good | Bad |
|---|---|
| 1. Warm, loving | 1. Too dependent on others to feel good |
| 2. Outgoing, makes friends easily | 2. Superficial |
| 3. Good sense of humor | 3. Dishonest |
| 4. Easy going | 4. Irresponsible |
| 5. Good looking | 5. Too concerned about appearance |
| *Now Add Some Of Your Own* | |
| 6. | 6. |
| 7. | 7. |
| 8. | 8. |
| 9. | 9. |

When your table is complete, you may discover that most of the items are value judgments rather than facts and that some of the things that were seen as "good" in one situation may also be seen as "bad" in another light. In any event, many of these images you will automatically discard as not valid because you do not believe that they are true. Keep the positive ones and build on them. The negative ones that you retain will probably be those which you fear are accurate. If you decide that they are parts of you which you believe to be true, *admit* them. Then decide whether you can change them or not. Some will be possible to change, others you will have to learn to live with.

The important thing to remember in building your own backbone is that all of your ex-love's viewpoints of you (or anybody else's for that matter) cannot be *totally* accurate or unbiased. Someone can say certain things about you which you decide are true, but that does not mean everything he or she says is gospel or would be true if you had a different kind of partner. For example, a woman may not be a nag if the man follows through on his responsibilities. Or, a man may not be unfaithful if his partner is loving and warm.

With practice you should be able to separate your ex-love's perception of you from your own feelings about yourself. As time progresses and you find yourself saying "She told me this was true" or "He always said I was like that," see if you can't stop yourself and look at whether the statement is really true or just your own fear, coupled with his or her opinion that it's a fact.

## Developing Your Own Self-Perception

If you have followed the advice in the first part of this chapter, you are already in the process of rebuilding your backbone.

The next step is to look at your self-image because whether you are aware of it or not, *this* controls your capacity to grow. It includes all of the different facts and roles of your existence: sex, age, nationality, religion, occupation, lover, friend, relative, plus your feelings about each one of them.

List *all* the different parts of you—and, across from each, state how you *feel* about it. For example, a man's list might look like the following table:

| Parts of me | My feelings about each |
|---|---|
| Male, Caucasian | Okay. |
| Late forties | A little scared of getting old. |
| Insurance man | Okay, but sometimes I worry about the money—takes a lot of energy to make sales. |
| Italian, Catholic | I'm a little too traditional and old fashioned. My head's filled with a lot of "shoulds." |
| Physical appearance | Not bad; worry a lot about my hairline and weight—feel fat. |
| Divorced | It's wrong. I feel ashamed; it's against my religion. |
| Father: 2 sons | I should be with them now; they need a man. |
| Intelligence | I'd like to be smarter; wish I'd gone to college. |
| Fears | Afraid of failure, getting in over my head, getting hurt. |
| Personality | Pleasant; usually kind to those I love. Dependable; sometimes short-tempered. |

Make your own *word self-portrait*, using this format:

| Parts of me | My feelings about each |
|---|---|
| 1. | 1. |
| 2. | 2. |
| 3. | 3. |
| 4. | 4. |
| 5. | 5. |
| 6. | 6. |
| 7. | 7. |
| 8. | 8. |
| 9. | 9. |

As your list expands, review it for self-condemnation. One of the ideals you may have to give up is your wish to be perfect. And what you might substitute is a compassionate self-acceptance that doesn't deteriorate into complacency but is receptive to growth and change.

In fact, you may also discover that your self-image varies from day to day. When things seem to be going well, you will feel better about yourself. When you're scared or feel rejected, it is natural to be more critical of yourself and therefore weaken your self-esteem.

The best way to gain an objective (and more accurate) picture of yourself is to complete your word portrait *twice:* once when you're feeling down and the second time when you're feeling good. That way you'll be able to see for yourself just how much your self-perception fluctuates with your mood.

When you fill out your portraits make sure to include *all* of the different factors that make you a unique individual. Many ex-intimates discover that they have gotten so wrapped up in their role as an ex-lover or a divorcee that they have forgotten all the other parts of them.

## Get Feedback From Others

Once you identify how you see yourself, look around and begin to notice how others perceive you. How do people usually react to you? Of course there are exceptions, but, in general, do they treat you with respect or are you normally stepped on by others? Do people ask you for your opinion or are you usually given someone else's?

Now, get a little more specific and list the names of your co-workers, friends, and family members and jot down how you think they treat you. Use the following format:

| Name | How he/she treats me |
|------|----------------------|
| 1.   | 1.                   |
| 2.   | 2.                   |
| 3.   | 3.                   |
| 4.   | 4.                   |
| 5.   | 5.                   |
| 6.   | 6.                   |

Take some time to reflect on the results. What can you learn from this? Do they treat others this way or only you? Make sure when you look at this information that you look at it with a fair amount of objectivity. Don't wait until you're feeling inferior to see if everyone else sees you that way too.

Ask friends how they see you in specific instances, i.e.: "Do you see me as quiet or outgoing?"; "Can you tell that I'm a warm and caring person?"; "I have the feeling I'm over my head in this project, what's your opinion?" Use your common sense and don't ask someone you're having a quarrel with or a person who is obviously involved in his or her own worries or fears. At first your friends may be caught off guard by your questions, but explain you are gathering information for your own interest to see how others view you. Tell them you're serious and you really do want to learn something about yourself and you think they can help you.

Although asking someone specifically how they view certain parts of you may be scary, the reality is we unconsciously make decisions about how others see us without finding out for sure how they feel. We assume a number of things about people's judgment of ourselves, and many of these assumptions are inaccurate. Usually we assume a much more critical stance than our friends would take. And, in building your own backbone, it is important to find out as objectively as possible how other people see you.

## Match Inner- and Other-Directed Perceptions

After you've gained some information about how others see you by asking them directly, study it. Choose a time when you think you can look at the comments objectively.

The first thing you will find is that each person views you in a slightly different light. This is true because no two people see *anyone* in exactly the same way, and, groups of individuals will see you in different roles. For example, an elementary school teacher will be viewed in a different role by his students than he will by his colleagues, family, or members of his bowling team. While his ten-year-old students may see him as a formidable figure, his mother may still view him as her little boy. In spite of these factors, you will find a consensus on how you generally come across in each role. Most students, for instance, will see their fifth-grade teacher in a certain way.

The next step in building your backbone is to match your own ideas of how you come across with other people's general viewpoints. The teacher, for example, might list the following:

| How I See Myself As: | How Others See Me: |
|---|---|
| *A teacher:* Pretty good; sometimes boring | *My students:* Good; makes learning fun |
| *A colleague:* Okay, but too quiet | *My colleague:* Bright, respected, dependable |
| *A son;* Good, but not loving enough | *My parents:* Proud of him; enjoy his company; trust him |
| *A bowler;* Average | *My bowling team:* Good bowler, fun, a leader |

Notice that the teacher sees himself much more negatively than others do, even when his overall perception is favorable. In every role he has focused more on his frailties than others have. This is a common human characteristic—to pay more attention to the parts of us that still aren't exactly the way we want them.

Following the example above, use the form below to list and compare your self-perception with the opinion of others.

| *How I see myself as:* | *How others see me:* |
|---|---|
| 1. | 1. |
| 2. | 2. |
| 3. | 3. |
| 4. | 4. |
| 5. | 5. |
| 6. | 6. |
| 7. | 7. |

Now take some time to reflect. What can you learn from this?

The purpose of matching other peoples' viewpoints with your own is to help you see a broader, more objective picture of yourself. In doing this, you will strengthen your self-esteem and, therefore, your backbone.

## How To Develop a Self-Improvement Priority List

In looking over your self-image and others' image of you, you may come up with areas that you feel need to be improved. It is important not to be overwhelmed by all the things you feel you *should* change. The easiest way to do this is to develop a priority list: a list of behaviors or specific personality traits that you *know* are self-defeating. For example, you might jot down: broadening your sense of humor, strengthening your ability to follow through on tasks you usually give up on, or learning to spend time alone creatively. List in the following manner those things you decide that you would like to improve:

*Things I could change*

1.
2.
3.
4.
5.

Choose one item from your list and begin finding ways you can change it. Let's say, for example, that the first thing you decide to change is your tendency to take things too seriously. Begin reflecting on all the ways in your daily living that small, really unimportant scenes in your life become major catastrophes. The toast gets burned, someone darts into your parking space, and you're ten minutes late for an appointment, someone doesn't call and ask you out for dinner and you hoped he would. Your response is really your own choice: you can make these very significant events in your day, or see them as unimportant. Why not try placing them in the realm of events which are disappointing but not catastrophic? Then, practice responding to them in that manner. Learn how to scrape off black toast and cover it with jelly. Learn how to put your car in reverse out of simple expedience rather than explosive frustration, and go look for another parking space. Practice the art of apologizing when you can't make an appointment on time. Find ways to spend your free time creatively by yourself without depending upon someone else's beckoning.

It will take time and a lot of effort to change a personality trait such as taking things too seriously. In fact, you will find that, initially, it's more automatic to revert to your old practice than to strengthen your new skill. Expect a certain amount of failure. If, in just one out of ten attempts you are able to change your habit of taking disappointments too seriously, that is an improvement.

Do things on a day-to-day basis and one at a time. That way you will be more effective, because the greater the number of things you try to change at once the less you will accomplish. Give yourself credit for each success—no matter how minor it might appear to be—because the task you are attempting is one of the most difficult, and yet most rewarding: self-determined growth.

## How To Build On Strengths

So far in this chapter we've spent a great deal of time talking about weaknesses and very little space on the parts of you that you already like. The first step in building on your strengths is to recognize that they exist. Use the space provided to jot down what you *like* about yourself: the physical parts of you that are attractive, your health if it's good, the skills and talents you have that you're proud of, and all the positive qualities that help make you special. Write them *all* down—this is no time to be modest or shy, you're the only one that will see the list and it should be as complete as possible to be useful.

Things I like about me
1.
2.
3.
4.
5.
6.
7.
8.
9.
10.

Once your list is complete, go through it and pat yourself on the back for each item. I know that may sound silly, but don't forget that you compliment others for their positive qualities. (If you don't, they feel unappreciated.) Well, don't neglect yourself with praise. Go ahead and give yourself some applause. Do that each time you notice in your daily living that you've done something well again.

Once you've discovered your strengths, begin to use them more often. Wear the clothes you look best in. If you're a good cook, bake sonething for a friend or treat yourself to a gourmet meal. If you like the part of you that helps people, volunteer or get a job helping out at a hospital, children's home or convalescent facility. If you appreciate nature, spend extra time at the park, down by the river or out in the country. If you enjoy a sense of humor, read, write or tell comical stories.

Learn to put yourself in situations where you *know* you will do well. Nothing builds up your confidence more quickly than doing something well and giving yourself a pat on the back for your own success.

## How To Corral and Tame Frailties

Learning to corral and tame your frailties involves five major steps: recognizing what they are, putting them in proper perspective, understanding and forgiving yourself, changing the frailties that you can, and learning to live with the rest.

For our purposes I will define a frailty as a piece of behavior that gets you in trouble with yourself or other people. Your frailties are parts of you that are most often criticized by yourself or others. Included among frailties are: drinking excessively, overeating, a quick temper, hiding from people, lying, failing to follow through on responsibilities, putting off decisions, getting others to make them for you, or, at the other extreme, expecting too much from yourself or being too critical. Almost any behavior or trait that you have which you see as a "fault" can be included in this category.

The *first* step is to recognize which ones you have. You will find some of these on your priority list of things you would like to improve. To show step by step how you might conquer a frailty, let us say that one of your faults is a quick temper.

After you have identified that this is a problem for you, the second thing you need to do is look at how often you lose your temper and what happens when you do. Do you fly off the handle every time someone says something that you don't like or any time you don't get your way? Or are there times when you feel like exploding, but control it? Look back over the last week and see how many times you actually exploded versus the times you did not. This will give you an idea of just how big and uncontrollable the problem is for you. Now look at what you do when you lose your temper. Do you physically strike out or explode verbally? How often do you stomp away from a fight? There are a number of ways in which people lose their tempers, and it is important for you to understand *specifically* what you do when you've lost yours and whether that behavior varies. Once you have answered these questions, you will not only have an understanding of the specific problem, but will surely recognize that you do not, in fact, have an uncontrollable temper and that your temper is not your total personality. This is an important realization because it sheds some reality on the fear you may have that your temper always controls you and that there is nothing you can do about any part of it.

The *third* step in taming a frailty is to understand and forgive yourself for owning this "fault." Developing an understanding requires finding out why you do what you do. In the case of a quick temper, look back over each incident during the last week and determine what you were fighting for. You may discover that you were fighting for someone to recognize your opinion as valid or to see you as someone to respect, not to use or put down. If this is the case, it should be easy to forgive yourself. All of us want to feel that we're valuable, and damning yourself for having human needs will not make them go away. You will find that most faults, when you understand *why* you have them, are easy to forgive because they are usually defense mechanisms we develop to protect ourselves from pain.

After you understand and forgive yourself for a frailty, the *fourth* step is to see how you can change it. Even though a quick temper, for example, may be understandable, it can get you into more trouble than it's worth. In fact, some of your frailties may actually *compound* the problem and make it worse. The more often you fly off the handle, for example, the more frequently you are given disrespect by others. Therefore, admit the value of changing a behavior that gets you in trouble. If you don't think it's worth your effort to change—you won't.

Learning to change a frailty is a matter of finding out what value the behavior has for you and then finding constructive ways of attaining the same goal. If, for example, you found yourself shouting at your boss last Wednesday because he questioned a decision you made, you may want to look at what you can do to feel better about yourself as an employee. There are other ways to gain respect from your boss besides shouting at him for questioning you. Or maybe you threw down a ceramic pot you were making because it didn't turn out the way you wanted. Perhaps a better idea would be to learn how to walk away from tasks that are frustrating until you can calm down or figure out exactly how to do them. Or, if the goal in ceramics is to create something which thereby helps you feel worthwhile, it's a better idea to find something that's more suited to your talents. The point is that once you find what the goals in your behavior are, it is possible to gain the same goals by altering your behavior.

There will be times when, no matter how hard you try, you will continue to have the same frailties. Some of them you will be able to tame but not get rid of entirely. You will have to learn how to live with these. In the case of a quick temper, you learn to live with this by knowing that you have one and trying as much as possible to keep yourself out of situations where you'll lose control of it.

Try these suggestions faithfully for a week or two on one of your frailties. You will begin to notice that you have the ability and power to change or improve almost any "fault" you own.

## How To Protect Your Vulnerable Spots

Learning to protect your vulnerable spots is a worthwhile skill for anyone and especially for ex-intimates who may feel emotionally fragile. Vulnerable spots are the wounds in your self-esteem, pride, or identity which have been reopened or were created by the ending of an intimate relationship.

The first step in protecting your vulnerable spots is to

recognize that there are certain scenes which will cause additional pain to your pride—at least until the wounds are healed. Seeing your ex-love with someone new, hearing your children call someone else Mommy or Daddy, listening to your old love songs, seeing the old house that used to be yours, going back to your favorite places alone or, oddly enough, trying to love someone new too quickly.

The best way to protect yourself from these additional blows to your pride is to *avoid* as many of them as you can. Do not purposely place yourself in any of these scenes before the wounds begin to heal. Those that you cannot avoid, face with an understanding friend or relative, if that's possible. Take someone with you for moral support when you have to go back to your old house and pick up your furniture. Don't go alone to your favorite old haunts unless you have decided that you really want to feel extra pain again.

Finally, there will be times when you can neither avoid a scene nor take someone with you to cushion the impact. When those times occur, prepare yourself by doing something that helps you feel worthwhile. Make sure that you at least feel as if you look well for the scene. And, after it's over, go visit a friend or reward yourself with a special treat. For example, plan beforehand what you will do *after* you see your in-laws for the first time. That way you can go automatically from the painful scene to a pleasurable one.

Gradually, as the wounds begin to heal, you will no longer need to protect them from additional blows. As time goes by and your backbone strengthens, you will discover that less from your past causes pain in your present.

## How To Develop Your Latent Talents

A hobby, even if it's training your dog, gives you a chance to focus your attention outside of yourself. Additionally, it can act as a diversion when you're feeling down—a vehicle for the expression of pent-up feelings and frustrations—and be productive or creative, thus giving you an ego-building end product.

Take the time to develop a new hobby or go back to an old one. Dust off the old paint brushes, crochet hooks, or wood-carving tools and get busy making something again. If you've never had a hobby before, visit an arts and crafts store for ideas or leaf through the leisure-time magazines at the supermarket. Many department stores, local "Y's," adult-education centers, craft centers, local colleges, and high schools offer classes in leisure-time activities.

Initially you may hesitate to try something new, figuring that you don't have the time or assuming that either you won't do well or you'll get bored. But, as you begin actually doing something new (whether it's making grandfather clocks, casting jewelry, or tinkering with your car), you'll discover that you are enjoying it and you will begin taking pride in those latent talents you didn't even know existed.

## How To Use Anger To Get You Moving

In spite of the fears you may have about anger, it can be a very constructive energy source. It is the energy your pride calls on to help you stand up for yourself and meet new challenges. It is the strength in your backbone that keeps you straight when you would otherwise collapse. It is, in fact, such a valuable source of personal power that all of Chapter 12 is devoted to it. For the purposes of this chapter, however, let's look at some ways you can recognize and use your anger to help your strengthened backbone walk away from people who stomp on your feelings or poke holes in your self-esteem.

By now you should know that you are neither as bad nor as helpless to change your sadness as you sometimes fear. With that knowledge, you may begin to feel a surge of energy, a flash in your gut, or to hear a voice in your head that periodically tells you it's time to stop feeling bad and start living again. Even *you* are getting tired of cutting yourself down or letting other people do it for you. Gradually this feeling will come back again, even louder and stronger, until you finally decide on a conscious level to do something about it. Each time you do something to build up your self-esteem, it will grow stronger until finally your need to punish yourself for losing your ex-love will be defeated by your natural desire to feel better.

All of this takes time. Your feelings will come and go. One hour you may be wallowing in sorrow and loneliness, and the next you may decide that you need to get out of your house and go to the park or visit a friend. Use your energy to do that. Don't just sit there until the idea is buried with self-doubt again.

Every time you stop demoralizing yourself, shake off a nagging self-doubt, or walk away from someone who's cutting you down, your anger is the energy that helps you. It acts as a defense mechanism to protect your self-confidence from unfair blows. The voice in your head that tells you to try something new or to fix yourself up will need your anger to get you moving. Ambition, some say, is merely the direction that anger takes in the spirit of revenge.

**Experiments and Exercises**

Below is a list of ways people build their self-esteem: Check (✓) those you are currently aware of using and put an (x) beside those you decide to try in addition.

——— Take care of my health.
——— Keep physically active.
——— Keep myself well-groomed and physically attractive.
——— Wear clothing I feel good in.
——— Compliment myself when I do something well.

___ Treat myself as I would my best friend.
___ Take pride in my traits and strengths I enjoy.
___ Stand up for my "rights."
___ Understand and accept myself for making mistakes.
___ Refuse to condemn myself for frailties.
___ Do one thing a day that makes me feel good about me.
___ Entertain friends at my house occasionally.
___ Help other people.
___ Allow others to help me.
___ Develop my talents.
___ Increase my job skills.
___ Develop my interest in the community.
___ Enjoy a hobby.
___ Use my anger as motivation and ambition.

Now look at those you have marked:

- What can you learn from each?

- Pick one or two items to begin practicing this week.

As you read through the book, periodically review this check list to evaluate how constructively you are trying to build up your self-esteem. When you find yourself "slacking off," take the responsibility to invest more energy in you.

List ways you have lowered your self-esteem in the last 48 hours (for example, agreeing to someone's criticism of you without looking at whether it was factual).
1.
2.
3.
4.
5.

Now take some time to reflect on your list:

- What can you learn from this?

- In the next two days try to be aware of how you make yourself feel bad about you.

- What can you do about this?

On a separate sheet of paper make a word portrait of how your ex-mate sees you. Are you seen as happy or sad? Bright or dull? What colors would be used to describe you—warm? cool? earthy? natural? What parts of you are emphasized—your mind? eyes? ears? mouth? back? hands? genitals? legs? what? Is your total body acknowledged or just part of it? Are you on a pedestal? level with others? below everyone? Are you standing up straight or bent over?

Use separate sheets of paper to make word portraits of the way other significant people in your life see you (your parents, children, co-workers, friends, etc.) Use the same format as before.

Make a *self*-portrait the same way as you did the others.

After you have finished these word portraits take some time to reflect:

- What can you learn from these "drawings"?
- Is there a pattern in them?
- Are the "other" portraits consistent with how you see yourself? How do they differ?

Increasing self-confidence and self-reliance is often a matter of becoming aware of your own inner strengths. Before going to sleep each night repeat one of the following statements until you can feel it in your body.

"I am courage."

"I am a loving being."
"I am pride."
"I am creativity."
"I am important."
"I am peace."
"I am optimism."
"I am safety."

The following exercises will help you develop body awareness and/or learn to relax. Choose a time and place that is physically comfortable for you—where you will *not* be distracted. Read these instructions into a tape recorder; then play them back while you practice. You may need to practice these exercises several times before you can actually allow yourself to experience them. Practice them when you genuinely want to and *don't* push yourself to relax. Set aside 30 minutes or so to experience any of the following:

## For relaxation

● By focusing your attention on the automatic process of breathing, you can achieve a blissful state of deep relaxation and detached body awareness.

1. Become aware of how you breathe. Allow yourself to inhale and exhale as you normally would. You may discover that you breathe smoothly or hesitantly, deeply or shallowly, rhythmically or erratically. *Don't change how you breathe.* Just become aware of it.

2. Now notice whether you inhale and exhale smoothly with balance and rhythm. Try to *smooth* the irregularities in the flow without strain or force.

3. Notice how deeply you breathe. Try to gradually *increase* the depth of your breathing.

4. Now concentrate on the rate at which you are breathing. See if you can *gradually slow down* your breathing. Continue this experiment for a few minutes to establish a pattern of smooth, deep, slow breathing. Then, just flow with your calmness.

● You can relax with relative ease by physically tightening and releasing all the muscles in your body.

1. Sit on the floor and curl up in a ball. Then contract—tightening all the muscles in your body. Scrunch up your face, squeeze closed your toes, fingers, arms, legs, thighs, etc.. Hold this position until it becomes absolutely unbearable. Keep tightening all the muscles that loosen.

2. Now release and instantly do the reverse: stretch on the floor as much as you can. Arch your back. Spread your toes and fingers. Pull apart your elbows, shoulders, ankles, knees. Stretch your face. Open wide your eyes and mouth. Stick out your tongue. Hold for a minute or two.

3. Release and breathe deeply and slowly. A great wave of peace is almost certain to come over you.

**Releasing tension**

● Emotional tension in the form of body tightness/pressure houses itself in many parts of the body: temples, jaw, back of the neck, shoulders, arms, legs, knees, etc.. To release your own internal tightness, focus your attention on your body. Become aware of any internal stiffness or pressures. When you discover your tense or pressured "spot," concentrate on that area and gradually increase the tension until it is as "tight" as you can make it (as you did in the tighten and release exercise). Then hold that tightness until it becomes unbearable. After a minute or two release the pressure. Then take a few minutes to breathe slowly and deeply. Many people find that with practice, they are able to let go permanently of their internal tightness.

**Anxiety**

Anxiety is often experienced physiologically as a "shakiness" which many people attempt to control by trying *not* to shake. To effectively release your anxiety, try the following:

Become aware of where your anxiety shows up in you—hands shaking, nervous tic, "butterflies in stomach," arms or legs shaking. Once you are aware of your shakiness, concentrate on it and exaggerate it. Try to let yourself go until you are shaking all over and meanwhile try to give up all your rigidity. When you're through you are likely to feel refreshed and relaxed. Take a few minutes to breathe slowly and deeply.

# 6

## GAINING STRENGTH OUTSIDE YOURSELF

Some of the special qualities about people who have loved before are their abilities to care about others, trust in the value of relationships, and have a basic belief in the intrinsic value of life. It may be difficult to see these qualities as helpful, when you're feeling demoralized by your loss or sabotaged by your heart. Initially, many ex-intimates damn their vulnerability and vow they will never care about anyone or anything again. "If only I hadn't loved and trusted so much, I wouldn't be hurting now" is the common thought to have, as in the desire to die or give up on ever feeling good again. But, in spite of this pain and emptiness (or maybe because of it), ex-intimates will discover they almost instinctively begin searching for someone or something outside of themselves for additional emotional support to make them feel better again. They turn to everything from liquor to religion, with people in between.

## How To Get Emotional Support From Old Friends, Family, and Acquaintances

One of the reasons that saying good-bye to an old love is so painful is that we usually say good-bye to some of our old friends in the process. But, in spite of losing some friends, there will be those whose friendships you will keep and cherish all the more.

If you know how to gain their support, old friends, family, and acquaintances are a valuable source of emotional strength during the mourning process and especially in the first few weeks. They can help you soothe your shattered pride and fill up some of the emptiness by letting you know that you are still lovable and worthwhile—and not totally alone in the world. They do this by their words and actions, and by being "friends." Some will take the initiative to contact you. Others, because of their uncertainty about how you feel, will wait for you to make the first move.

It's important for you to decide what kind of relationship you want with your friends now. This may be easier for you to decide with the friends that you know separately than those who are mutual friends with your ex-love. Friendships with people whom you know from work, school, or other outside interests and those whom you knew before your "marriage" began will probably be the easiest to maintain or nurture. These friends will automatically offer you emotional support because they have little or no connection with your ex-love, and, therefore, feel no pressure to "take sides" or get the two of you back together again. You are their friend, and since you are hurting, they will want to reach out. You will need to do little to encourage their support besides maintain your usual charm and accept their concern. Listen to the positive feedback they give you and give yourself permission to believe it. Do not abuse their support by constantly complaining about your plight or expecting them to take total responsibility for helping you feel better again. Also, beware of pushing your old friends away by burdening them with your expressions of bitterness or self-pity.

Mutual friends that see you as part of a pair may have trouble viewing you as a separate person. They may feel the need to take sides or to support one of you by attacking the other. Although this may initially feel good if you are the one they support, you will find in the long run that their opinion about whether you're the "good guy" or not will actually do very little to build up your self-esteem or fill up your emptiness. With mutual friends it will be important for you to clearly define what kind of relationship you want, and then see whether that's possible. You may say, for example: "Even though John (or Jill) and I have ended, I would still like to have a relationship with you—maybe have dinner together or see a show occasionally. How does that sound to you?" It will be important to let your friends know directly that you do not want them to take sides. The break-up of your "marriage" will affect your mutual friends, and it may not be possible for the friendships to continue. Perhaps you might wait for some time to pass before you decide to resume certain friendships—especially with other couples. After all, the first few times you see another pair that the two of you used to enjoy seeing together, you might discover that many of the memories of your ex-love will surge painfully forward again.

Relatives, like your other friends, can be extremely helpful to your shattered ego or your feelings of being disconnected from the world. Your own relatives, with few exceptions, will no doubt stand by your side, even if they do not approve of the "divorce." In fact, many ex-intimates actually move in with their relatives during the first few weeks of grieving or count on their family for financial support. As with your friends, it's important not to abuse your family and to use your own backbone plus any strength they may offer to help you feel better again. You can quickly wear out your welcome by taking their friendship for granted.

Relatives of your ex-love are another matter. Don't be surprised or feel personally assaulted if relatives of your ex-love, who used to be warm and caring to you, suddenly turn cold and rejecting. Unless there is a definite reason, such as children, to maintain a relationship with your ex-inlaws, it's better to sever the relationships—at least until the wounds are healed and *both* of you have started a new life.

## How To Get Ego-Building Feedback From New Friends

One of the scary but worthwhile adventures of saying good-bye to your past and your ex-love is the opportunity to meet, develop, and enjoy new friends and relationships. With the change in your status (and maybe even your environment) and the loss of many old friends, making new friends will be a necessity. What's more, just the act of making new friends will give your ego a boost by proving to yourself in the practice that people like you.

But obviously, before you can make new friendships, you will first have to be in a position where you can meet new people. If you move to another neighborhood or get a new job, the opportunity is there. Apartments are filled with a number of ex-intimates in a similar position. Choose an apartment rather than a house in the country for meeting new people. If you stay in your neighborhood and continue with your old job, look for leisure-time activity settings as a place to meet new folks: classes in night school or college, volunteer organizations, political parties, singles clubs, churches, and last, but most tricky, night clubs and bars. All of them can provide the settings.

Once you are physically in situations where new people are present, give up fighting for emotional support in a loud demanding voice. Practice a smile and an attitude which will signal to others that you are worth meeting. Give up feeling sorry for yourself or complaining to new friends about the "raw deal" you got from your ex-love. Few people are instantly attracted to pessimists or complainers, and your new friends aren't going to know that your total personality isn't gloomy if you don't also let them see the positive parts of yours. As an ex-intimate, you have the advantage of caring about others and believing in the value of relationships, or you would never have gotten involved with your ex-love. Use this strength in developing new friendships. Let the caring side of you show. Learn how to be interested in others and practice that skill; it's a marvelous way to make new friends and get outside of yourself and your worries.

A relationship (new or old) should be developed with people you like for mutual enjoyment rather than from a desire on your part to meet someone new to abuse or drain. With a mutually satisfying bond, you will automatically gain emotional strength as well as pleasant company to enjoy leisure-time activities.

## How To Make Yourself Look Better

Attracting new friends or retaining the old ones will not be easy if you feel unattractive. So, if you feel like hiding rather then meeting new people, it might be a good idea to refurbish your physical appearance. Actually, it's a good idea to improve your appearance even if you don't feel like hiding because a new beginning justifiably demands it! With the exception of major overhauls, like gaining or losing excessive amounts of weight, there are things that you (and most people) can do rather quickly to help make you look better.

Begin by taking an inventory of yourself and your wardrobe. Start at the top with your hair and end with your ankles. Take note of your good points as well as the parts of you which could use some improvement. Think about changing the style of your hair, going on a diet and toning up your muscles by getting in some physical activities. Go to a hairstyler, join a physical fitness program, or leaf through some magazines for ideas about accentuating the positive parts of your appearance and de-emphasizing the negative ones.

Now for your wardrobe. Go to a color analyst and have your colors done. Add a little flair! Brighter colors make you look livelier; dull colors can make you look washed out or drab. Keep looking around and trying on clothes until you find something that helps you look absolutely smashing!

## How To Gain Positive Feedback At Work

An occupation can be an invaluable resource for gaining additional strength and emotional support. It is especially valuable for ex-intimates who feel like a failure at the end of a love relationship and have a tendency to withdraw into themselves. Many ex-intimates acclaim the value of working as a resource that saved them from despair. "If it wasn't for my job, I think I would have gone crazy or killed myself" is a common statement. Work gives you a routine to follow, a place to go during the day, and a feeling of still being connected to the world.

If you don't have a job, think about getting one. In spite of fears you may have about not being qualified, you will find, if you put enough energy into actually becoming employed, that it can be an invaluable resource for helping you to feel better again. There are several employment and training agencies available to help you, and day-care centers for your children.

If you already have a job and find it emotionally satisfying, keep it for awhile and utilize whatever ego-building support it may offer. Try not to change jobs immediately after you've said good-bye to your ex-love. You will find that the stability of a known routine will be helpful emotionally during the first few days or weeks. This is not to suggest that you remain stagnant professionally. The ending of an intimate relationship often acts as a catalyst for people to examine their lifetime goals. Many ex-intimates change or develop careers after they've grown through the grief process. One lady I know went back to college and subsequently became an elementary school teacher—after twenty-four years of marriage. Another woman, age twenty-five, with two little children and eight years of a self-destructive marriage, enrolled in nursing school and became a registered nurse. A forty-five-year-old man was kicked out of a twenty-one-year marriage and subsequently evolved from an office manager in a large computer business to an agent opening his own insurance business.

To ensure getting positive feedback from a job, make sure that you work in a manner which will merit approval. Keep yourself physically attractive, be punctual for appointments, put effort into improving your skills, and follow the suggestions for gaining support from your friends in relating to your co-workers. Avoid the natural tendency of allowing everything to fall apart, including your job, while you wallow in feelings of self-pity and rejection. At first, you may need to concentrate on doing your job well. But you will find that the energy is well spent for the rewards you will earn.

## Getting the Most Out Of Inspirational Literature

Many people who are down gain emotional strength by reading and applying inspirational literature to their own lives. Inspirational literature can include everything from sagas of people who overcome handicaps and the power of positive thinking to philosophical writings by nineteenth-century transcendentalists like Henry David Thoreau and Ralph Waldo Emerson, who spoke on the merits of individualism and self-reliance. Humanists from the 1970s, such as Dr. Carl Rogers who acclaims the idea of accepting yourself as a person, and armchair philosophers like Dr. Jess Lair who authored the book "I Ain't Much Baby, But I'm All I've Got" offer people-oriented ideals which inspire millions.

Perhaps you'll be inspired to look for the beauty in others and in your world, despite the disillusion or disappointment you may harbor from the death of an intimate relationship. Look beyond the phoniness in others or yourself for the parts that are honest and real and nurture them. Set aside your broken dreams of love everlasting with your ex-love and begin replacing them with dreams for the future you can build on today. Be realistic and cautious in selecting your dreams or planning for your future, but always strive to be happy. Each day of your life, take the time to see the beauty in yourself and the world.

## Gaining Strength From Others In a Similar Situation

Getting together with people who have similar problems and sharing ideas about how to feel better can be a tremendous source of strength. Anyone who has ever confronted a problem or felt hurt and confused, isolated, or scared can tell you what a relief it is just to *share* his feelings with someone else who "knows what it's like to feel that way." Ex-intimates often gain a great deal of emotional strength and practical support from others who are in the same psychological "boat."

It's hard to feel alone in the world if the person you're talking to knows exactly what it's like to feel a failure at love—or to be rejected—or to walk out of a relationship and feel guilty. It's emotionally uplifting to meet someone else who looks "okay," but is also living alone again. It's easier to talk with someone who has gone through the same thing. You don't have to feel foolish or embarrassed—to feel the need to justify your actions. Some things you don't have to divulge painfully all at once. You say, somewhat hesitantly, to the man you've just met, "I'm divorced," and automatically you can see in his eyes that he knows some of what you may be feeling. There's a sense of relief that settles in your body when he replies, "So am I," thereby lifting the pressures of self-condemnation and the fear of how your listener will judge you. You can then begin talking about what it's like for you to be single again. Maybe later, he'll share a couple of answers that worked for him when the question of

"Will I always be alone?" arose, or perhaps he'll offer his friendship because he feels a kinship with you. Definitely, this is a source of strength! You can gain empathy for your scary feelings, companionship when you're alone but don't want to be, courage from watching others in the same predicament feel better, knowledge on how to help your children cope with their feelings about divorce, and a sense of being needed again when you help someone else.

The strength you can gain from other ex-intimates while you're growing through the grief process can be invaluable if, as with any other resource, you know where to seek and how to go about getting support, as well as how to filter out the "garbage" (their own cynicism, bitterness, or self-destructive behavior, like alcohol abuse).

There are a variety of settings where you can meet other ex-intimates who are already giving and getting additional emotional strength and practical advice on problems that arise from being single again. Singles' clubs and national organizations like Parents without Partners, the Singletons, and the Junior Officers and Professional Association are just a few of the groups that are designed specifically for you.

Another resource for helping ex-intimates gain strength from each other is group therapy sessions specifically aimed at the problems of being single again. These sessions are usually led by a mental health professional and are available through community agencies such as the YMCA or through private clinics and counselors. The time and cost of these sessions may vary from 1½ hours a week for a specific number of weeks to all-day or weekend marathons, with prices ranging anywhere from free to very expensive.

Community colleges have begun to offer classes for single adults on living alone. Such subjects as loneliness, human sexuality, housekeeping for men, and mechanical skills for women are just a few of the courses available through night school.

If there are no singles' groups available in your town, start one yourself. Check with community agencies, churches, and clubs to see if they will help you begin one. Contact a national organization like Parents without Partners (7910 Woodmont Ave., Suite 1000, Washington, DC 20014) or Junior Officers and Professional Association (3286 M St., N.W., Washington, DC 20007), and begin your own local chapter. This will provide a perfect opportunity to meet others who are single again.

## Gaining Courage From Religion

Many people gain courage through their religious beliefs. Their faith that God will provide or see them through a crisis, even the death of an intimate relationship, gives them additonal strength during a time when they may feel the most rejected and alone. Those who have had a strong religious background turn to their faith to help them understand and accept the change in their status. Even when you have forgotten your faith, you may find yourself automatically turning to God for additional strength during the mourning phase for your past love.

If you have a personal faith in a divine power, you may find it helpful to use it for extra courage or strength. In a world that is often seen as godless, there are still a number of people who call on their faith to help them through crises they are unable to understand by themselves or feel helpless to handle without divine power. In spite of the cynicism in our land, people still do ask for God's help to give them additional strength—and many will tell you it helps them to feel stronger.

## How To Find Competent Professional Mental Health Support

Emotional stress may lessen with guidance from mental health professionals. Whether you can use the additional help of a

## Gaining Strength Outside Yourself

therapist is a personal choice. Contrary to the common belief, you do not need to be "crazy" to talk to a "shrink." A counselor can help you understand some of the inter- and intra-personal conflicts you may have about ending, help you work through a depression and find direction for your present and future life. A therapist cannot take away your pain and suffering or give you a magical answer, but may be able to help you discover some answers for yourself. When you find yourself stuck in a painful phase, you may want to contact a professional in the guidance field for advice and support.

Since there is such a wide variation in the theoretical concepts and training that a counselor might have, it's a good idea to ask whomever you see about his or her general approach in practice.

A psychologist, clinical social worker, or a licensed counselor might treat an individual exactly the same, with the same amount of expertise, in spite of the formalized differences each may have had in training. To tell you that one is better or more qualified to help you in therapy would be folly. You can, in general, feel confident that all have had enough formalized training to know how to help you, but your own common sense must tell you that some are more insightful than others because all of them are human.

Another consideration that you should probably look at consciously before you decide on a therapist is your own feelings about the therapist's sex. Some people find it easier to trust someone of their own sex—others rely more automatically on the viewpoint of members of the opposite sex. To a minor degree, your own prejudices about a therapist's sex (or age and race) might affect how much advice you are willing to accept.

Once you know in general which of the professionals you would like to see and whether any of your personal prejudices would hinder your choices, probably the most effective way to find a competent therapist is through the recommendation of someone you know. A friend, co-worker, relative, minister, doctor, or boss may be able to recommend one or several therapists near your home.

It is natural to feel frightened or apprehensive at your first session. For this reason, don't make a decision that therapy won't help or that this therapist won't work for you until you've seen the same person at least two or three times. If you feel that therapy might help, but you don't get along with your therapist, it's a good idea to change. People have different personalities, and it's time-consuming to work on a personality conflict with your therapist when you need help in coping with your feelings about being single again. So, try another therapist. If you discover with your second—or third—therapist, that you don't like any of them, you might want to look at the possibility that your dismay has more to do with the idea of seeing a mental health professional, or with what they are saying to you, rather than with them as individuals. If this is the case, I suggest that you stick with one of them and continue. While there is a certain amount of validity in therapy shopping, no therapist can help you feel better if you never get involved in the process.

As you can see from this chapter, there are a number of ways to gain strength and emotional support other than relying totally upon yourself. Every time a friend, relative, or acquaintance tells you directly or shows you through actions that you are loved and appreciated by others—even in the most minute fashion—your confidence expands, if you give yourself permission to believe it.

**Experiments and Exercises**

Move quickly through this list and check (✓) whether you are Likely (L) or Unlikely (U) to do the following:

                                                                                L   U

1. Invite a friend over for dinner on the spur of the moment.   ___ ___
2. Plan a week in advance before you invite someone over for an evening's entertainment.   ___ ___

## Gaining Strength Outside Yourself

                                                                     L   U

3. Call up a friend on Sunday afternoon and suggest going to a movie.  ___  ___
4. Sit alone on Sunday because you have nothing to do.  ___  ___
5. Call up a friend just to say "Hi."  ___  ___
6. Start to call someone and then decide against it for fear you'll be intruding.  ___  ___
7. Invite friends over for a drink after work.  ___  ___
8. Ask a friend if you can come over to visit.  ___  ___
9. Invite yourself to a friend's party.  ___  ___
10. Have a spur-of-the-moment party on Tuesday.  ___  ___
11. Initiate a conversation with a stranger.  ___  ___
12. Drop in on a friend unannounced.  ___  ___
13. Initiate a weekend "vacation" with someone you like, but don't know very well.  ___  ___
14. Send "divorce announcements" to your friends and acquaintances indicating you would still like to be friends.  ___  ___
15. Go to a singles' club by yourself.  ___  ___
16. Share your feelings with other ex-intimates.  ___  ___
17. Ask for guidance from another ex-intimate.  ___  ___
18. Seek professional counseling even though you could handle your feelings yourself.  ___  ___
19. Tell a friend you're feeling "down" and would like to talk.  ___  ___
20. Talk to a minister about your problem.  ___  ___
21. Seek strength through religion.  ___  ___
22. Ask your family for their support.  ___  ___
23. Move in with a friend or relative.  ___  ___
24. Look for guidance through literature.  ___  ___

Now look at your responses.

- Is there a pattern?
- Are you missing out on some emotionally supportive experiences because of fears?
- Which ones would you like to change?

# 7

# SEPARATION PITFALLS AND HOW TO AVOID THEM

Most ex-intimates unwittingly *add* to their pain and *prolong* their grief by falling into certain traps during the early stages of their separation. In this chapter I will describe the most common pitfalls, tell you why it's natural to become ensnared, and explain what you can do to rescue yourself.

## Trying To Help Each Other Through the Crisis

This is a popular trap for nice, kind, intelligent people who are afraid of getting angry at their ex-love, uncertain about burying their dead relationship, and frightened of beginning a new life. It is natural to feel all of these and to want support and reassurance that you're a worthwhile person.

When you try to help each other through the crisis, you are saying: "I still feel love, commitment, or obligation to you and I'm afraid to let go." Obviously, still needing to hold on makes it very hard to say good-bye.

## Separation Pitfalls And How To Avoid Them

When you offer to help your ex-love through the depression and loneliness caused by the ending of your relationship, you are saying one of three things:
1. I want you to need me.
2. I feel responsible for your pain and obligated to help you.
3. I'm scared and still count on you to take care of my emotional needs.

Although all of these fears and feelings are natural, to *act* on them when you're feeling so vulnerable will prolong your pain. To fall into the trap of trying to help each other through the crisis, one or both partners must *still* be dependent on the other to the extent that at least one member acts as an emotional rescuer.

A friend of mine was divorced for three years before she finally quit calling on her ex-husband to wipe away her tears. The sad part about Evelyn depending on Sy all the time was that at the end of the three years, she still had to start over and learn how to find a new love to comfort and support her. Unfortunately, by this time, she had wasted three years of her life holding on to Sy who, after the first six months, was involved with someone else.

To save ourselves emotionally we *have* to let go of our past loves and their support in order to gather our strength and eventually develop new loves. Sometimes it takes a few weeks or months to learn that going forward is *much* more exciting than backing up and clinging to the remaining shreds of an emotional attachment.

So what do you do when you feel you just *have* to talk with your ex-love? Call someone else, or visit a friend, or join a group of other recently single folk. The question you need to ask yourself when you reach for the phone is: "Can I *really* go forward if I keep clutching at yesterday?" The answer is obvious.

And, what do you do if your ex-love keeps clinging to you? Explain that you can no longer be counted on for support. It prolongs the pain for both of you and even though you were once very important to each other, neither can afford to back into the future with an eye on the past.

## Getting Back Together With Your Ex-Love

> After 30 years of separation, the aged couple gazed lovingly into each other's eyes. In that moment, they knew what they had always known: that they were meant for each other. And even though the years had dragged slowly by, at that very second they were young again and life was once more worth living.

It is *not* emotionally healthy to wait all of your life to recapture that moment when you can once again be in the arms of your lost but not forgotten love. Many recently single folk try to get back to their "other half" and sadly learn that the idea of together again only works in the movies. There are too many roadblocks in real life to make recapturing an old flame workable.

To begin with, there are usually lot of arrows flung at each patner during the ending and the exit speeches. Even though each may hope to forgive and forget what was shouted in the past, usually neither can fully trust the other not to be hurtful again.

A friend said:

> "I thought that we could forget all the hurt we had caused each other. But I discovered that we just couldn't. Each time we got into a small argument, like any couple does, we made it worse, by pulling in *all* the past hurts—including who had suffered the most during our separation. I guess you can't start anew with someone you've already begun and ended with before."

There is little doubt that you cannot start fresh with an old love. Much of the appeal is that you already know your old love's moods, strengths, weaknesses, habits, and favorite foods. You, therefore, save yourself the embarrassing awkwardness of a new relationship. At a time when you may feel fragile and vulnerable, it is quite natural for you to want to protect yourself from any additional hurt a new romance may offer. But to go back to your past love (even if that is possible) may be more painful then moving on.

Another major roadblock that causes rekindled flames to burn out quickly is that there is usually little fuel to keep them glowing. The relationship died and was buried the first time. The same old issues that were there before will still be there when you go back. As soon as the honeymoon period is over, they'll return to haunt you.

Remind yourself that going back rarely works out and refuse to kid yourself that it will be different this time. It wasn't good before, and, there's little that's changed except that you're lonelier now. Use your loneliness constructively to help you *risk* meeting someone new.

## Trying To Be Friends

George and Alice had been together for seven years when they finally decided to end their relationship. They lived in a middle class "bedroom community" near a northern California city. Alice worked as a teacher and stayed there when George moved out. It was Alice's idea that they separate. George moved closer to his work in the city.

He felt lost and empty without Alice and came to a mental health clinic for counseling.

During one of the therapy sessions George was talking about his relationship with Alice and how it ended—five months ago.

"We weren't angry at each other when we parted. We'd fought in the past, but decided that neither of us were 'bad' people. We'd just grown apart. I remember when I left, Alice said she'd hoped we could be *friends*."

"I remember the feeling I had when she said she wanted us to be friends. It was as if someone had kicked me in the stomach! But in a strange way, I wanted that too—because I didn't want to lose contact with her."

"It suddenly occurred to me that I didn't answer with more than a grunt. I wondered if I could ever stop needing her. And, if I did, whether I'd choose her as a friend. I knew I would feel too vulnerable for a long time to let myself feel very close to her. I thanked God that we didn't have children! So, having to be friends would be our free choice, rather than a necessity."

"I could never imagine hating Alice, but I couldn't see myself confiding in her like I do with some of my other friends."

"It saddened me to think that after all she'd meant to me, a friendship with pleasant smiles and 'Hello—how are you?' would be the most we could expect from each other in the future."

"I wondered if it was worth it. I'm still not sure."

George's commentary exposes a lot of internal conflicts that many ex-intimates battle:
1. Why do I really want to be friends with my ex-love?
2. What are the advantages and disadvantages for me?
3. If I'm objective and look at what's *best* for me in my future, will "being friends" really be helpful?
4. Is my ex-love someone I *want* as a friend once I feel better about myself and my future?

Each single-againer has to answer those questions individually. Trying to be friends with your ex-love is possible *if* your wounds are healed and *when* you no longer need the love that your former relationship provided. For George to try and develop a friendship with Alice while he is still feeling the pain and vulnerablility of being alone would be silly.

Of course, we've all heard stories about ex-intimates who are the best of friends. A male co-worker of mine takes pride in the fact that he, his present wife, and the children of his former marriage, often go on picnics with his ex-wife. I'm sure that's a cute family portrait, but I often wonder how the two women feel about it—and why his ex-wife never remarried.

Before you jump into the pitfall of trying to be friends with your ex-love, ask yourself how much it will cost you emotionally. If the cost is holding on to yesterday so that you cannot find someone new today, don't do it.

When you have children, work toward the goal of feeling neutral. In general, if you have to *work* at being friends and there are few advantages with lots of disadvantages, avoid the trap altogether. How? See your ex-love *only* when you have to, and reach out to others for friendship and love. No one is really so desperate for friends that it is necessary to remold an old love into a new friend.

## Saving Old Love Letters, Mementos, etc.

Saving old love letters and mementos is about as helpful or productive as saving Confederate money after the Civil War! So don't wait around a hundred years, with your hands full of faded paper! For the love of your own sanity and peace of mind, *don't* save memorabilia. You can't reach out to someone new with your hands (and heart) full of old love letters from your last love.

## Pulling In Memories To Fill the Emptiness

Ex-lovers build on past memories (and selectively gloss over the problems) partially to protect themselves from hurt again. But it serves other functions: to help them wallow in self-pity and to stop them from living, growing, and loving again. How? By filling the emptiness immediately, and, thereby not making it crucial for the lonely single-againer to risk loving someone new.

In fact, most psychologists say that without anxiety and discomfort a person will stagnate or regress. Having a memory close at hand to pull in any time you feel lonely will limit your motivation to love again.

> John D. was readmitted to the psychiatric hospital for the twelfth time in seven years—following a suicide attempt.
>
> Life had little meaning for John since his wife left him. He spends most of his days reminiscing about the past, feeling sorry for himself, and damning his fate. He rarely goes out and has no close friends. Nothing he does compares favorably with what he used to do. And, almost all of his statements start with "I remember when Marge and I used to _____." John is a very lonely man and will probably die, many years from now, as depressed and unhappy as he is today. Even John knows his past love is dead, but, he refuses to bury it.

Maybe there's a lesson in his tragedy for those who have loved and lost and feel empty now. Sure, there will be times when *all* of us harken back to a happier time in our lives. Especially if we're feeling lost and lonely now. But watch yourself. Don't let it become a habit. Whenever you find yourself spending a whole evening reminiscing about the glories of your lost love, remember some of the less pleasant things, too.

Handle your nostalgia for what it is: discomfort with today. Then, spend the next evening in your life filling in the emptiness with new memories.

How did you get the last memories? You found somebody, and enjoyed yourself, which means that *you* have the ability to do it! So go out and create new memories! (And leave the reminiscing to those to aren't as brave as you.)

## Checking Up On Your Ex-Love

Checking up on your ex-love is a painful, self-destructive but natural trap for many ex-intimates. Especially for those who were not the first to initiate good-bye. Although few ex-intimates spend an entire day tracing the steps of their last love, many *do* drive by his or her apartment or just *happen* to find themselves in their ex-love's neighborhood and decide to drop in for a visit.

The object of this detective game is to find out whether your ex-love is as lonely as you are which is almost *never* the case. Most detectives are motivated by their insecurities and usually hope that the discovery of a rival will motivate them to let go of their hopes for reconciliation.

Unfortunately, this trap causes more wounded pride than emotional growth for the one who plays amateur detective. Moreover, it wastes precious time that you *could* be using to enjoy life or find someone new. You'll never meet your new love by staking out your old love's apartment. So, instead of playing detective, get on with the business of living—and, put your old trench coat away. Anytime you find yourself accidentally cruising by your ex-love's apartment, quickly make a "U" turn and dash to someone else's door!

## Trying To Get Friends To Take Sides or Pumping Them For Information

> "Yes, Madge, I saw him at the party last night. *No*—he wasn't with anyone in particular. I didn't ask him, Madge! You're *absolutely* right! It was his fault. Harry's a Bastard. I'm on *your* side, Madge. *Now* can we go play tennis?"

Madge doesn't know it yet, but she just lost a friend. She slid right into two common pitfalls for the recently single: trying to get friends to take sides and pumping them for information about her ex-love. If you need an ally or sympathizer, **don't use your friends.** You'll lose them that way.

What are friends for? *Not* to use as a judge or jury to decide whose fault the break-up is. Not mutual friends, anyway. There will be enough friends who fall by the wayside when you separate anyway.

You won't lose all of your mutual friends by pumping them for information or asking them to take sides. In fact, there will be some who will pump you for all the gory details of the break-up, readily offer their verdict of guilty on your ex-love, and call you the *minute* they hear any gossip about what your former love is doing! As you might have guessed, these are the same folks who follow fire trucks to watch the buildings burn. When you get tired of talking about your "ex" and want to get on with the business of living again, you may find these friends dropping by the wayside—or you may want to shove them.

So to whom can you talk about him/her in your hour of need? Probably your best bet is any friend you don't have in common. If you don't have separate friends, this is a good time to make some. In the meantime, another resource might be an outsider like a mental health counselor or your minister who might help you to see that trying to place blame is of little value and that constantly keeping "tabs" on him/her drains energy that you could be using on *you*. In addition, it usually keeps your wounds open.

What will help you feel better is to set aside the issue of who's to blame and admit to yourself that it really is over. In spite of that (or maybe, because of that) you really are a worthwhile person. That's what all the energy you've spent pleading your case is all about anyway—trying to prove to yourself that others still see you as worthwhile. Maybe now that you know that you're fighting for your self-esteem, you can figure out other ways to win. (For ideas, see Chapter 5.)

When you pump your friends for information about your ex-love, you are competing because each time you find out what your ex-love is doing now, you quickly make a mental note of how that *compares* with what you're doing. If he or she seems to be happy, you may find yourself bemoaning your fate or getting angry. Obviously, watching someone else's progress or damning yourself for *still* being lonely isn't going to help you out. What will? Take your eyes and ears off your ex-mate (quit pumping your friends) and work on getting your own life together.

Whether you feel worse off, by comparison, or guilty because you're enjoying life more than your ex-mate, don't sacrifice friendships for your curiosity or wounded pride.

## Wishing It Hadn't Happened and Hoping It'll Change

Have you ever noticed how little gets done when you sit around and wish something hadn't happened or hope it'll change? Sometimes it's pretty easy to just fall back and feel sorry for yourself and wish this hadn't happened to you. With all the energy it takes to carry your self-pity around, it's hard to have the guts to do much more about your plight than just hope it'll change.

When you're in that pit, what are you hoping for? A miracle? Hoping you were back, living in the good old days, perhaps? Have you forgotten the horrible fights you used to have? Or the put-downs? Or the hurt feelings? Or how little you had in common when you left? Probably you have, or you wouldn't be slumped in your chair wishing it wasn't over.

You really haven't been forgotten down in that pitfall. You're just recovering from a serious injury and, at times, you'll fall back into feeling sorry for yourself. It's easy to do. And natural, too. Not only are you not the only one who has ever fallen in this pit—but, you've probably been there before.

This time put a time limit on how long you're going to wallow in your misery, feel helpless and "pass" on life. A week? Better yet, how about just the rest of the day? You decide—you're the one down there.

It's a natural part of the healing process after the death of an intimate relationship to become depressed and immobilized at times. So you don't need to panic. Actually, if you're at a point where you hope your feelings will change, you're beginning to look for ways out of this pit. All you have to do is remember that you can pull yourself out when you've had enough.

When you decide that it's time to leave Gloomsville for awhile, tell a friend how you feel. Just getting the feelings off your chest helps.

Probably during the first year, you will slide into this "wishing it hadn't happened and hoping it'll change" pitfall a number of times. You'll notice, though, as time goes by, that you hit it less often and for briefer periods because you'll start climbing out of the hole by reaching out to others or pulling on your own strengths.

## Beware Of Anniversary Dates

You're having an absolutely marvelous time, enjoying the new exciting you and all of a sudden—ZAP! For no apparent reason you've gone from the top of the roller coaster down to the bottom again. As you pick yourself up, you shakily ask yourself, "What happened? I thought I was getting over **him (her)**." Then, you look at the calendar and discover that tomorrow *would* have been your anniversary—or your ex-love's birthday—or any one of a dozen used-to-be red-letter days.

What happened? You have been belted by the *Syndrome: Anniversary Date* (S.A.D.). And almost every recently single gets clobbered by this syndrome several times during the first year.

It operates in one of two ways: on or around the date of an important past event in your life, you may have the *same* feelings as those experienced earlier; or, because of loss of a loved one, you may experience feelings that are the exact *opposite* (feeling sad about a past event that was happy).

Examples:

● Feeling sad on the anniversary date of a loved one's death.

● Feeling down on the anniversary date of a divorce.

● Feeling dejected on the anniversary date of your former wedding day.

● Feeling sad and lost around the time of year that you and your ex-love used to go on vacation.

The best protection is an offensive tactic; that is, attacking S.A.D. before it can sneak up and belt you. Go through your calendar for the next month or six weeks and circle the dates that are likely to be troublesome. (Don't go much farther than this because it could be overwhelming—or, in six weeks you may be so busy with your new life that the plans you make now will be outdated.)

Dates that you need to circle are the red-letter days you can remember, such as: your first date, first time you vowed eternal love, last time you fought, first time you "made up," the day you ended it, vacation time, and special "togetherness" holidays.

There will be a certain amount of sadness in remembering these events, but since you really can't forget them anyway, you might as well allow yourself to go through the painful feelings now—when *you've* decided to feel them.

There are several different things you can do with these special days. Plan a party. Invite a few single friends over for dinner. Go to an art show, play, music festival, or antique auction. Plan a short trip. Get involved in a hobby or project. Go to a singles' club dance. **Be with people. Do something!!!**

Make it a part of your Sunday routine to browse through the entertainment section of your newspaper and note the coming events in your town. Fill these special dates on the calendar with your plans. Then, most important, *carry them out!* Gradually you will find that the original objective (to attack the S.A.D. by filling up the time with people and activities) has been replaced by a genuine enjoyment in doing more exciting activities and meeting new people.

If you use this plan of attack, few anniversaries will be able to sneak up and clobber you. There will, however, be times when you've forgotten to plan ahead. When that happens, reach out to someone or some project to help you through it. None of us can avoid feeling some pain and sorrow about the loss of an ex-love, but we can, by turning to other people and events, keep the S.A.D. from immobilizing us.

## Panicking With Free Time: Weekends and Such

Weekends can be lonely and painful for the recently single. Any free time can be very scary, in fact, and it's quite common to panic over an upcoming holiday, or Heaven forbid, a two-week vacation.

Whoever said we need *more* three-day weekends? Certainly *not* a recent single. In fact, employers usually count on their employees who have recently ended an intimate relationship to volunteer for extra work during the evenings, holidays, or weekends.

There's a private club in San Francisco called T.G.I.M. (Thank God It's Monday) comprised of single people who get together on Monday nights to celebrate that they've made it through another weekend.

Armed with anxiety, it is natural for recent singles to do one of two things: schedule so many activities that they hop from one to another or be so panicked that they end up immobilized and, unable to make any decisions, sit at home all weekend vegetating.

## Separation Pitfalls And How To Avoid Them

Carol panics with free time and usually avoids being alone, if at all possible. She spends her week programming overly active weekends. Week nights are spent at singles' bars or working late at the office. She stays away from her apartment until it's late enough to get ready for bed.

Whenever she is unable to fill up her weekend with activities with other people, she packs up her parakeet and visits a nearby relative.

Mike vegetates on weekends. He spends most of the week dreading Friday night to Monday morning. Everyone he knows is married and unless his friends suggest that he do something with them, he usually spends the weekends at home alone.

Through the week he can keep busy and, being around people, he sometimes forgets that he's lonely. But on the weekends, he feels like one of the walking wounded.

On Monday he usually vows he's not going to spend another weekend alone, but by Friday night he's usually come up with zero plans. Mike handles his fear of being alone on the weekends by getting so overloaded with dread and misery that he does nothing.

How can Carol and Mike learn to enjoy their free time?

First of all, most single-againers say that it takes from 3 to 9 months to feel good enough about yourself that the prospect of being alone with free time doesn't throw you into a tailspin. You can speed the process along by planning some activities with people for your weekends. But stagger this with some time to be by yourself and get to know and like you again. (You really aren't very good company for you or anyone else until you let go of the panic.)

Use the time alone to develop some of your talents, such as decorating, indoor gardening, cooking, painting, crafts, reading, playing a musical instrument, or singing in the shower. Take walks—in the country, at the beach, through the city parks and streets. Begin looking at the beauty and comedy around you as you stroll. In your travels, gather in new ideas for things you'd enjoy. Go to an art or craft exhibit. Talk to the artisans about their wares. Smile at strangers and be friendly. Remember, wherever you meet people you have a chance to make a new friend. Gradually you will find that the pain and panic over the free time will lessen.

## Falling In Love With the First Person You Meet

Falling in love with the first person you meet can be just as emotionally destructive as refusing to ever love someone new because it does not allow you the healthy experience of dating again and growing through the grief process. Worse than that, it may set you up for another painful ending. As we have seen from Chapter 1, many experts believe the ending of an intimate relationship *begins* at the start. That is, intimates join together blindly because of neurotic needs and fears rather than emotionally mature choices.

Ex-intimates often fantasize about finding someone to sweep them off their feet or take them away from all their pain from good-bye. Often they desperately search for a "new" love to fill up their emptiness and protect them from hurt, and occasionally they fall in love with the first—or second—person they date. But usually this leads to disaster, and a few months later, they are dealing with the death of *two* intimate relationships and are numbed by the overwhelming fear that they cannot "make it" with anyone.

Instead, date and enjoy a number of different individuals. Give yourself the time and experience to grow through good-bye and learn to enjoy being a separate person again before you decide to commit yourself to someone new.

## Summary

The common theme of most pitfalls is a pull back to the past. The antidote is obvious; *force* yourself to let go of the past and move forward. That takes the courage and wisdom growing within you now.

## Experiments and Exercises

Below is a list of pitfalls. Check (✓) those you have *not* fallen into.

\_\_\_ trying to help each other through the crisis
\_\_\_ getting back together with your ex-love
\_\_\_ trying to be friends
\_\_\_ saving old love letters
\_\_\_ pulling in memories to fill the emptiness
\_\_\_ checking up on your ex-love
\_\_\_ trying to get friends to take sides or pumping them for information
\_\_\_ wishing it hadn't happened and hoping it'll change
\_\_\_ getting slugged by S.A.D. (Syndrome: Anniversary Date)
\_\_\_ panicking with free time
\_\_\_ falling in love with the first person you meet

Now ask yourself:

● How do I avoid these?

● What can I learn from my own experience that will help me get out of any I may be stuck in now?

● Are there times when I'm vulnerable? When? What can I do about it?

● Am I getting anything out of holding on to the past? What?

Go back to through the above list and place a big "X" near one pitfall you *do* get stuck in and are willing to give up. Write the following on a piece of paper:

   I'm tired of _____. (Write the pitfall *and* your ex-love's name.) For example: I'm tired of trying to get back together with _____.

Read what you have written out loud. Repeat this again and again until you can *feel* the words in your body. (This may take several rehearsals.) Once you have finally acknowledged your own desire to stop hurting yourself, crumple up the paper and throw it in the garbage—or burn it.

Take a few moments to feel your relief. Then, pat yourself on the back for your decision.

Make a commitment to yourself to follow through on your decision to begin feeling better. *Force* yourself to avoid that pitfall and *plan* how you'll do this during the next week.

# 8

# FOR THE ONE WHO WAS LEFT BEHIND

Most everyone agrees that when a relationship dies, the first person who says its over has an easier time with saying good-bye and burying the past than the one who is left behind. You may or may not have been the one who physically left but emotionally you were the one who was *still* in the relationship, or at least felt that you were, when your partner announced he/she was leaving—or had already left. You, who felt committed to or dependent on the relationship or slightly dissatisfied but too frightened to act, will probably suffer the strongest feelings of rejection, hurt feelings or abused pride.

If you are the one who feels left behind, this chapter will teach you how to get on with your life. You will learn how to take charge of your self-doubt, self-pity, and resentment and replace them with self-confidence and independent thinking.

You will need to *risk changing* and your progress will be slower if you are overly self-critical. So, keep that in mind as you practice what you learn in these pages. In spite of your fears, if you *genuinely* want to give up feeling victimized or abandoned and start living again, you *can* do it!

## How To Put a Limit On Self-Pity

The one who feels left behind at the end of a love affair will be the one who is most likely to engage in self-pity. To some extent, this is natural and is nothing to hide from yourself or feel ashamed of. When someone leaves you, you may feel like a victim: abused and abandoned with no control over his/her leaving and less control over your future. You may not have people near you to help salve your wounds—or, if you do, you may push them aside, declaring that only your ex-love can help you feel better again. Because of all this, you may find that you are the only one left to give yourself comfort.

But the problems sneak in when you become so wrapped up in self-pity that it gets in the way of your growth and becomes the reason that you cannot reach out to others for support or be interested in anything or anyone outside yourself.

Limiting your self-pity first requires that you recognize it exists in you. In pure form, it may be difficult to spot because it usually travels with the feelings of self-doubt or bitterness. So how can you learn to see the self-pity in you? Any time you find yourself thinking, feeling, or doing any one of the following, you are engaged in feeling sorry for yourself:

• Bemoaning your fate and not looking at how you can change it.

• Deciding that your ex-love always used you—"I took care of him and he never did anything for me."

• Thinking about how other people always have a good time—and you always get left out.

• Letting the telephone ring because it's probably a wrong number—or just someone wanting to use you.

• Nurturing feelings that you were born to lose—nothing good ever happens and no matter what you do, it ends up in failure.

• Remembering all the bad things that have ever happened in your life and ignoring or minimizing the good ones.

- Reminding yourself that no one has ever felt so alone or been so abused.
- Imagining what a good time your ex-love is having without you.

The list could go on and on, but that should give you some clues about the kind of thoughts and feelings you may have that are signals of self-pity. Any time you become the focal point of the world and its suffering, and you wipe out any possibility that someone else may care or feel the same way, or that you can do something constructive for your pain, you are stuck with feeling sorry for yourself, sometimes feeling bitter, but usually feeling resigned to your fate.

Once you're aware of the self-pity in you, begin looking at what's going on at the time (or just before) you began feeling that way. Did you hear a depressing song on the radio or see a "couple" that look like they have what you want? Or, maybe, you heard your ex-love is living with someone new, or dating a friend? Whatever the catalyst, see if you can find it. One lady I know told me that during the first six months after her divorce, every time a weekend drew near and her co-workers talked about their plans, she found herself slugged with a surge of panic, then settled back into feeling sorry for herself because she had nothing to do and no one to be with.

When you discover which scenes set your self-pity in motion, figure out how many times during the day you turn to self-pity and how long you wallow in your suffering before you decide to get out. Once you know this, try to cut it down to one or two times less each day and limit the wallowing by 1/10th. By slowly limiting your self-pity, you will be able to recognize that you do, in fact, have some control over that part of your grief process.

## How To Fight Self-Pity and Self-Doubt

Self-pity and self-doubt can be demoralizing. Self-pity says,

"Isn't it awful that this has happened to you—no one else suffers as much," and self-doubt comes along and tells you, "Go ahead and feel sorry for your plight if you'd like to because there's *nothing* you can do to change it. Anything you try will end up in failure."

Often the ex-intimate who has been left behind has both of these feelings simultaneously—especially during the first few weeks of the ending process—because much of his/her pride and self-confidence has been shattered by his/her partner's rejection. This reaction may be magnified if your partner has a new love or you felt insecure before the relationship began. These feelings are also enhanced if you only confided your feelings in the one who left—or looked primarily to your ex-mate for comfort and support. With the ending of the relationship, your only source of nurturing, however unhealthy that might have been, is gone. And so, you are left feeling sorry for yourself; not knowing how to let go of your pain, and doubting your ability to do anything constructive for yourself.

In order to fight self-doubt and self-pity you must first admit that they are more natural at this time in your life than ever before and that they seem to penetrate every aspect of your existence.

As one man related, after his wife of seven years filed for divorce, "I found myself double-checking everything I did—even though I know that I'm good at my job. I panicked when I had to meet someone new—or try something different." The woman who shared that her weekends were filled with self-pity for the first six months after saying good-bye to her ex-husband, discovered that barricading herself in her apartment with plenty of Kleenex and stacks of sad books was her way of handling her self-doubt about being attractive to anyone. She was afraid that if she asked her co-workers to come over for dinner or to go to a movie, they'd turn her down. The thought of being attractive to another man, or having the ability to make new single friends, frightened her, too. So, she stayed in her apartment and felt sorry for herself.

How long this self-doubt and self-pity will last varies with a number of factors: the length of your relationship; how insecure you felt before it began; how self-destructive the relationship became; how dependent you were on your ex-love; and how soon you allow others to help pull you out.

The only way to fight these two villains is to begin *proving to yourself* by your actions and applause from others that you are a worthwhile person. To speed this process along, you will need to give yourself permission to feel more confident and risk making mistakes or being rejected occasionally in order to give yourself opportunities to be successful. The man who was unsure of himself and afraid to meet anyone new or try anything different minimized his fears by finally corralling his hesitation and actually doing the things he feared. Then, with each success, he knew for himself that, in spite of his self-doubt, he really could do his job well, learn new skills and meet strangers successfully. Each success gave him more confidence. The lady who stayed home for six months' worth of weekends found, when she actually invited people to her home, that they accepted her invitation and many new men she met did find her attractive.

The point is that you can fight self-doubt and self-pity by *doing*. Thinking about how scared you are to try something new and feeling sorry for yourself because you don't have the energy or desire to try any more will only build up your fears. Doing something constructive will help them vanish quicker.

## How To Clear Your Eyes and Look At Whom You've Lost

During the first few days or weeks after you've said goodbye it is natural to go through a self-purging process, which includes romanticizing the one who initiated the parting. Your ex-mate becomes all that you ever wanted or a much better person than you really deserved—out of the "people" category and up on a pedestal.

The lady who spent six months by herself often talked in our singles' group about how wonderful her ex-husband had been to her and how happy she'd be if he came back. The man who was left behind after twenty-one years of marriage would speak of his wife as a strong woman who finally got fed up with his weakness. Even many married couples in counseling will speak of their old loves (the ones who left them) as the love of their lives.

It is important, then, not only for your pain during the grief process, but also for your next intimate relationship to take your current ex-love out of the "god" category. No one, including you or your new love can compete with the ideal of perfection.

How do you stop caring for someone who no longer loves you? *Decide that you want to enough to do something about it.* See differences in your ex-love and new date as just that: differences in people, not proof that your old love was better. (Make sure that you're not suffering from the syndrome of never respecting someone who could care for a person like you.) Remember when comparing your old love to someone new, that you felt more at ease with your ex-love because the two of you had already gone through the anxiety-provoking stage of getting to know one another.

Remember your ex-love's faults as you gaze lovingly at your past. See them as the problems that they actually were for you then, rather than trying to minimize or forgive them so quickly right now. If you couldn't tolerate your ex-love's flirting with others, or spending more time at work than with you, or drinking too much, or acting irresponsibly, or whatever the faults, remember the stress or unhappiness it created for you then and don't whitewash the problems so quickly. Each time you flash on how wonderful your ex-love was, remember some of those imperfections as well.

If you're unhappy or lonesome now, it's easy to minimize the loneliness and hurt in your past. See your idealization for what it really is—your own desire or need to love someone again. Once you can look at your ex-love realistically, it will be much easier for you to give your love to someone new.

To increase your objectivity in viewing your ex-love, list the traits or behaviors you did *not* like:

*Traits or behaviors I did not like*
1.
2.
3.
4.
5.

## How To Determine What You've Lost

Looking at what you have really lost is just as important for your mental health and emotional growth as taking your ex-love off that pedestal. Initially, you may feel overwhelmed with your loss, as if the rug has been pulled out from under you and there is nothing left in your life worth caring about.

Unlike your partner, you have not had the opportunity for serious forethought in unhooking emotionally from your ex-mate, planning where to live, what to give up, or how you'll replace whatever you are losing. So, the loss can feel overwhelming at first. But gradually, as the days and nights pass, you will begin the sometimes painful process of saying good-bye to the past and replacing the objects, ideals and people that have gone.

To help you go through this process in a healthier, more productive way, you will need to determine, somewhat objectively, what you have really lost compared with your fears or fantasies of losing everything. This may be a painful process at first, especially if you've decided to feel like an absolute failure. But many ex-intimates discover, upon close examination, that even though they have lost an intimate relationship with a specific person, they have won the freedom to have a healthier, happier relationship with themselves and with someone new.

Begin by looking at what you still have and what you have gained by saying goodbye to your ex-mate. List these below:

| What I have left | What I have won |
|---|---|
| 1. | 1. |
| 2. | 2. |
| 3. | 3. |
| 4. | 4. |
| 5. | 5. |
| 6. | 6. |
| 7. | 7. |
| 8. | 8. |

Be sure to include things like your job, if you work; some friends, and the support from your family; material possessions that you've kept; your children if they are with you; your health, intelligence, talents, personal warmth, *and,* although you may not be aware of it at first, your ability to care about someone and probably love again. Keep all of these factors in mind and add any others you think of from time to time. In the column of what you have won, be sure to include freedom from hassles with someone whom you could not please, nor could he or she please you. Those who were in a self-destructive relationship will find that in saying good-bye, no matter who says it first or how scary it is, they have won the freedom to develop a healthier relationship the next time around. Take for example, the man who, after fifteen years of marriage and twelve of alcohol abuse, finally quit drinking when his wife left him. The people who marry their parent figures often end up becoming adults when Mommy or Daddy finally moves out. So, in looking for what you have won, look at the negatives that were in your former relationship and applaud the fact that you have won your freedom from those.

Now that you are aware of some assets you still have or have won in saying good-bye, begin to look at what you have actually lost. Be careful not to romanticize or overgeneralize. You have not, for example, lost your reason for living, or everything in life that's worth caring for—even though it is natural for you to feel that way at times. You have lost *specific* people, roles, and routines. So, make sure in determining what you are saying good-bye to, that you put down concrete examples. Much of what you have lost you will want to replace at some future date and it will be much easier to do this if you are specific about what you have lost. The *key* in making your list *is your attitude.* You must genuinely want to determine what you have actually lost and not just use this to bemoan your fate or prove to yourself that you are a failure. It may take some time to obtain the objectivity you need to evaluate your losses fairly, but it also takes a genuine desire on your part to look realistically at your current position. This will be easier to do if you can curb your self-doubt, self-pity, and the tendency to glorify your ex-mate while examining your losses with an eye toward replacement.

## Accepting Responsibility Improves Self-respect

> "One of the things that bothers me the most about our divorce is that it was Laurie's idea. Our marriage wasn't all that great, you understand. All it gave me was a housekeeper and an occasional bed partner, but I stayed there and took it. She at least had the guts to end it—I must not feel very good about myself."

That was part of a statement that Vic, 34-year-old insurance salesman, made in my office several months ago. He and Laurie had been married for eight years and while neither one of them was acutely miserable, both had gradually settled for a strained, mildly unhappy marital relationship. They had a seven-year-old son, Scott, who often seemed like the sole reason for staying together.

"This is the first time I have ever lost at anything—and, I don't like it at all. If only I had been the one to come up with the idea of divorce, I might have felt better."

Vic's lament over not being the first to announce that it's over and his resultant loss of pride is not unusual. Many ex-intimates who are in the same position express feelings of embarrassment, hurt pride, low self-esteem, rejection, and depression because they were left by their mates. In fact, the majority of those who attempt suicide or spend a long time feeling empty and staying alone are those who did not initiate the ending process. Often they view their ex-mates as better than they are: more desirable or emotionally stronger because the ex-mate is either involved with someone new or has the strength to leave an unhappy union without the security of another love affair right away. They see themselves as still committed to the relationship while their ex-mate was someone who needed something better. In some instances, this viewpoint plus anger and a feeling of helplessness can create a sense of being victimized with no control over what happens.

But few love affairs end with one mate still emotionally committed to the relationship and the other one out. Typically, what happens is that one person (usually the one that's left behind) deals more indirectly or passively with the unhappiness in the relationship and, therefore, confuses emotional commitment with fears of ending.

> Although Vic recognized that he did not feel the relationship was that good, he chose to deal with his discomfort by passively accepting the coolness and distance which settled over their marriage a long time before he ceased courting Laurie or viewing her as a primary love. His job became more important after Scott was born, and gradually he turned to his friends or held the feelings inside that he initially shared with his wife. Laurie was always around, and

he no longer felt that he had to keep trying to please her. It was easier to take her presence for granted and spend his charm on customers instead of on his wife. By taking her out of the category of someone worth pleasing and putting their relationship in the position of something that can take care of itself, Vic was instrumental in quietly pushing his wife away from him.

And, at many of those times, he was consciously aware of what he was doing. In fact, he could remember telling himself that Laurie was unhappy, and if he didn't work harder at showing his love she would probably leave him. Usually at those times he would find himself thinking: "She's not trying to please me, why should I bend over backwards for her?" or "She doesn't care, why should I?" Sometimes he found himself rationalizing that she expected too much from him, but that excuse didn't hold much water because he knew that if he really thought it was worth the effort, he could do almost anything. It just wasn't worth changing to please her or save the relationship. But, in spite of the years that Vic spent wondering about how much affection, courtesy, and respect to show Laurie, when his wife finally announced that their relationship was dead, he felt totally abandoned and shocked by her statement. "She rejected me—I'm not man enough to keep her," he wailed.

With time and professional counseling, Vic was able to recognize and admit how often he consciously (but indirectly) rejected Laurie. With each awareness, he discovered that he was not victimized by Laurie's announcement. In fact, in looking back, he discovered that quietly through the years he had begun rejecting Laurie's affection by tuning her out or deciding that keeping a close relationship with his wife just wasn't worth the time and effort to change his behavior. By admitting the choices that he also made to end their marriage, Vic was able to feel more in control of its death, and, therefore, not as helpless or inept in guiding his future.

To facilitate letting go of your feelings of being victimized, you need to go back through your memories and identify the times that you subtly declined to help strengthen the bond or actually weakened it. Whose final announcement actually began the burial procedure is irrelevant. Your judgment about whether good-bye was the "right" or "wrong" decision will vary. When you're feeling good, it will be the "right" one, when you feel unhappy, it may be viewed as the "wrong" decision. But, either way, the decision to end the relationship was a mutual one. So, you need not wrap yourself up in self-doubt or place your ex-love on a pedestal for having more guts or being more desirable than you.

Going back through the past and accepting your choices to end the relationship can be helpful. You had and still have just as much control as your mate over how close or how lasting an intimate relationship will be. Acknowledging those choices and making a constructive self-examination of when you said "no" will provide the tools to help guide yourself into a healthier, more permanent relationship the next time around.

## Self-Induced Traps and How To Avoid Them

Most traps come from feeling inadequate, rejected or abandoned, still being emotionally tied and dependent on your ex-mate to take care of your needs. If you knew that the relationship was dying and consciously made efforts to unhook from it while your ex-mate was still present, you will probably not go through all of these traps as intensely or as often.

1. *Viewing your old love affair for what it might have been rather than what it was.* Part of saying good-bye to your old love

affair is saying good-bye to your dreams of what it might have been—your fantasy of love ever after. A choice to see the ending as a tragedy and your ex-love as a god or goddess is a painful trap to fall into because any dreams of feeling as good again—or maybe even better—with someone else are automatically doused. To fall into this trap, you must still feel emotionally connected to your ex-mate and must either be alone or unhappy with someone new.

Avoiding this trap is a matter of allowing yourself to mourn the death of your old friendship as it was: feeling sad about saying good-bye to the good times, but relieved that you will not continue enacting the bad scenes. Of course, there were times that were good—that's why it began—but there were also the painful, lonely times and that's why it's over now. So, mourn the death of your old love affair as it was, not as it *might* have been. Use your legitimate anger to *stop* your nostalgia.

2. *Remembering the good times and forgetting the bad.* Similar to the trap we just mentioned, this one can also be painful and lead you into a future of emptiness if you stay there too long. Poets say this is a trap for romantics who find the painful memories too hurtful to recall; mental health professionals declare it's a tool ex-intimates use to punish themselves and remain dissatisfied; your best friend may tell you it's silly and you should stop torturing yourself, and your own good sense will tell you that you're not being totally honest. In spite of all this knowledge and advice, there will be times when, in looking back over your old love relationship, you'll remember the good times and choose to forget the others.

Since you may do this anyway, despite your good sense, utilize this experience as an awareness that you have the ability to laugh and enjoy someone else and remember that when you are through the grief process, you can do that again—with someone new.

3. and 4. *Holding on to your ex-love by trying to get even or trying to get him/her to come back.* These two traps may sound

different but, in many ways, they are the same. Both can be harmful to you because the energy you waste on your ex-love could be spent on someone much more important to your happiness—you! Both traps are the results of the same factor: still being hooked on your past and a love that is gone. You are just as emotionally hooked on someone you love and try to get back as someone you hate and want to see suffer. However, you may need to try some of your tactics at getting your old love back or at revenge to find that truth out for yourself.

You will know that you're trying to get your old love back when you find yourself doing any one of the following:

> Calling your old love when you have no legitimate reason, just to see how he/she is doing
>
> Changing some of your habits or attitudes that your ex-love didn't like and then reporting that fact
>
> Going out of your way to contact or please your ex-love
>
> Inviting her out to dinner, or having him over for a home-cooked meal

Some of these traps can also be a way of getting even with your old love. In fact, many ex-intimates who have been left behind, often speak of their fantasies of getting their old love back and then dropping them, as a way of getting even.

Other tactics which are part of the revenge fantasy are:

> Spreading lies or harmful truths about your ex-love among mutual friends
>
> Turning your children or family members against your ex-mate
>
> Flaunting your new love or success since the "divorce" in front of your ex-mate
>
> Finding out your ex-love is unhappy, then rubbing it in with unkind remarks

Both of these traps, whichever form they take, should be

avoided if at all possible. It probably isn't worth your time and effort to try getting your old love back. Spend that time and energy on someone new.

Getting even with your old love for rejecting you can be more harmful than helpful. One of the reasons you may feel vengeful is that you are still hurting. But revenge won't make your wounds heal any faster. Use the anger you feel in constructive ways to help yourself feel better again, rather than wasting it on your ex-love.

5. *Still caring more about your ex-love than about anyone else.* If you've found no one new to replace your ex-love, it's natural to be scared of trying to love again but to still need someone to love. The easiest solution for many (at least at the beginning of the grief process) is to idolize their ex-love. "I never knew how much I loved him until he was gone" is a common lament for ex-intimates. But someone who is easier to love at a distance cannot be a love you can live with, no matter how lonely you are or how scared of your future. And all of us need to love and be loved by someone who is present and available to touch or to hold in real life—not in our memories.

Caring more about your ex-mate than about anyone else is a way of protecting yourself from getting hurt again. Your ex-love cannot possibly hurt you any more than that person already has, so there is no risk in still loving him or her. Someone new whom you're willing to trust with your love does have the power to hurt you, however. The problem with this is obvious, of course. In protecting yourself from being hurt too deeply, you also shield yourself from feeling the strength of new love.

It's your decision. Choose wisely. To relinquish the "love at a distance" for your ex-mate, you must deliberately decide to let go and then work to make it really happen.

6. *Daydreaming about your ex-love's new life.* If you're unhappy, you may find yourself daydreaming about what your ex-love is doing—who your replacement is now and whether they are happy together. Sometimes you will hope that their

relationship lasts so that you can finally give yourself permission to bury your old love, and other times you will find yourself wishing it would fail so the two of you can get back together again. Your feelings may fluctuate back and forth between these two extremes from day to day.

You need not be terribly concerned about falling into this trap, because you will find that it tends to be self-limiting: that is, gradually it dies out, either because you become aware that it leads nowhere or you find someone new.

You can speed up the process by finding someone new to daydream about or filling your boredom with creative projects and personal goals to attain.

## Ways Of Reaching Out To Others

Since you may be more passive or dependent than your ex-mate, it's important not to demean yourself or allow fate to control your destiny. You will need to *actively* reach out to other people. Your ex-love will look very good to you (no matter how unavailable or destructive the love) if the choice for your present and future is between your former mate and nothing. Even if you feel that you're not ready to replace the old love with someone new, it's important to at least begin developing new friendships and give your emptiness a chance to be filled by kindness, respect, and support from others.

Let people know that you need them. Show them and tell them directly how important they are to you. Take the time to smile and say hello to strangers. Initiate getting together with friends. Spend as much energy building friends for your future as you do trapped in the past. Use the charm that you used on your last love to find someone new and the insight you've developed about yourself to make the effort to change. If you discover that in your last relationship you were always too scared to risk saying, "I love you," or, "You're important to me," gather the strength to say it this time. Don't let your insecurity get in the way of accepting and giving the warmth and the love that all of us have to share with each other.

At first you may have to force yourself to break out of your shell. But, gradually you will find that your awkwardness and fears will vanish and in their place will be a sense of pride, self-confidence, and the warmth from your friends.

## On The Thought Of Moving

Many ex-intimates who are not the first to initiate the ending remain in their former homes. "If you want a divorce, you move out! I'm staying here." At first it may seem like a triumph. At least, you kept the family abode or are still in familiar surroundings. Everything in your life has not changed. But after a few weeks, you may notice that the comfort of being in the same scenes is gradually beginning to make you uneasy. Going to the same grocery store seems different somehow. The buildings in your neighborhood or trees on your block remind you of your ex-love, and when you sleep in your old bed alone, the memories rush back. This time you're alone in that space; last time you were part of a pair. Sometimes staying in familiar surroundings or following the same routines will make it harder to bury the past because it prolongs the mourning process.

And while, practically speaking, it may be easier for you to remain in the same house or community, if, after a while (say six months or so), you find yourself just as deeply entrenched in the home situation as you were when he/she left, you may want to make a concerted effort to change your environment. You need not move all the way across country, and it's true that you cannot run away from your past or its memories, but you can de-emphasize them. Think about moving from your home. If you own it, maybe selling the family homestead will give you the cash to launch yourself into a brighter future. If you're renting, isn't about time you thought of moving into a smaller house or apartment?

If you decide, for whatever the reasons, to stay in the same house—or in the same community—begin rearranging your house and saying good-bye to the memories that flash back when you look at the old, familiar "scenes." Use different routes to drive to the store. Experiment with shopping at different times of the day, days of the week—or at different stores entirely. Change or reorganize as much of your old environment and routine as you can. It will shorten the mourning process and help you feel better.

**Summary**

Even if you are not the first one to say that it's over, you can learn through the process of ending that being without your ex-mate could be the beginning of a happier future for you. Sure, there will be times when you feel you've been abandoned and rejected by someone who's better, but, as you begin looking more realistically at whom and what you've lost and admitting your choice to end it also, you may find yourself wishing that your partner had left sooner.

**Experiments and Exercises**

Consider the following when you have uninterrupted time:

● Say in a sentence what you imagine your ex-love thinks of you.

● Is your current self-appraisal related in any way to your ex-mate's opinion of you? How is it different?

● If you have "bought" his or her opinion of you, how long do you plan to keep it? What will you have to do when you are ready to give it up?

For those who are filled with self-doubt:

● Ask yourself, "How was I ever convinced that I'm inadequate?"

- Look back in your memory and watch the scenes which influenced this decision. Evaluate them *now* as you would for a friend.

- For the next 48 hours be aware of all the ways you put yourself down. Then, for the following two days stop yourself from judging you so harshly.

- List all the things you do well:
  1.
  2.
  3.
  4.
  5.

- Become aware of those competencies during the next few days. Pat yourself on the back when you do well.

- Imagine that you are in a conversation with your ex-love. Share how you felt during the latter part of your relationship and use any "unsaid" words you've kept inside. When you have expressed everything you've buried inside, say "Good-bye."

This exercise will help you to say good-bye to your ex-love. Do it when you feel strong, not "down," and have some quiet time to yourself. Let yourself re-experience those feelings as you can tolerate them. You may need to do this several times until you feel "finished."

# 9

# FOR THE ONE WHO FINALLY CALLED IT QUITS

Generally ex-intimates who are the first to say good-bye have less trouble getting through the grief process than their ex-mates. There are a number of reasons for this: their ego-strengths (pride, self-confidence, independence and ability to adjust) are usually stronger; often they are not as dependent on the relationship for emotional or physical survival; in rare cases, they are not committed to a permanent relationship from the onset; and, finally, they are the ones who actively decide that burying the relationship will be better.

In spite of all this, if you were the one who first declared that your love was dead, you will not avoid the mourning process. Typically, the grief will strike *after* you have physically separated. You can also anticipate that you will carry *more* than your share of guilt and responsibility for how well your ex-mate adjusts to the dissolution. This is especially true if you were in a parent-child relationship and you believe that you are emotionally stronger than your ex-mate. The longer your relationship existed, the more difficult the ending will be.

Deborah and Tom were married for twenty-six years when Deborah filed for divorce. Tom was an alcoholic whose drinking got progressively worse. During the last twelve years of their marriage Deborah supported the family more often than Tom did.

Throughout the marriage, both Tom and Deborah tried to improve their relationship. Tom was in and out of A.A., admitted to psychiatric hospitals and seen by a number of therapists—with no success. Deborah joined *Alanon* and participated in her husband's therapy. After several years of indecision about remaining together, Deborah finally decided that she could no longer live with Tom.

The ending process was painful to both. Tom continued to drink, using his failure at marriage and "life" as his reasons. Deborah continued to support him, at times, financially, and to periodically bail him out of trouble. She also became increasingly more depressed about her own situation and guilt-ridden by the responsibility she felt to Tom.

Nine months after their divorce, I met Deborah in my office, and through the course of therapy she was finally able to let go of her depression and guilt feelings and learn to feel better about herself and her life than she had felt in years.

This chapter is written for men and women like Deborah who, somehow, through the course of a "marriage," end up parenting their partners and feeling responsible for their ex-mate's survival and happiness.

## Moving Is No Picnic, Either: Problems Encountered By Those Who Left

As we've already acknowledged, many ex-intimates who are the first to say good-bye can have just as much pain in leaving a relationship as their ex-mates. If you physically leave and take with you the burdens of financial support for your ex-mate and children, as well as for yourself, you may struggle with all the problems of poverty—plus. Typically, in our society, this happens to the man: "If he wants a divorce, he'll pay through the nose!" vows his rejected spouse. Often the lawyers and judges agree. Sometimes even the man, who feels guilty, may concede: "If I can't give my wife and children the love they deserve, at least I should see that they're financially secure." So, one of the problems that often comes up is the financial strain. An ex-intimate may agree to pay more in money just to avoid a hassle or to ease a guilt-ridden conscience.

Another type of payment an ex-intimate may agree to accept is harder to see but more difficult to avoid: self-blame or the judgment of others that ending the relationship was selfish and "wrong." Any time it looks to you as if your ex-mate is suffering or you are faced with some of the problems of dissolution such as loneliness or fear of your future, you may find yourself "paying" for the decision to leave by condemning yourself for your choice.

> Deborah spent many hours condemning herself for being too hard on Tom—not understanding and supporting him as much as she felt she should. "When I married Tom, I vowed to stay with him for better or worse, in sickness and in health. Alcoholism is a sickness and I broke my vows. I deserve to feel unhappy. God knows, I wasn't a perfect wife—and he stayed with me, anyway."

Relatives and friends who are close to your ex-spouse may also judge you harshly at times, especially if your former partner wants to continue the relationship but you won't agree. In this type of scene, your ex-spouse is seen as the underdog. And, whether that is accurate or not, many onlookers will automatically be on the "underdog's" side and, therefore, against you for saying good-bye.

The payment of self-blame or negative judgments from others can be a high price to pay for your freedom—and one that, beyond constructive self-criticism, will serve no earthly purpose in helping you to feel better again or become a healthier person. Still, it's a problem you may encounter after you've decided to bury the relationship.

Occasionally, an emotionally unstable ex-intimate will resort to threats of suicide or other forms of emotional blackmail in a desperate attempt to reconcile. Although this problem is rare, if your ex-mate has convinced you that life isn't worth living without you, get professional counseling to help *both* of you separate constructively. Learning how to feel better after you have said good-bye will be difficult enough without the voice of threatening doom hanging over your head.

Another problem that is not quite so treacherous, but occurs more often, is the problem of having your ex-mate periodically contact you for continued emotional support or occasional questioning regarding your decision to end it. Each time this happens, you may feel a slight urge of annoyance, mixed with ambivalent feelings about your decision and a small amount of guilt if the choice remains unaltered. In time, your ex-mate will cease contacting you to continue the relationship and begin turning to someone else. (Incidentally, when that finally happens, you may feel some sadness.) In the meantime, direct, honest communication that you plan to stay with your choice of ending will help your ex-mate let go of the past.

Most special problems that arise for the first one to end the relationship are self-induced traps which are caused by your feelings of ambivalence about ending the relationship, plus guilt and responsibility for the welfare of your ex-mate.

## Causal Factors Of Guilt

Guilt is a form of self-punishment or blame that we apply to ourselves when we have done something that we believe is "wrong" or fail to do something that we think of as "right." It is a tool that we use to control our behavior. Any time your behavior is *different* than your value system, you will feel guilty. If you have a value that says fidelity is important, infidelity will cause you to feel guilt. If "marriage forever" is part of your value system, divorce will be seen as an act of shame and something to hide.

There is a wide variation within each person's value system and, therefore, different degrees of guilt that each person may experience. For example, while I may have a strong value for maintaining honesty with those I trust or respect, I may have only mild guilt pangs when not being totally honest with a used-car salesman. Knowingly harming a person through an act of unkindness may cause me sleepless nights of remorse; accidentally hurting a friend through a casual remark can be mended by an apology. Within my own value system, there are ideals I feel are extremely important to uphold and others which I would like to follow but understand and forgive when I don't. We each gain our sense of values from our religious background, cultural heritage, family, and friends. Because of these variables, each of us has a highly individualized value system. But there are some general values that most of us growing up in a our culture have in common: the value of treating others as we would like to be treated ourselves, viewing adultery as something less than honorable, or seeing the destruction of human life as a crime. Some people's value systems are so rigid and narrow that even *thoughts* of going outside their system cause tremendous feelings of guilt. Others have such broad value systems that almost nothing they say or do creates any feelings of remorse. Most of us fall somewhere in between.

Many ex-intimates who initiate good-bye feel pangs of remorse or intense guilt because of any one or a combination of the following:

> Divorce is against their value system.
>
> Leaving their family or mate just because of their own dissatisfaction feels "wrong" or "selfish."
>
> They believe they have a responsibility to take care of their ex-mate.
>
> Their behavior during the relationship was less than honest or went against their value system.

Whatever the specific causal factors of your own guilt feelings, you will need to identify which personal values you have violated by your behavior. In doing this, you may discover that you can let go of some of the guilt just by knowing how you have let yourself down, or by recognizing the need for change within your value system.

## Healthy Ways To Deal With Guilt

People can do a lot of harmful things to themselves in the name of self-punishment—suicide attempts, excessive drinking, drug abuse, self-condemnation, withdrawal, and isolation from friends and family. The best way to deal with guilt is never to do anything that will make you feel bad about yourself. But the reality is that sometimes we human beings let ourselves down— do things we feel ashamed of or wish we hadn't done.

There are two things you can do with your guilt feelings: beat yourself over the head with self-condemnation or learn from your mistakes and, perhaps, modify your value system. Many people vow that they will never let go of their guilt feelings about something they've done because what they did was so horrendous to them. While a certain amount of guilt may be healthy and help prevent you from repeating a behavior that lowers your self-esteem, an extensive amount can be harmful. You will know for yourself how many pangs of remorse you need to keep buried inside in order not to let yourself down in that manner again. It will be hard for you to accept yourself and learn to grow or feel better if you judge yourself unworthy because of your past mistakes. The man who beats himself for divorcing his wife because of religious beliefs will find that he may be stuck in loneliness for the rest of his life if he decides he cannot go back to his wife, and that he doesn't have the right to find happiness with someone new. Letting go of your guilt and learning from your mistakes or altering your value system can be a long and complicated process.

This process is even more difficult for people who don't know how to say no without feeling guilty. If your partner begs you to reconcile and you *normally* sacrifice your needs to avoid hurting someone else's feelings, you will have trouble feeling good about yourself while your ex-mate seems to be suffering.

Vague, generalized guilt feelings can only be handled by vague, generalized regret and self-punishment. The more *specific* you are about what actually triggers your guilt, the better your chances of growing beyond it. Therefore, the first step in this process is to figure out *specifically* what you feel guilty about. Was it how you acted in the relationship or the fact that it ended? One lady felt guilty about ending the relationship because her ex-mate still loved her and wanted their love to continue. Her recognition that she did not love him and subsequent decision to dissolve their relationship were directly opposed to her values that she *should* feel the same way about people as they feel about her and that she *should not*, under any circumstances, hurt someone's feelings. Once she learned why she felt guilty, she could begin the process of dealing with her guilt in a healthier manner. One man suffered a great deal of guilt and self-blame for divorcing his wife who was psychiatrically disabled. In spite of the fact that she spent most of her time in hospitals and had for years, the man felt like a villain. His decision to end their relationship was directly opposed to his values of staying with his ex-mate (through sickness or health), wanting to be someone who was loyal and loving no matter what the circumstances, plus feeling responsible for causing her illness or not helping her become healthier. Once he was able to recognize why he felt guilty, he, too, was able to begin the process of dealing with his guilt in ways that were healthier for him.

After you have identified specifically why you feel guilty, begin to figure out what it would take for you to forgive yourself. This is the *making up* or penance phase of the process. This is only necessary for those actions or decisions you feel guilty about *after* you understand specifically what they are. Go through each item that you feel badly about and determine what behavior that is healthy and helpful to you will salve your conscience. Would an apology to your ex-mate be helpful—or, perhaps a vow to learn from your mistakes and try not to repeat your behavior? One man who left his wife lessened his guilt about leaving by helping her get some occupational training and then her first job. Another man who felt guilty about leaving his children learned to lessen his guilt by making it a point to be the best part-time father he could. The list of examples of how to absolve your "sins" in a healthier manner than beating yourself with remorse is endless. Any kind of "repayment" which will help you obtain self-forgiveness will do, but be careful not to include excessive self-sacrifice or self-denial as part of your penance.

The third step is the hardest to do, but the easiest to explain. Once you have decided specifically what you need to do to let go of your guilt, get busy and do it. No need to punish yourself any longer by procrastinating. If it's saying "I'm sorry" or making an effort to change your behavior for the next time or whatever it is, grab hold of your courage and get on with it. The sooner you've paid for your feelings of shame or for letting yourself down by some actions, the more quickly you can give up your feelings of guilt.

The final step is learning to forgive yourself. Once you have gone through the process of constructive self-examination and have learned specifically why you feel guilty—the reasons you had for your behavior or decisions at the time—and have developed a way of "making up" for the action that you cannot forgive just through understanding and accepting yourself as a person with faults, it should be a simple matter for you to say to yourself—"I forgive you." It may sound silly to you now, but practice saying those words or something similar while looking at yourself in the mirror. Repeat them until they *feel right* to you. Forgiving yourself for mistakes you have made or broadening your sense of values will help you feel a whole lot better through the grief process. Also, you might just find you'll be a healthier person for the next time around.

## How To Get Yourself In Proper Perspective

One of the major reasons ex-intimates who are the ones that initiate good-bye feel guilty is because they mistakenly see themselves as *the* ones who are totally responsible for the dissolution. While this may give some people a sense of power and importance, it can also hand them sleepless nights of regret or self-condemnation if they decide, for whatever reason, that the decision to end was wrong—or much more difficult than they had planned.

But the death of an intimate relationship and its eventual burial is the handiwork of two people, *not* one. If you're an ex-intimate who currently believes that you are solely responsible for the ending of that last love, you may find it helpful to get yourself in proper perspective and take a more realistic view of your own power, responsibility, and blame (if you must) for the burial of your old love.

To help you more clearly evaluate your control over and responsibility for the demise of your love, take a few minutes and answer the following questions for yourself.

1. How much of my decision to announce "it's over" came from my partner's failure to change or compromise with me?

2. How many times before I pulled out did I hear my partner indirectly say he or she didn't care any more?

3. When it comes right down to it, what are the reasons our love died and how many times was I responsible compared to the number to times it was within my ex-mate's control?

4. Why do I need to feel as if it was my sole decision, anyway? What would I do differently now if I didn't?

5. If I'm so powerful, why couldn't I have changed the relationship into something more satisfying?

6. What actually killed my commitment to stay with my ex-mate—did I stop loving and respecting by myself?

7. What good does it do to "blame" one of us more than the other?

By answering these questions you will discover that the choice, no matter when you consciously made it, was also guided by your ex-mate. There is a strength in finally deciding to bury a relationship that is dead, but do not damn yourself into believing that this strength makes you strong enough to carry the entire burden of dissolution for both of you.

You have the strength to make your own decision on what you are willing to settle for in an intimate relationship and what you are not. You will need to nurture those strengths to help you feel better now that it's over—do not zap them by carrying the entire blame for the ending whenever it feels that the decision was somehow wrong or scary.

## How To Equalize Blame For Dissolution

Self-blame and negative judgment from others, including your ex-mate, will occur if the dissolution of an intimate relationship is viewed as unfair or somehow "wrong." Because of the nature of ending, the subsequent grief process, the sociological and religious pressures, it will be impossible to escape *some* blame for the death of your relationship.

There is nothing wrong with accepting part of the responsibility for the dissolution of your relationship. Basically, this just means that you had some influence within the relationship. The problems occur when you assume *all* of the responsibility for the relationship and condemn yourself for how it turned out. In doing that you discount the fact that you were in a two-person relationship, and you encourage your ex-mate to feel inept.

Blame is a negative reaction to the normal insecurity and feeling of helplessness that comes with major separations. Some of this will automatically lessen with time and as each person begins feeling more secure and self-confident.

As the one who initiated good-bye, you may accept the extra burden of "fault" for any one of the following reasons:

1. Since you were the first to suggest ending, you may *appear* tougher and more able to handle everyone's displaced anger—including your own.

2. Your mate may take on the wounded-puppy stance and beg you to stay. (Few people have the heart to blame or get angry at a puppy.)

3. You will be less emotionally committed to the relationship at the time of ending and will, therefore, probably adjust more quickly to a new life. This quicker adjustment can be confused with being coldhearted.

4. You may see your ex-mate as fragile and, therefore, protect him or her from being responsible for certain behavior. ("It wasn't his fault that he couldn't support the family, he's always been afraid of responsibility.")

Thoughts like: "I *should* have been more understanding—or given in more often—or changed my expectations" will be natural for you to have occasionally, even if you are the one who initiated the dissolution and you tried everything that you could think of at the time to make the relationship better. Many ex-intimates who take on most of the blame for the ending do this because of their own self-perception. They see themselves as people who are never satisfied with less than perfection and somehow, maybe because of that, have the ability to destroy or cause harm to those whom they love. Most clients I see who divorce a spouse that's an alcoholic, for example, often blame themselves for their ex-mate's drinking problem. "He wouldn't be an alcoholic if I hadn't nagged him so much—I knew he had a drinking problem and I just made it worse."

To help equalize blame for the end of a love affair, you must admit that *both* of you are adults and that *each* of you contributed to the death of your love. The fact of the matter is that the relationship is dead and you are now in the process of burying it for yourself.

## Common Self-Induced Traps

If you initiated good-bye, you may fall into some of the following self-induced traps because of your own mixed feelings about ending the relationship.

> Feeling guilty each time you have a good time or when you begin feeling better.
>
> Acting on ambivalence: going back and forth about your decision to end and acting on it.
>
> Continuing to meet your ex-mate's emotional or sexual needs out of guilt.
>
> Screaming at your ex-mate to "shape up" and become independent so that you no longer need to feel tied down or guilty.
>
> Seeing yourself as emotionally stronger or more prepared to cope with the ending and, therefore, not seeking support for yourself from friends and family.

All of these traps are a natural part of the grief process and it may be necessary for you to slide in and out of some of them in order for you to feel better about yourself and finally let go of your dead love affair. Each time you fall into one of these traps, your energy is spent on trying to unhook from the past or expunge your guilt. It's important to remember that some of your energy must be focused on developing a creative future as well. And even though you had the strength to initiate goodbye, you, too, will need to nurture your strengths and gain support from others to grow through the grief process.

## Utilizing Strengths To Handle Obstacles Coming Up

Every ex-intimate, whether the one who initiated good-bye or not, will run into a number of obstacles once he or she is single again. Just learning how to date again can be a frustrating and awkward experience of trial and error at first. If you've been married for twenty years, you may discover that being single again is a lot like being back in your adolescence—only this time with a slightly dumpy body, graying hair, a battered self-image, and a somewhat provincial moral code. You will need a great deal of courage, flexibility, and determination (plus maybe a good sense of humor) to tackle this challenge all over again—especially on those first few dates.

One lady I know confessed that she spent all afternoon and part of an evening getting ready for her first date.

"I cleaned up the house, shuffled the kids off to grandma's, spent over an hour putting on makeup and combing my hair, then another hour dressing and undressing. Nothing I put on seemed to look exactly the way I wanted it to—I hadn't realized that my wardrobe consisted mostly of clothes to work around the house, rush to the supermarket, or drive the kids to the dentist. I settled for a five-year-old dress that I bought for a PTA installation and a vow that I had to lose ten pounds and buy some new clothes. All through the day, I was nervous and no amount of telling myself to relax seemed to help. Twice I thought about calling my date and telling him one of the kids was sick, but decided that I had to start dating again sometime. I'm glad that I did; we had a good time. I can look back on that scene with a smile and some pride at how confident I've gotten since then."

The awkwardness of dating isn't confined to just the female gender, of course. Many men also find it nerve-racking to go back to the business of asking a woman for a date, figuring out where to go, how to be entertaining, whether and when to make sexual advances, as well as how many times he can see one woman before she expects some sort of exclusive relationship. The chances are that both dating partners have had a previous relationship and will, therefore, feel equally awkward and uncomfortable about these issues in dating again.

Dating is just one of the challenges of being single again. Some of the others which will require your strength, determination, and ability to roll with the punches are:

> Figuring out what you want to do with your life now that you have your freedom
>
> Constructive insight and change, including the resolution of some old "hang-ups"
>
> Learning how to take care of everyday tasks that your ex-mate handled, such as: cooking, washing, ironing, shopping, and housekeeping, if you're a man; or, taking care of mechanical, electrical, and maybe even financial matters, if you're a woman—plus, perhaps, learning how to support yourself for the first time

No wonder ex-intimates sometimes feel lost or overwhelmed with depression and decide to crawl into a hole. Hiding can be mighty tempting at times. Especially in the beginning.

To creatively conquer these obstacles, it is important to use *every strength* that you have and learn to build more. If you spend a lot of time worrying about your ex-mate or punishing yourself for initiating good-bye, you will have little motivation or energy left over for getting yourself ready for dating again or meeting any one of the other challenges of being independent. You have already begun to use your courage, pride, and common sense to announce the end of a relationship that was already dead. Now, it is important that you continue to devote your energy to you and building an emotionally healthier future.

## Experiments and Exercises

The ex-intimate who initiates goodbye often gets "hooked" on guilt and resentment. For those who are stuck in these feelings, the following exercise will prove beneficial. As with any of the exercises, choose a setting where you are physically and emotionally comfortable and will not be interrupted by noise. Make sure you feel strong, and not "down."

Close your eyes and look back in your memory for the last scene which gave you an invitation to feel guilty. Remember who was there and what was happening. Allow yourself to feel the guilt and resentment.

When you are ready, imagine that you are in a dialogue with the person you feel guilt/resentment toward. Share how you honestly feel and make sure that you express the resentment tied to your guilt. For example, "I resent you telling me that you want me back because then I feel guilty about not wanting you any more." Continue repeating this final assertion until you feel that it "fits" for you. (This may take several rehearsals.) When it finally feels right, close the dialogue with an announcement that you are no longer going to feel guilty about that issue any more.

After this exercise take some time to reflect.

- What can you learn from this

  About your relationship with that person?

  About your relationship with other people?

  About your relationship with yourself?

During the next 48 hours be aware of when you find yourself feeling obligated or responsible for someone else.

- What do you get out of it? (Does it help you to feel better than everyone else, for example?)
- Is there some other way you would like to feel?
- What would you have to do to change it?

List all of the reasons you deserve to take care of your own needs first.
1.
2.
3.
4.
5.

# 10

## HEALTHY WAYS TO MOURN

It may seem strange to include a chapter on healthy ways to mourn; after all, isn't this book designed to help you feel *better* after you've said good-bye? Nevertheless, in order to grow through the grief process and let go of the past, you will need to go through a mourning phase. In fact, part of this chapter will include constructive ways you can help yourself get in touch with your pain, because, paradoxical as it may sound, your mental health demands it. If you cared about your ex-love and the life that you had, you will need to feel the grief when it's dead in order to let go of your pain and start living again.

The process of grieving over the death of an intimate relationship, like grief for the death of a person, involves five stages—denial, depression, anger, resignation, and acceptance or proceeding with your life. It is necessary to go through *all* of these stages in order to finally reach the fifth, which involves going on with your life. There are thousands of people walking around who have never completed the grief process and, therefore, have never really gotten over an old love affair. These people continue to carry their hurt feelings or anger into their next love relationship or live the rest of their lives alone.

No one can tell you exactly how long it will take to finally accept that it's over and to proceed with your life without carrying a lot of unresolved hurts. It varies for each person. Do not expect yourself to go through the mourning process in a simple 1, 2, 3 fashion. Human beings and their feelings are more complicated than that, and you need the time, plus regressions, to help heal them. Consequently, there will be times when you go from the first stage of the grief process to the second, to the third, then back to the first or the second again. This cycle will repeat itself again and again as long as you need to go through it—until you have finally resolved all the questions and problems that arise in each stage—or learned to finally set them aside.

There is one sure thing, however. Whether you acknowledge your grief to yourself or not—it will be there. If you deny the existence of that pain, you will wipe out your only opportunity to learn how to control the sorrow and let go of the grief. If, for example, you tell yourself that you really don't have a cold, it doesn't change the reality that it exists; it only alters the way you deal with it. Ignore a cold and continue with your daily routine and you may find yourself lying in bed with pneumonia. Ignore your sadness and continue with your regular routine and you may find yourself feeling numb inside and therefore unable to love someone new.

## How To Give Yourself Permission To Grieve

> "I don't need to learn how to feel sad—that comes naturally. I need to learn how to turn off the pain."
> —Anonymous divorcee

Being able to naturally feel sorrow over your loss helps you grow through the grief process and learn to feel better. For,

## Healthy Ways To Mourn  157

without feeling sad, you cannot bury your dead love and constructively seek out a new relationship to overcome the loneliness.

We are taught as children not to feel sorrow or any kind of negative feeling. "Don't get angry, it isn't good for you." "Don't feel sad about your dead kitten, we'll get you another one." "If you can't say something nice, don't say anything at all." "Come on, soldier, big boys don't cry." By the time we're adults, we not only do not share painful feelings directly with other people, but sometimes do not allow even ourselves to know what we feel.

The dangers in this "avoidance" are phenomenal:

● By cutting off negative feelings from your awareness, you also diminish your ability to feel the positive ones.

● Unacknowledged hurt festers inside and may turn into anger or a sensation of not being aware of any feelings.

● When you deny your right to be aware of your painful emotions, the emotional hurt can lodge in your body and become physically translated into ulcers, heart attacks, colitis, or headaches.

Children rarely have ulcers or tension headaches; parents often do because adults are taught to think out their problems—children quite naturally *feel* them. An emotionally healthy adult learns to do both: feel the pain and then problem-solve and adjust. If you are an adult who has somehow forgotten how to let yourself feel, the first thing that you need to do is give yourself permission to grieve over the loss of your ex-love. You will not fall apart. Remind yourself that you weren't always so afraid of your feelings—even the painful ones—and that you have a right as an ex-intimate who feels sad to directly acknowledge that pain to yourself. There are some things that you just can't think away. Math problems can be solved by logical abstraction; hurt feelings begin healing after you've given yourself permission to acknowledge that the wounds exist.

## Ways Of Allowing Yourself To Feel Pain

If you find it difficult to feel the grief from good-bye, consider these suggestions. First, develop an understanding of why feeling your pain is so scary. For some people, it is foreign to take the time to acknowledge their own hurt feelings. They have learned throughout their lives that their own feelings are not as important as other peoples'; discounting themselves has become automatic. If this is the case for you, begin standing up for yourself. Be as concerned about your own feelings as you are about your friends'.

Others shy away from the feelings because their experience with grief has been traumatic or second-hand. They have known or heard about individuals who became so overwhelmed with hurt, self-pity, depression, or anger that they stayed stuck there forever. If you have no real-life practical experience of your own, the fear of falling into the same trap forever can put the skids on your willingness to experience your grief. But you must have faith in your own ability to grow—and let go of your pain when it becomes too intense. With practice you will discover that when you take control of your grief and allow yourself to feel the pain, you also have the strength to shut it off when it becomes overwhelming.

Another quite obvious hesitation in allowing yourself to feel the pain is that it hurts! And most of us don't like to hurt. But the fact of the matter is that the pain is already there from saying good-bye. Your only decision at this point is whether to let yourself feel it directly and then learn to release it; or to carry it around inside your gut for the rest of your life and gingerly avoid caring about anyone again because of the fear that you can't take any additional hurt.

Once you have a basic understanding of why feeling pain is so terrifying to you, the next step is to see how you currently keep yourself from feeling the grief. Usually people avoid admitting their hurt by either keeping so busy that they don't have time to be alone and feel, or they rationalize that they shouldn't feel any sorrow. "There's no reason to feel badly, it won't help" or "I don't know why it should bother me to lose him—he's a bum anyway." When you find out how you avoid admitting your grief, you can allow yourself to feel some of the pain by curtailing the techniques you use to deny it exists. Usually this is the easiest way to get in touch with your feelings. Just ask yourself, "How do I feel when I'm not hiding from me?"

If it's been several weeks since you've separated and you have not allowed yourself to experience your grief, the first recognition of your hurt may come out like a flood. One woman shared that the first time she actually sat down and decided to cry over her divorce, she spent the entire weekend in tears.

"The only other things I did that weekend was periodically fix something to eat and occasionally sleep. I've never been so exhausted in my life. Tears just flowed. At first my whole body felt tight, like there was a bomb inside ready to explode. But once I finally began crying, the pressure inside disappeared. I can't even tell you what I cried about or all of the different thoughts that raced through my head. And just when I thought I was through crying, the tightness would come back in my chest or stomach and I'd start all over again. At one point I remember thinking that I had to quit this and get control of myself, then I remember telling myself that I had nothing else to do, and I deserved a good cry. I haven't cried as intensely or as long since. I guess the feelings had to come out—I even remember deciding sometime during that weekend, that once I was over this, I had to find some new goals for my life. I'm just beginning to look at that now—I'm not sure yet what I'll do, but I know now that I'll make it."

A man related a similar experience, adding that in order to finally allow himself to begin feeling grief, he literally had to force himself to look at old family pictures, listen to sad records, and remind himself that his marriage was over.

> "The last time I remember crying was when I was seven and my grandfather died. My mother said she was surprised because she didn't think I felt that strongly. It's funny, I really don't know why I never shared my feelings very much. Probably it would look funny for a middle-aged businessman to burst out in tears when he loses an account. But knowing that I actually do have feelings makes me feel so much better about me. I've gotten a lot closer to me and my friends since then. Just by being what I've always been but afraid to admit—a human being with feelings."

The point is that once you allow yourself to feel the pain from your loss, you will discover some very valuable rewards:

- There is a relief in allowing yourself to experience your pain.
- It will hurt and feel scary at times but will never be quite as intense as the first time.
- Allowing yourself to grieve makes space in you for positive feelings.
- Feeling pain will help motivate you to proceed with your life.

## Getting the Proper Perspective On Loss

One of the major reasons that you may feel overwhelmed by your loss at first is because the death of a love affair, like the death of a person, immediately gets you in touch with your own mortality. A death or the loss of anything major in your life leaves you feeling disconnected. People who are emotionally prepared for dissolution or for the death of a loved one and what they'll do next with their own lives will suffer less intense feelings of being alone and abandoned than their unprepared counterparts.

When you first get in touch with your grief you may be trying to cope with an overwhelming fact of life that you could not have been aware of at first—your unconscious fear of death. For a while, life may seem to have no meaning to you. On a conscious level that meaninglessness might derive from the loss of your ex-love, parts of your identity, and your former lifestyle. On an unconscious level you may be dealing with the death of the **you** that you have known. The longer you were "married," the harder it will be for you to see yourself as a whole person outside of your relationship. That is why you may automatically begin evaluating your life up until the present (or quickly condemning it), find yourself wanting to return to a nurturing family or someone who can give you comforting and, then, slowly, begin to decide, as did the lady in my group, that you need to develop new goals for yourself or a reason to make your life meaningful.

Getting your loss in proper perspective in this case means not only looking realistically at whom and what you have lost, but, also, recognizing on a conscious level that you are still alive. There are many crises in our lives (saying good-bye to our childhood, or our children's dependency on us, or a career, or an intimate relationship) that trigger our need for constructive self-evaluation and future goal planning. After careful examination, some people decide that they want to continue with their life career, but change parts of their personalities or methods of coping so that they can truly feel good about themselves for the first time. Personal growth and positive change during a divorce is much more rapid than it is during a marriage. People feel more anxiety during a crisis, which becomes the impetus to grow, than they do when they are dissatisfied but safe in their ruts.

Some people decide at the end of a relationship to change professions or maybe develop one for the first time. Businessmen look at their computerlike lifestyle and decide that they want a career that's more meaningful for them. Housewives decide to go back to school and create a career outside of the home.

When you begin to look realistically at what you have lost, don't forget to pinch yourself and revel in the fact that you are still alive. The grief over your loss will become less overwhelming when you allow yourself to recognize that your life isn't over yet and you still have a lot more time to grow creatively. You might discover tht life can become much more precious when you recognize not only its tenuous quality but also your own potential for its control.

## Techniques That Help You Let Go Of Pain

In order to let go of your emotional pain, you must first allow yourself to experience it totally. The idea of diving into a bad feeling—precisely what you want to be rid of—may sound like needless torture. However, becoming vividly aware of a painful emotion helps you come to grips with it. When you can experience exactly how severe it is in you, how it affects your body, and what its dimensions are, then the pain is no longer an overwhelming ogre you must run away from. Now you know the pain and choose to touch it or sense when it has been touched by some person or situation. It is, therefore, yours—to do with as you wish but certainly no longer to fear.

Emotional pain can be caused by feeling scared of your future, feeling abandoned, rejected or worthless, alone in the world with no one to comfort you, or any number of things. If you genuinely want to know for yourself where the sources of your pain are buried, purposely force yourself to admit your feelings.

Put on some comfortable clothes, pick a spot in your house which is quiet, and begin to relax. See if you can feel in your body where the hurt lies. Is it in your stomach or throat? How about your neck or the muscles in your back? Some people discover they've been swallowing hurt feelings or "garbage" from others for years and, with the ending of an intimate relationship, they swallow a little more just so they can get through the separation scenes. But now is the time to experience that pain. Really feel it and begin releasing out loud the words and the feelings that are knotted up inside of you. Let your words ramble. Say anything that comes to mind. Cry when the tears come. Scream when you're hurting or angry. If you genuinely want to get rid of what's bugging or frightening you, you can when you feel it.

One way to strengthen emotional awareness is to say what you're feeling over and over again until you actually *feel* the words in your body. One man in my group practiced saying "I'm lonely" over and over until he shouted "My God, I really am lonely—I'd better do something about it!"

When you're first trying to identify your feelings, avoid the common tendency to block emotion by trying to understand it or think about something else. Many people have trouble experiencing what they feel because their mind is somewhere else. They walk in the country but think about their problems in the city. They begin to feel pain and quickly think themselves out of it because of their fears.

If you find yourself pulling out of a feeling or stopping yourself from experiencing it totally, relax and don't push yourself. You can come back to it some other time because your feelings stay inside of you until you release them. In learning that you can stop yourself from feeling more pain than you think you can handle, you will discover for yourself, once again, that you have control over your feelings.

Once you have experienced your painful emotions, you will discover that some have diminished. Allow time for reflection after you have gotten in touch with your feelings. Look back on your experience and see what you have discovered about yourself; the opportunity for insight at this point is bountiful. One lady found that she kept herself in pain by constantly trying to get her ex-husband back. She did this, she discovered, because her own father had died when she was a young child and she had always felt that he rejected her, but never had the opportunity to resolve it with him. As an adult, she somehow felt that if she could get her ex-husband (who had been harsh and rejecting) to take back his words or tell her he was wrong about leaving her—which she couldn't get her father to do—she would feel better about herself. Once she discovered on a conscious level what torture she was putting herself through for unconscious reasons, she could quit giving her husband continued oppotunities to reject her.

In your reflection, make yourself admit how you continue adding to your pain in everyday life. All of us have the same feelings and fears, but some of us build on them. Some people keep themselves in a position of feeling like a doormat by always letting other people's needs come first and taking care of everyone but themselves. Some ex-intimates discover that they keep feeling rejected by reaching out again and again to the same people who refuse to meet them half-way or are unwilling to accept them. Others discover they continue to feel overwhelmed by taking on more problems than they can possibly handle. Some discover they build on their feelings of loneliness by isolating themselves and not allowing their friends or family to comfort them. Look at yourself in your own situation and take the responsibility of finding out how you build on your pain—then change some of those patterns.

To summarize, the techniques that will help you let go of your pain are:

- Taking the responsibility to admit your painful emotions.
- Experiencing the pain and discovering its size.
- Releasing part of your hurt, just by letting it out.
- Reflecting on your experience and discovering how you continue to build on parts of your pain in everyday life.
- Changing some of your current behavior which is self-defeating or needlessly hurtful.

## How To Get a Little Help From Your Friends

Although it is essential for you to dive into some of your painful feelings alone, it is equally important to reach out to others for emotional support and comforting after you've experienced the pain. Close friends or family members can help you feel better during the grief process by offering you their love and concern, an ear to hear how you feel, a hug to help you know that you're not alone in the world, and sometimes helpful advice for your problems. You will know when you need to seek others for comfort and support. In general, it is not a good idea to go for more then two or three days of "bad" feelings alone before you make the following conscious efforts to encourage the friendship and soothing of others:

1. Recognize your own need and the value of gaining emotional support from someone outside yourself. Admit your feelings of isolation, abandonment, lack of self-confidence, and hurt, and accept the fact that as long as you stay by yourself and hesitate to call up a friend you will continue to feel isolated—because you are. The minute you allow someone else to experience your world of feelings, you are no longer totally alone or abandoned. And when someone accepts your invitation (no matter how briefly) to hear how you feel, that act, in itself, tells you that you still have value to someone.

2. Deliberately determine who in your current life will be able to give you emotional support and who will refuse or be unable to do so. People you know separately from your ex-mate are probably the most ideal—and, relatives you have always felt close to are another source. Avoid the tendency to eliminate everyone because of your own fear of rejection. Do, however, eliminate some people from your list—at least during the first few weeks—your ex-intimate's best friends and family. Occasionally, reaching out to mutual friends can also be hazardous. All of these people will be affected by the death of your love affair; for some it will mean a threat to their own "marriage"; for

others, an event to judge or choose sides in. In any case, it is best to give them and yourself some time to feel better before you decide to get back in touch.

3. Take the responsibility of contacting others (those you've decided might help) and ask them for their friendship in person, by telephone or through writing a letter. Having the names in your head of a few friends and relatives who *would* help you feel less isolated and alone is of little value if you don't contact them. People who are near can give you immediate comforting just by their physical presence. Writing a letter expressing your feelings can also be quite helpful.

4. Admit your need for someone to listen to you, care, and be concerned about you as a valuable person—make a conscious effort not to turn off your friends by getting them to take sides. It's natural, especially if you were not the one to initiate good-bye, to see your ex-intimate as responsible for your pain, or to spend a lot of energy trying to prove you're okay by getting others to judge your ex-mate as the person to blame for the dissolution. The analogy can be made between healing a broken heart and mending a broken leg; at the time that they're broken, the circumstances which led up to the crash are of only *secondary* value. The primary concern now is getting it mended. When you're feeling abandoned, it's important to reach out to someone who will accept you and care. Later, when you begin feeling better, you can constructively reflect on why the relationship died.

## How To Bury the Dead

The whole mourning process is geared toward acceptance and continuation of your life after you have said good-bye to a dead love affair. Obviously, if you refuse to say good-bye emotionally, you will never proceed with your life and learn how to love again. Each time you attempt to rekindle your old relationship, you are denying the reality that it is over and setting yourself up for a little more heartbreak. Still, it is natural for many ex-intimates to periodically slip back into the denial phase of mourning and attempt trial reconciliations. One couple I know spent two years of their three-year marriage saying good-bye to each other and then making trial reconciliations. Both partners were afraid to bury their love and feel the pain of good-bye.

Burying a dead love affair involves accepting that your old love is over and no longer attempting to rekindle the sparks by dating your ex-love, trying for reconciliations, or fooling yourself into believing that someday the two of you will be together again. It is a painful process accomplished with neither speed nor ease.

Ex-intimates who have children in common may have more trouble burying their old love than their counterparts who do not; especially if the parent who does not have custody of the children visits them often. The reason for this difficulty is that most ex-intimates still do care to some degree about their ex-mate, and continuing to see an old love makes it difficult to bury that fondness. Especially if neither of them has developed a new love relationship yet. The children may try to get Mommy and Daddy back together again—so that they don't have to go through the mourning process themselves. If you find yourself in this situation, avoid private contact with your ex-mate as much as you can. Have a friend with you when it's necessary to see your ex-love.

Burying your dead love affair requires getting rid of all the old love trinkets and mementos that were part of your relationship when it was alive. If you're a sentimentalist and have saved old love tokens, letters, and cards from the "good times," go through your closets and drawers and throw them away. Do this with any object that you find yourself keeping "just in case we get together again." With each article that you toss away, go through the process of literally saying good-bye to it first and allow yourself to feel the sadness you may have. It's hard to pretend that your old love is still alive if you actually allow yourself to emotionally bury each dusty memento.

Another way to help you bury your dead love affair is to tell yourself out loud again and again that it is dead. As with the heightening of any emotional awareness, sometimes repeating reality to yourself helps your head and gut to finally acknowledge the truth.

As much as possible, avoid other people in your life who refuse to believe that the two of you have ended your intimacy. Obviously you cannot do this with your children or close friends and family members, but many of your mutual acquaintances who seem to have a stake in denying that the two of you have decided to go separate paths should be avoided. Especially in the beginning if you are having difficulty accepting it's over yourself. For those in your life that you will continue to see who deny the burial of your old love, you may explain that the relationship has been dead for a while and your "divorce" is merely a part of facing that fact. Sometimes when you tell others this, it helps you to acknowledge it, again, for yourself.

Remember that you are not dealing with the death of a person; you are groping with the death of an intimate relationship. Your ex-mate will still be alive and occasionally look good to you. Each time you say good-bye to an old memento, let someone else know that your old love affair is definitely over and feel it yourself; you are throwing another shovel of dirt over the casket of your dead love affair. Soon, you will be able to walk away from the graveyard.

## Unhealthy Mourning Practices

Many ex-intimates go through an unhealthy mourning process because there is not a socially acceptable, clearly defined procedure to help them deal with their grief. When an individual dies, there are funeral rites to bury the body and clearly defined mourning rituals to help the bereaved. Widowers or widows can expect expressions of sorrow over their loss, invitations for social activities during the convalescent stage and offers of assistance from the very beginning. A widower will automatically receive help with the choking, cleaning, shopping, and care of his children if he needs it. A widow will no doubt receive offers from the men in her life to work on the house, keep the car mechanically safe, act as a substitute father for the children, help her move, find a job, and whatever else she may need—without any "strings."

But with the death of an intimate relationship, there is no automatic support you can count on from others and few, socially acceptable, clearly prescribed mourning rituals. There is no funeral and no specific bereavement process. If you were married, there is a divorce decree and the trips to the lawyers and courts which can be used as official ending rites. But most of these rituals are handled alone or with strangers. You cannot automatically expect anyone to offer emotional support or assistance in helping you adjust to your loss. In fact, many of your friends and family (including your priest or minister) may actually avoid you or talk about "what's wrong" with you behind your back, now that you've ended an intimate relationship. If you go out with friends for a "good time," you may find some of your loved ones denouncing your behavior, instead of encouraging you to get away from the house. If you're a woman and one of your male friends offers his help, you may find there are sexual "strings" attached—or, you may discover that his wife will discourage your friendship for fear you are "after" him.

Because of these signals and their own mixed feelings, many ex-intimates believe that there is something "wrong" with grieving over the death of an intimate relationship, and, in fact, they should not feel any hurt at all, since they are the "villains" that killed their love. If this happens to you, you may hide your grief from yourself, mix it up with excessive self-condemnation, or handle your grief with emotionally unhealthy mourning practices. Do not be unduly alarmed if you find yourself mourning in unhealthy ways. The key issue is not whether you grieve in an unhealthy fashion, but for how long and to what extreme.

1. *Enshrouding yourself in black and assuming the role of the "bereaved" as your total identity.* This practice is easy to slip into and quite natural for many during the first few weeks or months of the mourning process. Especially for those who were not the ones to initiate good-bye. However, you can carry this bereaved mourner role too far. If you make absolutely no effort to be attractive or develop the parts of your wounded ego that will help you want another intimate relationship someday, you could get stuck as a permanent mourner.

A little of the "bereaved lover" can go a long way! To avoid staying in this mourning ritual longer than is healthy, set up some definite length of time to mourn in this fashion. Build up the other parts of your identity, such as employee, parent, son or daughter, friend, member of the community, etc., even during your bereavement phase. That way when you are ready to begin living again, those parts of your identity will not be lost or forgotten entirely.

2. *Burying yourself in self-pity.* If you decide that your life is over and there's nothing you can do to change it, you may succeed in beating down your natural instincts to continue enjoying your life. There are some similarities between this mourning practice and the one above. It is natural to feel a certain amount of self-pity and to periodically slide into hours or days of bemoaning your fate—especially during the first few months. However, some people have a tendency to withdraw into themselves and refuse to take the responsibility for changing their situation. Others spend so much of their energy trying to change their loneliness by getting together again with a dead love that they do not give themselves the opportunity to gain love and acceptance from someone new.

If, after the first three months, you are as wrapped up in feeling sorry for yourself as you were in the beginning, you'd better accept the fact that the next three months aren't going to be any different unless you take the responsibility for changing your way of dealing with the loss. The longer you wallow, without relief, the harder it is to do anything constructive with your wounded pride.

3. *Drowning your sorrow in liquor or drugs.* Unfortunately, one way to gain temporary but immediate relief from painful emotions is to numb yourself with booze or drugs. Both of these escape routes are easily available to all of us and, although every person who gets hooked on drugs or alcohol as a tool to deal with life may tell you that it really only *adds* problems, that person has discovered a way to gain temporary relief and the motivation to resolve the troubles and obtain permanent relief somehow gets lost. The reality is that you need to feel your pain and anxiety in order to let go of the hurt. If you develop the skill of "copping out," you will not be able to develop the art of "coping through" the mourning process. Do not encourage the coward in you to escape each time you feel pain.

4. *Giving up your interest in the rest of the world and focusing only on your losses and personal sorrow.* It is natural for a short period of time to avoid contact with or interest in the outside world and focus your thoughts and energy entirely on whom/-what you have lost. But set up a definite period of time to withdraw from the world and bemoan your loss. Then, at the end of that time, make a conscious effort to resume the business of living again. It's difficult to tell you exactly how long you should give up your interest in the parts of your world that are still alive. It varies for each individual. But probably you should not allow yourself to remain cut off from your natural interests and sources of pleasure for any longer than a few days at a time. This mourning practice can become self-destructive practice, if, after the first three months, you are still mourning the loss of your old love by focusing all of your energy and thoughts on its demise.

5. *Avoiding feelings of grief entirely and throwing yourself totally into your work or the children.* A common practice for many ex-intimates who are afraid of their own emotional pain is to avoid feeling entirely and begin devoting all of their waking

hours to a "cause." Men often do this with their business; women sometimes dive head-on into the lives of their children. But this practice does not help you grow through the grief process. In fact, it encourages you to put off your grief, until your "cause" is completed or the children are grown. Many ex-intimates who decide to handle their pain in this way find themselves feeling not quite fulfilled and, years later, overwhelmed with their losses. Just at the time when they are saying good-bye to their youth and productivity, it becomes apparent that they have no one to share their personal lives with any more.

Rationalizing that you don't have the time to "get involved" with someone new can be an excuse for you not to try. You can protect yourself from ever getting hurt again by love, but you also give up your chances of once again (or maybe for the first time) feeling the warmth and happiness that loving someone can provide.

6. *Consciously devising ways to end your own life, so that you can be buried with your dead love relationship.* I don't know how many ex-intimates actually decide to kill themselves as a way of dealing with their grief. Although it is said that each of us at one time or another will contemplate suicide; but for those who are especially insecure, the thought of death may become more than just an idea to consider. If you feel so overwhelmed by your loss that you actually begin contemplating taking your own life, you need to contact a local mental health clinic or suicide prevention center immediately. You will find a "crisis line" or "suicide line" listed in your telephone book. Better yet, contact someone before you get to that point.

## How To Stop Grief From Overwhelming You

Even though it is literally impossible to become overwhelmed by grief, there are times when it *feels* as though you will never get over your sorrow, that there will never be light in your life or warmth in your heart again. No wonder people try to avoid feeling their grief. Grief hurts—and it's scary! And, sometimes, ex-intimates make it worse by overreacting to their fears, overloading their ability to cope with sorrow, or immobilizing themselves.

You can avoid becoming overwhelmed with grief by admitting your sorrow and refusing to let yourself become a victim of your feelings, as follows:

1. Accept the reality that it is natural to feel sadness about the death of your old relationship. Expect to feel some pain. Don't be afraid of your feelings. Remember that all feelings, including the hurtful ones, are transitory. You are in a *process*, it is not the end of your life!
2. Don't overload yourself with past hurts or losses. Sometimes ex-intimates immobilize themselves by pulling in their memories and unresolved grief from all of their past losses: the deaths of other relationships, important people in their lives who are gone, good-bye to their own youth, or life patterns and ambitions they have given up. Grief over the loss of their old love affair gets mixed up with the pain from other losses.
3. Do take the responsibility of reaching out to others for comfort and support.
4. Don't be surprised if you unexpectedly feel sorrow after you have gone for days or even months of feeling good again.
5. Do take the initiative to build up your own backbone and self-esteem. Build on your strengths and use them to make a better life for yourself.
6. Don't overload yourself with excessive amounts of self-condemnation. If you feel that your life is empty and bleak, avoid cutting yourself down with harsh judgments that will only immobilize you and make it more difficult to begin practicing ways of feeling better again.
7. Do take one day at a time. Avoid the natural tendency to try and predict how you will feel a year or two from now—especially

when you're feeling hopeless. Stay with today and your immediate future.

8. Avoid the eleven common pitfalls described in Chapter 7. They will prolong your grief or stop you from becoming a healthier person.

9. Don't psych yourself out with your fears. Panic promotes panic. Many people become immobilized by "what ifs": "What if I fail again?"; "What if I get rejected?"; "What if nothing I try helps me feel better?"; "What if I'm always alone?" It's natural to wonder, but don't do it when you're feeling scared.

10. Do take the initiative to help yourself feel better. Don't sit and wait for your ex-mate to come back or for a miracle to happen or use up all your energy feeling sorry for yourself. Decide what kind of realistic action would help, then do it.

**Summary**

Often saying good-bye to an old love affair is a blessing in disguise. It offers you the opportunity to grow emotionally stronger, resolve old hang-ups and learn to effectively plan a happier, healthier future for yourself. It's important not to let your fears of letting go stop you from becoming free. If you use your courage and the knowledge you have already gained to help you, soon you will feel better. If you do not, there is a very good chance that you will stay stuck in one of the stages of grief—or choose another intimate relationship *exactly* like the last one—with the same ending.

**Experiments and Exercises**

This exercise is designed to help you bury your dead love affair, accept that it's over, and proceed with your life. Repeat it whenever you feel that you need to "unhook." Choose a time when you feel "strong" enough to say good-bye and will be uninterrupted. Place a sheet over the "body" of your dead relationship. Talk about the relationship as if this were the funeral. Express all the words and feelings that you have kept inside. Feel your grief.

Talk as long as you want and when you are finished with the "funeral rites," say good-bye and walk away.

After this exercise, take time to reflect on the following:

- What can I learn from this experience?
- What do I want/need to do with my future?
- How can I begin working toward my new goals?

The five stages of the grief process are listed below. Identify the one you are currently in.

Denial/ Depression/ Anger/ Resignation/ Acceptance and Proceeding

Now take some time and ask yourself the following:

- What can I learn from objectively looking at where I am now? Can I see an end to my grief?
- Have I developed any constructive insight about myself through this process?
- Am I stuck in one stage?
- If so, list *specifically* what you do that keeps you stuck:

1.
2.
3.
4.
5.

- Put a time limit on how long you plan to continue the above behaviors or attitudes. What will you need to do differently when you decide to proceed?
- Pick one that you feel would be easiest to change and consider doing so.
- Estimate a time when you believe you will have completed your grief. 3 months? 6 months? 1 year? 5 years? When?

# 11

## DEPRESSION: THE ENERGY CRISIS

I call depression the "energy crisis" because most people who are feeling depressed complain of changes in their energy levels. The majority describe themselves as feeling fatigued, "run down," or "too weak to move." Statements such as: "I can barely drag my body out of bed in the morning—and, I go back to bed whenever I get the chance" are typical. A few individuals who are depressed experience the exact opposite; those who are normally calm suddenly develop great bounds of energy and are unable to sit still for any length of time without fidgeting in their chairs. Some people fluctuate back and forth—with no energy on one day and excessive amounts on the next.

Much of this redistribution and loss of productive energy comes from some of the side effects of depression itself: loss of appetite, lowering of body resistance to viral and bacterial infections, insomnia or change in sleeping patterns, feelings of being torn apart inside, dissatisfied, desperate, and angry (but internalizing the energy from anger).

People who complain of depression often say that they are

tired of feeling badly, but they do not have the energy and/or motivation to change. The conscious decision to do something about their sadness gets shoved back by a heavy sense of helplessness and hopelessness. Anything that could be done to climb out of the pit of depression seems like too much trouble and not worth the effort. For some people in this emotional state, suicide appears to be the only solution. For everyone, the feeling is bleak and scary.

How long depression lasts and how far down you will fall varies with a number of factors, such as your own ego-strengths, sense of insecurity, ability to adjust, dependency needs, religious or philosophical attitude about ending, age at the time of good-bye, readiness for ending including other options available, physical stamina, unconscious commitment to continue the relationship, self-destructiveness of the "marriage" itself, length of the relationship, and number of role identities that were tied up in the union. The more independent and self-assured you are as a separate person, the less intense your feelings of depression will be. If you initiated good-bye, you will probably feel less depressed during the mourning phase than your counterpart who still felt committed to the relationship when it was buried. Passive, polite or stubborn people who did not want the relationship to end will stay depressed much longer then those who assert themselves and their feelings with relative ease.

Depression is usually the first painful emotion that ex-intimates feel. Normally it is self-limiting and, in time, will ease. However, many ex-intimates increase their sorrow by unconsciously (or consciously) preventing themselves from adjusting and growing through this crisis or prolong their depression by fighting it with fear.

It is natural for depression to come and go during the first six months to a year on a relatively sporadic basis. Initially the pain will be more intense and more frequent, then gradually diminish in size and duration. The more effective you become in dealing with your depression, the easier it will be to let go of your sadness.

The theories of feeling better are of little personal value until you put them into use. It will take a great deal of effort on your part to pull out of depression, and require energy you may not feel you have any more. But the more energy you begin mobilizing to work your way out, the more you will find you have and the stronger you'll feel. At first you may have to *force* yourself to do exactly the opposite of what you feel like doing.

## Origins Of Depression

Depression is caused by internalized anger and a sense of helplessness. It is a passive reaction to a situation which is unsatisfactory or unpleasant. It is often a reaction to a loss which is initially viewed as irreplaceable. The more important the loss, the deeper the depression. If you get angry about something, but do not express it (to the degree that you feel it) and keep the anger inside, you will become depressed. Because depression is a reaction, it is mixed with a number of other feelings such as feeling inadequate, put-down, helpless, abandoned, hopeless, scared, trapped, insecure, lonely, or sad. These painful feelings, and others, if "sat on" will cause you to feel depressed—in addition to whatever else you may feel. If someone says something to you that hurts your feelings and you passively take it to heart, you will not only have hurt feelings, but you will also feel depressed. If a man is left with the responsibility of being a single parent, doesn't feel capable of parenting, and deals with his insecurities by doing nothing, he will not only feel anxious about his parenting, but also be depressed about letting his children down.

Depression is a passive way of dealing with negative feelings and the situation which set these feelings in motion. It requires no action. If you take whatever negative feedback other people may hand you without asserting yourself, you may get depressed immediately afterwards. The man who passively accepts his uncertainty about learning to care for his children and does not make the effort to try, develops a sense of defeat and depression. A woman who refuses to push herself to learn how to drive reinforces her feelings of helplessness and despair.

There is a natural tendency in all of us to desire that life be exactly the way we want it and to try and effect change when it is not. This desire is sometimes manifested as anger, self-assertion, determination, motivation or drive. When you decide to "sit on" this energy and do nothing to change an unhappy situation, you will become depressed.

Ex-intimates often become depressed from any one or several of the following reasons:

● They have accepted the harsh judgments their ex-loves have handed them as if they were "truths"; for example, they believe themselves to be inadequate lovers, parents, or "marital" partners.

● They feel rejected by their ex-loves and assume rejection means that they are "losers."

● They are frightened of being single again and are unsure of their ability to adjust and proceed with their lives.

● They are dependent on their ex-loves to make them feel "whole," and now that it's over feel helpless about feeling like "total" beings on their own.

● They are afraid of ever being loved or loving someone again and immobilize their efforts to try for that goal.

● They get wrapped up in self-pity or become martyrs about the loss of their love.

● They remain emotionally tied to their ex-loves and are afraid to get angry for fear of further alienation.

● They have never developed goals outside of the marital relationship.

● They feel responsible for taking care of their ex-loves, feel guilty about leaving, but refuse to return.

- They have lost most of their friendship circle in saying good-bye to their ex-loves and feel isolated—but fear making new friends.

If you don't like being alone, but feel helpless to change, you will probably slide into the trap of depression. Some will feel this reaction before they actually separate physically; others will experience it after—a few will feel sporadically depressed about the death of their love years before they leave each other.

Scenes that trigger depression once you're alone are innumerable: being alone at dinner time, fixing meals for one, going to a party by yourself, festive occasions like Christmas, waking up to the sound of silence, hearing your voice echo in the hallway, or listing your mother instead of your ex-mate on the line that says: "In case of emergency, please notify."

People who are afraid of their anger or feel that they do not have the right to assert themselves may automatically deal with disappointments by passively accepting their plight.

## How To Figure Out Why You're Depressed

Ex-intimates become depressed during the first part of the mourning phase because they experience a number of unpleasant feelings which they are unprepared to deal with in an active or constructive manner.

To figure out exactly what you are reacting to, you will need to learn what you feel *beneath* the depression. During the first few days, it may be difficult for you to sort through your feelings. Your depression may feel too overwhelming—and your mind may dart rapidly from one painful scene to another. Within a short period of time, however, you should be able to begin looking at the feelings beneath your depression.

If you find yourself at a loss, it may be helpful to reread the first part of this chapter and see which causal factors and underlying feelings appear to be relevant for your own situation. Usually, there are a number of reasons for a depression, with, perhaps, one or two predominant issues underlying the majority of it.

For example:

One lady who was married for twenty-seven years to an alcoholic found that she was extremely depressed after she finally filed for a divorce. Although she had left her husband several times before she finally divorced him, she always returned because she worried about how he would live without someone taking care of him and felt responsible for helping him. Intellectually, she knew that he was responsible for himself, but, in spite of that knowledge, she still felt obligated. Each time he called her or she found out he had lost another job or lurched into trouble again, she would return. When she finally left him permanently, she was depressed for several months. The feelings and fears she reacted to by depression were her sense of obligation, worry, and guilt about not taking care of her ex-mate, internalized anger at both of them for being in a position of divorce, a sense of helplessness to change either her own feelings of responsibility or his alcoholic behavior, and a fear of never feeling better again.

A man found that much of his depression after saying goodbye to his love of three years had to do with his desire to continue their relationship because he still cared about her. Part of him hoped that they could reunite, and so he refused to directly get mad at her or use the energy in his anger to find someone new. He ended up feeling very lonely and empty but chose to "sit on" his needs to love again in hopes his old girlfriend would return. Her departure had shattered his self-confidence and, for over six months, he stayed alone every night and on weekends waiting for his ex-love to telephone or write.

Questions that you can ask yourself which help you identify which feelings you are reacting to with depression are:
1. What's going on in my life that I don't like right now?

2. What would I have to do to feel better?
3. Why don't I do it?

The answers won't come easily at first. But, eventually, you will find that gaining this insight will be well worth the effort—for without that knowledge, it will be impossible for you to ever win your battle with depression completely. Treating the symptoms of emotional pain is one thing; finding out what causes it is the start of curing that pain.

## How To Fight Depression

Depression is a self-inflicted pain. No one makes us cope with our hurt feelings or dissatisfaction with passivity. People choose this way of reacting because they do not want to risk becoming assertive or angry, don't see any way to constructively deal with their pain, or feel they deserve to settle for less than what they want. A certain amount of depression is inevitable and a natural part of the grief process—or life, for that matter. Do not be afraid of it—or worry too much. With simple depression, sometimes just feeling sad for a while and releasing that pain through your tears will be all that you need to do to let go of your hurt. Disappointment and loss can often be handled just by feeling "bad" for a day or two. And, if you reflect upon your feelings and thoughts during that "sad time" or shortly afterwards, you may gain a great deal of insight and wisdom. Usually, *when you're feeling relatively good about you*, a depression will lift after it has run its natural course.

If you find, however, that depression has become your primary feeling and that it is beginning to get the best of you, you will need to *actively* begin fighting the "blues." Don't wait around for a magical answer or for someone to swoop down and take you away from your sadness. Fighting depression requires **insight** and **action** on your part with an eye toward feeling better again.

The *insight* you will need to develop consists of:

● Identifying what you're reacting to from the good-bye. (Like the lady who was married to the alcoholic or the man who was rejected by his girlfriend.)

● Understanding why you feel helpless to take care of the feelings beneath your depression in a more constructive manner. (e.g., placing the responsibility to *make* you feel better on someone else who won't help you; cutting down your self-esteem so that you don't have confidence in your ability to get your needs met; or deciding that you deserve to stay feeling "blue" as a self-punishment.)

● Learning what reinforces the depression in your present situation (blundering into the pitfalls, immobilizing yourself with self-doubt, isolating yourself from others at a time when you feel the most dependent).

The *action* part of your battle requires that you:

● Mobilize the energy in depression and turn it back into anger, motivation, determination, or drive. This may require a change in attitude from "Oh, well, who cares about my plight?" to "I'm tired of feeling down and I'm ready to do something positive." (You may find it helpful to keep repeating the second phrase out loud to yourself until you can feel that the words are true for you. Anyone who is depressed does have enough internalized energy to get mobilized again.)

● Give up energy-wasting double-binds you may be in, like wanting to love again, but keeping your feelings "hooked" on someone who doesn't care about you; wanting to stand up on your own two feet but looking for someone to help you get up; or, wanting to feel that you are a valuable person, but doubting your every action and the motivation behind it.

● Avoid situations which are set-ups for feeling depressed. Look at your own life and notice the scenes which cause you to react with depression. They will vary for each individual but usually they give you an invitation to feel inadequate, put-down, abandoned, hopeless, frightened, trapped, helpless, insecure, or lonely. Those you do not really need to be part of, avoid. Take a friend with you to others, if you can.

● Put yourself in situations which help you feel confident. These vary too, but usually involve being around friends and family who love you, or doing tasks you do well.

● Reach out to others for positive feedback; encourage them to be your friends.

● Build up your own backbone and self-confidence by using the advice in Chapter 5 plus any other ideas that you know work for you.

● Force yourself to eat balanced meals; get enough sleep and physical exercise. (It's difficult to "fight" anything if your body's worn down.)

● Clean out closets or rearrange cupboards. Taking charge of *small* parts of your environment helps you feel more in control of your life.

● Separate the issues you are unhappy about and deal with them one at a time. Don't overload yourself.

Every time you make a decision to do something about what seems like a bad situation, you will feel the depression lift from your shoulders. If, for example, you are sitting alone on a Sunday afternoon feeling blue and decide, "I think I'll go visit a friend." Then climb in your car and do it. Your mood will lighten. If, on the other hand, you decide that you would like to go visit someone *but* _____ and end up staying alone, the depression may deepen.

Part of fighting depression is to fight the "buts" in your life. "I could go visit a friend, *but*
● he may not be home."
● he could be busy with someone else."
● if he wanted to see me, he'd call."

- what good would it do?"
- I have to learn to stay alone."
- it's almost dinner time."
- I shouldn't bother him."
- it's not worth driving all the way over there."
- what if he's not happy to see me?"
- what will he think?"
- what do I say when he opens the door?"

You can probably add a dozen more of your own "buts" behind that statement and still end up in the same position—the position of staying at home, not visiting a friend, feeling lonely, helpless to change that—and a little more depressed. When you say "I could, *but* _____" to yourself, you are saying "there's a reason for my hesitation." Of course there is—*but*

- Do you need one?
- When will you give it up?
- How can you take care of that hesitation?
- Would it help to check your hesitations out with your friend?
- When will you do it?

## How To Find Ways To Win

Winning your fight with depression is similar to winning in a sports event. It requires practicing your skills and playing in a league where you can win. Any coach will tell you his trainees have a better chance of winning if he uses some common sense when matching his team. A high school football coach, for example, would never expect his team to win a game with the Miami Dolphins or any other big-name professional team. If he did, he (and his team) would be very disappointed after the match because their chances of winning are extremely slim.

If you can think about your fight with depression in a similar light and see your head as the "coach" for your self-esteem, you will quickly see how the analogy can be effectively used to find ways for you to win.

The "coach" part of you needs to use some common sense and convince the rest of you to put into action the insight you've gained about your fight with depression. If you're depressed because you feel lonely, your "coach" needs to give you a pep talk and convince you to practice reaching out to others and giving your kindness to someone who cares about you. If you cope with fears by huddling in the corner, your "coach" can help you figure out how to feel safer and remind you that you can overcome almost anything that is scary by practicing how to protect your vulnerable spots. Fear of getting in a car accident can be lessened by learning how to drive defensively. Fear of being alone at night can be reduced by making sure you have locked all the doors and windows, sleeping in a room with a telephone nearby and avoiding the game of psyching yourself out with "what ifs."

Just as the high school coach would not expect his team to beat a professional team, the "coach" part of you should not expect you to win in your battle with depression by overwhelming you with expectations. It would be unfair to expect *all* of your lifetime hang-ups or insecurities to be cured once and for all when you feel that your ego is shattered from saying good-bye. Sure, you may grow through some of your hang-ups while battling depression. Emotional change and growth often take place when you feel the pressure to change—but only when you can see your way clear to do something about it. If you overload yourself with unrealistic goals for success, you will give up the fight to feel better before you begin.

A good coach gives the team members immediate rewards, plus a sense that he is pleased when they try. The "coach" part of you should do the same. Reward yourself whenever you take constructive action to fight your depression. If you dress up to go visit a friend or apply for a job, praise yourself and do something kind for you as a reward. When you "goof up" or do something that deepens your depression, like begging your ex-love to

come back, give yourself a pep talk and try to avoid making the same mistake again. Forgive yourself and learn from your errors.
No coach has all the answers for developing a winning team. He learns from others in his field. The "coach" part of you can do the same. You are already reading this book for ideas. Another source is other ex-intimates who have also felt the pain from good-bye or almost anyone *but* your ex-love or people who may have negative feelings toward you. Many may have positive suggestions that you can use too—ask them. You might gain helpful suggestions *and* build a friendship in the process.

## The Art Of Feeling Better

Sometimes it surprises ex-intimates to discover that toward the end of the grief process they feel better than they have ever felt in their lives. Old hang-ups and insecurities that they have carried with them all through their lives have been resolved through constructive insight and behavorial changes learned during the grief process.

> If someone would have told me a year ago that I would actually feel better today than I could ever remember, I wouldn't have believed it. I take the time now to enjoy life—and I have a sense of achievement and self-confidence that I've never known before. Like I can do almost anything I want. It's fantastic! A feeling mere words can't describe.

That statement was made by a friend of mine who, less than a year before, divorced her husband of seven years. She divorced him, but he left her for another woman. And, for several months, her despair seemed unbearable to her.

If you're struggling with depression right now, it may be difficult for you to even fantasize a day in your future when you, too, will have mastered the art of feeling better. But most ex-intimates do—even the ones who, at the lowest point in their depression, contemplated or attempted suicide.

The art of feeling better is the combination of a number of skills suggested throughout this book and an ability to see yourself and your world in a positive light. As with any art, it requires that you master (through hard work and long hours) the skills necessary to practice it. Few people are born with a natural talent to do anything specific. Most of us have the potential to paint, write, sing, play an instrument, bake, sew, grow vegetables, drive an automobile, or feel good about ourselves and our world. It's just a matter of learning how to do something, then practicing those skills until we can do them with relative ease.

Your attitude and ability to adjust are the primary instruments that need to be perfected to learn the art of feeling better. Each time you successfully win a bout with depression or self-condemnation or fear, you will have a sense of self-confidence and pride. You will also have learned for yourself that you are in control of your feelings.

Ironically, those who feel the most pain in good-bye also have the ability to feel the most pleasure when they finally say hello to their new world. A woman who felt totally dependent on her ex-mate for survival can gain a tremendous sense of pride and accomplishment when she discovers through practice that she can not only survive without her ex-mate, but enjoys her achievements and accepts the choices she makes. A man who always falls in love with a helpless, deliberately inadequate female can learn through his own struggle with good-bye how to build up his ego without the aid of someone he sees as inferior. In doing that, he can discover for himself that he is worthwhile and, the next time around, he can choose an intimate whom he can not only love, but respect as an "equal."

The Alcoholics Anonymous prayer suggests an attitude and ability to adjust which most ex-intimates have the opportunity to attain: "God grant me the serenity to accept the things that I can't change . . . the courage to change the things that I can . . . and the wisdom to know the difference."

## Pitfalls That Reinforce Depression

Pitfalls that you may stumble into when you're already feeling depressed are traps that will increase your sense of helplessness or discouragement. In Chapter 7, several are mentioned which may deepen your sense of depression.

- Getting back together with your ex-love.
- Trying to be friends if it isn't necessary.
- Saving old mementos.
- Pulling in memories to fill emptiness.
- Checking up on your ex-love.
- Pumping mutual friends for information or trying to get them to take sides.
- Wishing it hadn't happened and hoping it'll change.
- Panicking with free time, holidays, and anniversary dates.

Others have already been mentioned in this chapter, such as immobilizing yourself with fears and self-doubt or internalizing and sitting on your own anger. All of these pitfalls can reinforce your depression, keep you in limbo, and extend the length of your grief. Although it is not necessary to panic when you fall into one of these traps (or the others mentioned in this section), it is important to avoid as many as you can. Sometimes acknowledging on a conscious level that you are in the process of deepening your depression helps to alleviate your feelings of despair. With that in mind, let us look at additional pitfalls which reinforce depression.
1. *Attempting to escape from your hurt by sleeping or numbing your body with alcohol or drugs.* During the first few days of your depression it is natural to feel overwhelmed with painful feelings and see your only salvation as some form of uncon-

sciousness. The trouble is that when you're conscious again, the problems are still there—and you still aren't any closer to constructive solutions than you were before you went to bed or killed that last glass of wine. In fact, you may feel more discouraged than before. Unfortunately, choosing a passive "do nothing" solution for a painful, real problem adds to your sense of helplessness. If, after the first week, you find yourself yawning and preparing for bed in the middle of the day, do some physical exercises to get your circulation moving again. Then use the energy you find to constructively fight a piece of your problem. As for numbing yourself with drugs or alcohol, we have enough scientific information to tell you that chemicals *cause* more problems than they solve; they increase a sense of impotence and are physiological depressants.

2. *Fighting your dependency needs by withdrawing from others during the deeper parts of your depression.* We know the human being is a dependent animal and cannot sustain feeling good in a vacuum. Yet, many ex-intimates during the first part of their depression actually heighten their despair, loneliness, and self-pity by purposely isolating themselves from any human contact. They see people at work, but avoid socializing during their "leisure" hours. It is a fact that when you are depressed, you will feel *more* dependent than at other times in your life. Ignoring your dependency needs will only make you feel worse. If at all possible, maintain contact with those who still love you. Share your home with someone else if that's feasible. If you feel that you have no one to turn to for friendship or are hesitant to talk over your feelings with someone, contact a mental health clinic or get in touch with a singles' organization. Getting at least some of your dependency needs met during your depression can save you from prolonging your grief, immobilizing yourself with self-pity, or making mentally unhealthy decisions for your future.

3. *Viewing yourself as a "victim" of fate or a pawn controlled by your ex-love.* This is a trap that many ex-intimates who were not the first to initiate good-bye, or those who see themselves as

fragile or inadequate may fall into. The longer you avoid taking responsibility for your life, how you feel and what you do, the easier it is to see yourself as a "victim" of fate—or your ex-love's whim. The sooner you practice admitting the choices you've made—about not nurturing your old love relationship, choosing unwisely to begin with, taking responsibility for helping yourself feel better now that it's over—the quicker you can pull yourself out of the "victim" pitfall.

4. *Seeing yourself as better than everyone else because you don't stand up for your rights directly and, therefore, never risk hurting someone by your words.* An ex-intimate who has a lifestyle of being a martyr is the one most prone to fall into this trap. Healthy anger and self-assertiveness are not utilized in a constructive manner; they are reshaped into self-sacrificing bitterness and depression. If you have the tendency to "turn the other cheek" when hit rather than slap back, walk away, or protect yourself in some other way, it is important for you to learn how to stand up for your rights. There are healthier ways to deal with your dissatisfaction than swallowing pain and attempting to soothe your hurt feelings with a noble sense that you are above mere mortal imperfections. Part of our "humanness" that helps us adjust and grow emotionally is our natural sense of anger when we are disappointed or hurt. Learn to use that natural emotion constructively.

5. *Setting unrealistic goals for yourself when you already feel depressed.* Many mental health experts suggest that one way to alleviate a sense of depression is to set up personal goals. There is nothing more satisfying than successfully completing a goal you have set. And, there are few things more discouraging than to fail at a personal goal. Therefore, it is important to set *realistic* goals with regard to your current strengths and abilities. Jumping into the collegiate scene full time when you're raising a family and haven't practiced the skills of effective studying for twenty years may be very unrealistic. Signing up for one night class on a subject that interests you and that you feel you can learn is much

more realistic. When you're depressed, you will be less sure of yourself, more frightened of failure, and, at the beginning, maybe even have trouble concentrating. Take those realities into account as you plan your goals. Don't use them as an excuse to sit back and do nothing, but accept the fact that you are depressed and, therefore, may not perform tasks with the same amount of self-confidence and ease that you may have before and will later on. Setting goals which can realistically be achieved is mentally healthy; reaching for unrealistic goals deepens depression.

6. *Dragging in all the past hurts and disappointments when you're depressed.* I'm not sure why people who are depressed do this, but there is a natural tendency to drag in from memory all of your past hurts when you're feeling low. Maybe it's because the gut feeling is always the same and therefore generates the memories. In any event, all those I talk with who are immobilized with depression admit that they began feeling overwhelmed by their depression after recalling painful past hurts and disappointments. A certain amount of reflection and constructive "ghost hunting" from your past can be healthy. Too much can be overwhelming. There's a fine line between wallowing in pain and choosing to acknowledge and feel its presence. You are "wallowing" when you make a conscious decision to give in to your fears of helplessness and self-pity and thereby refuse to constructively salve your wounds. Acknowledging your pain, feeling the hurt, and then initiating constructive action are healthy. You can tell for yourself when your reflection ceases to be useful and crawls into the harmful category. Pull yourself out of the painful memories when you find that you are beginning to feel devastated. The most effective way to do this is to acknowledge what you are doing and *force* yourself to focus your attention on the current problems you need to resolve.

7. *Using insight as a reason for no action.* It may sound strange for a mental health professional to list using insight as a pitfall which reinforces depression. But, even though I am firmly convinced that insight is necessary for lasting emotional growth and

change, it *must* be followed with action. There are some folks who use their intellectual knowledge of themselves as a copout to avoid change or taking the initiative to do something constructive about their own problems. Early childhood hang-ups or sociological pressures become their reasons for passivity. If you find yourself understanding that you are punishing yourself unfairly for the dissolution of your love affair because you feel guilty, but continue to punish yourself anyway—you'd better *force* yourself to stop looking at "why" and begin looking at "ways to change." Developing insight without putting it to a constructive use is counterproductive.

**Experiments and Exercises**

The following is a list of pitfalls which increase depression. Go through it and note those you currently fall into.

    Trying to get back with your ex-love
    Trying to be friends when it isn't necessary
    Saving old mementos
    Pulling in memories to fill the emptiness
    Checking up on your ex-love
    Pumping mutual friends for information or trying to get them to take sides
    Wishing it hadn't happened and hoping it'll change
    Panicking or dreading free time
    Dreading the future
    Being too critical
    Holding your anger inside; refusing to stand up for your rights
    Escaping your hurt by oversleeping
    Trying to numb pain with alcohol or drugs
    Withdrawing from friends and family
    Viewing yourself as a "victim"

Being excessively self-sacrificing
Setting unrealistic goals for yourself
Dragging in all your past hurts and disappointments through memory
Using insight as a reason for no action
Wallowing in self-pity
Letting your physical health or appearance slide
Giving yourself excuses to do nothing

Now go back through the list and study those you have especially noted.

- What can you learn from this study?

- Is there a pattern for you with disappointments?

- Are there any pitfalls you could avoid if you put an effort into doing so?

Pick a pitfall which you feel would be the *easiest* for you to give up or avoid. Then, on a separate piece of paper, develop your plan of attack:

- What *specific* actions will you need to take? (If the solution requires a number of steps, be sure to write them down.)

- Can you do it by yourself or will you need help?

- If you need help, whom will you ask?

- Now set a time frame including when you will begin and how long you believe it will take you to be successful. (Evaluate your progress every day initially and make revisions in your "plan of attack" occasionally.)

As you read through this book, periodically refer back to this list and review your progress. Work on other pitfalls as you decide you're ready.

# 12

# ALL ABOUT ANGER

Anger is one of our most misunderstood feelings or reactions—one that many people try to avoid or deny because it is scary to them. Most people don't want to feel angry because they associate that energy with destructiveness. They see it as something that causes more problems than it cures because they have only experienced the uncontrolled, hurtful forms of anger. They have not learned how to turn that energy into ambition or drive.

But feeling angry is not "wrong" and it need not be scary, destructive, or an end in itself. It is a natural part of the grief process and a phase that ex-intimates must go through in order to proceed with their lives. Anger is a source of energy: a normal reaction to painful feelings or anxiety. We experience anger during the grief process because saying good-bye to an old love affair or hello to an unknown future can be hurtful or frightening and most of us do not like to feel either way. If ending gives you an invitation to feel inadequate or rejected, it is natural to react with anger to protect yourself from feeling any other "hurt." A woman who feels she's been treated unfairly by her ex-mate may react with anger, vengeance to get back at her ex-husband, or a decision never to "trust" any man again. If a man's ex-wife judged him as "childish," he may try to get her to take back her evaluation of him by forcing her to admit she was wrong or take out his anger on other women so that no female will ever "hurt" him again.

The degree of anger you may feel during the mourning phase will vary with how frightened or hurt you are and how adept at dissipating that pain. The less intense your hurt feelings and fears, the milder your reaction of anger will be. The greater your ability to adjust, the easier it will be for you to turn that energy into motivation or drive.

You really do *not* have a choice about whether you experience anger or not. The fact that you have feelings and that some of them may be injured because of the death of your old love affair is enough to cause you some sense of anger. You *do* have a choice over how you deal with those feelings, however. You can direct them toward yourself through self-condemnation or guilt (which usually gets you back into depression). You can explode in physical or verbal outbursts toward anyone and everything— or just your ex-mate. You can quietly seethe inside and devise ways to "get back" at your old love. Or you can use the energy from anger to help you let go of the past and plan constructively for your future.

Anger can be an effective tool to help you create emotional distance from your ex-mate or it can keep you emotionally tied—depending on how you use it. If the woman who feels used by her ex-mate applies her energy to "get even" with him, rather than to help her "unhook" emotionally and go on with her life, he will continue to be the most inportant man in her life years after their divorce. The same alternatives are available for the man whose ex-wife judged him as "childish"; he can either spend the rest of his life trying to get her to take back her opinion or decide to use his energy to build up his self-esteem, realistically evaluate her opinion, and find a new love who will view him more kindly.

There are several alternatives you may choose in order to deal with your anger from good-bye. On some occasions you may choose to control your anger and utilize its energy to help you grow, and, at other times, you may find yourself screaming at your ex-love. Your methods of coping will vary, depending upon your mood, so don't get too worried if you don't always use your anger exactly the way you would like. The important thing is to learn how to release it and utilize the energy to move forward. Holding on to your anger or reinforcing it will keep you stuck in the middle of the grief process. Attempting to skip this phase will keep you emotionally tied to a love that is dead.

## Understanding Your Anger

Anger is a secondary feeling. A feeling that comes *after* you have experienced anxiety or pain. If your child gets lost in a super market, the *first* thing that you will feel is anxiety. Once your anxiety is relieved by finding your child, you may *then* feel anger. Whenever you fail at a goal, get your feelings hurt, or feel anxious, it will be natural for you to react by feeling *either* depressed *or* angry. While depression is a *passive* reaction which says: "Oh well, what's the use?," anger is an *action* response that shouts: "I'm *not* going to take this!"

Anger, as an attempt to control our own lives, is an emotion which all of us experience. During the grief process it is more pronounced. There are several reasons for this. First of all, all ex-intimates experience loss when they say good-bye; not only the loss of an intimate relationship, but the loss of familiar surroundings, mutual friends, self-image connected with that person, routine, and, probably, the sexual relationship with a familiar partner. Until those "empty spots" are refilled, it is natural to feel anxiety *and* some form of frustration. Even refilling those empty spots or learning how to live without an ex-mate can create anger. It isn't easy to find a new love, live in a new area, make new friends or learn to take over tasks that your ex-love used to perform. A man who has never cooked for himself may feel a mild sense of irritation each time he opens a can because mealtime will tap his unconscious fears that he cannot survive without depending on someone else to provide for his nutritional needs. A woman who has never managed her own finances before can become livid with rage when the checkbook seems to be fighting with her desire to have it balance and to feel in control of her financial security.

Calling it quits, no matter how wise or emotionally healthy, will give each ex-intimate an invitation to feel like a failure. And there is nothing more anxiety-provoking *or* aggravating than feeling inadequate. The first person who pronounces the relationship dead usually feels less like a failure than the partner who is rejected. The one who assumes the most responsibility for its demise will accept a greater sense of failure than the one who feels "innocent." Ex-intimates who believe that togetherness is "good" and singleness is "bad" will experience more intense feelings (including anger) over good-bye than will others. Those who *always* accept an invitation to feel inadequate will greedily grab at the chance, then roar with their low self-esteem. Whatever the degree—mild, moderate or severe—all ex-intimates will feel some sense of inadequacy and failure at the end of a love affair and will, therefore, react with frustration.

Saying good-bye to an old love and lifestyle means that you must say hello to an unknown future and a sense of uncertainty. If you have not made future plans, your anxiety will be heightened. Many ex-intimates know that they want "out" but are unclear about what they want to do next. "Do I want to jump into another relationship right away?" "Where do I want to live?" "What do I want to do with the rest of my life?" All of these questions, and more, will come up. Answering them causes uncertainty, ambivalence, indecision, fear, and, surrounding them all, some sense of anger. When these questions are resolved, your frustration level will lessen. But until you have successfully gone through this "Who am I and what do I want next?" crisis, your frustration will be greater.

Anger in a relationship creates emotional distance. Obviously, to develop that necessary distance from a dead love affair, you must *not* continue to feel tied to or dependent on your ex-mate for emotional nurturing. Anger, then, as a natural phase in the grief process, helps ex-intimates begin to let go emotionally of their old love affairs. When you are angry at someone, it means that you care enough to be hurt. You still feel dependent on that person but are creating some distance. This is not an end in itself. Ex-intimates who stay stuck in the angry phase *never* fully let go of their old love; but it is an important and a positive step in the direction of letting go. The first person who says good-bye probably has reached this stage in the grief process already. Although he or she may slide back into an earlier phase when the relationship is physically severed, one partner must be at this point to finally end the relationship.

## Traps That Increase Anger

Even though it is important to feel anger after ending a relationship, it is not necessary or wise to reinforce or build on that emotion. Any pitfall that could reinforce depression may also increase your anger—depending on whether you hold that irritation inside or spit it back out. According to many ex-intimates, however, the following traps are more likely to promote anger than others.

1. *"Carrying a chip on your shoulder" and getting into verbal or physical battles with everyone.* Anger promotes anger or at best creates distance. Any time someone vents hostility toward you, you will probably find yourself either reacting back with your own anger for protection, or avoiding further contact. Although it is easy to understand why an ex-intimate would feel angry at the end of a love affair, those who take out their anger

on everyone with whom they come into contact will find that they have more anger at the end of the day than they did at the beginning. If you carry a chip on your shoulder, you will find many opportunities to react with hostility: getting caught in traffic, a constructive but critical remark from a co-worker, a negative statement from a friend, or a frown from the grocery store clerk. All of these scenes and more provide the perfect chance to overreact. In fact, in my practice as a therapist, I have met many ex-intimates who feel so defensive that almost any reaction from me other than smiling support is seen as a "put-down" and another reason to get angry. Unfortunately, this spontaneous hostility toward everyone creates additional hurt feelings for the person who carries the chip. Usually other people react by rejecting you, which will leave you feeling even more alone and misunderstood than before.

2. *Attempting to "get even" with your ex-mate.* This is a common trap to fall into but one that is hard to climb out of. One ex-intimate hurts the other, then the other retaliates, then back to the other, again and again. Ex-intimates sometimes get even in ways which promote additional hurt feelings and anger. For example, she dates one of his friends, so he dates one of her girlfriends, or he doesn't visit their children at first, so she refuses visitation rights when he finally asks to see them. The trouble with getting even is that it's hard to finally stop the cycle and it does not promote any healing effect. You won't feel any better after you've gotten even because you know that your ex-partner will retaliate. The only way to stop promoting your anger in this fashion is to refuse to take your turn.

3. *Fighting over custody of the children.* This is a very destructive trap for adults and particularly for children. Happily for all, it is rare, but it does exist. Those who get involved in this battle over custody reap nothing but additional hurt and anger. It's hard for a parent to lose custody of the children (and for the

children to physically separate from one of their parents), but in a divorce someone usually does. And, although it is becoming increasingly popular to split up the family and have each parent assume custody for some of the children, only heartache and anger can result from battles over this decision.

4. *Fighting over the division of property.* If you're going to fight over anything with your ex-mate after the relationship is dead, the safest battleground issues are material possessions: houses, land, cars, furniture, and dishes. At least these things won't get hurt in the process, as would a child, and usually there is an end to these battles, though they can be quite drawn out and expensive. Most divorce lawyers will tell you that fighting tooth and nail over every piece of property (including who gets the can opener) can lengthen the divorce proceedings and run up the costs. While it's important to split property fairly, when a couple fights each division with vengeance this will promote more anger than it resolves. In fact, you will literally need a referee (the judge) to help you let go of the battle and proceed from that point.

5. *Fighting over whose fault the ending was.* Although it makes absolutely no sense and neither can possibly win in this fight, some people battle with their ex-mates about who was the most responsible for the death of their love. This trap can keep you emotionally "hooked" on your ex-love and prolong your anger. I suppose there may be some amount of satisfaction in hearing your ex-love tell you that you were "right" and he or she was "wrong"—but even if you hear that, what do you do then? To consciously become aware of your own decisions to quit nurturing your love and constructively use that insight is mentally healthy. To argue with your ex-love about who killed your love will only keep you emotionally connected, give you an invitation to feel like a victim, and promote more hostility.

6. *Purposely recalling hurtful scenes.* It is not unusual to hear an ex-intimate talk about how anger-provoking it is to purposely remember a painful event.

- Every time I think about what that Bastard said to me I get angry.
- It makes me mad, just to think about....
- I still remember how she *used* me; what a Bitch!
- Each time I think about seeing her in bed with him, I feel like killing them!

Certainly it's unhealthy to rationalize away or try to forget your anger before it's resolved, but purposely recalling painful events and fulminating over how unfairly you've been treated by your ex-mate will only promote more anger and keep you stuck in that phase.

7. *Trying to pretend your anger doesn't exist.* It is just as unhealthy to deny that you are angry as it is to purposely hold on to it with memories—both traps actually build up anger rather than diminish it. The "nice guy" who never allows himself to acknowledge his anger can be a walking bomb of rage. He can't control a feeling which he doesn't admit exists—even to himself. People who have nice, friendly divorces often continue to hold grudges against their ex-mates several years after the final decree. Many fail to develop another intimate relationship because they have not truly let go of their last—or have denied so many of their feelings that they no longer feel much of anything for anyone. Some people describe this as "cold" anger because they literally can't feel warmth toward anyone any more.

8. *Dealing with your anger indirectly.* If you deal with your anger indirectly by dreaming of your ex-love's demise, using sarcasm, getting headaches each time you feel frustrated, being "super sweet" to your ex-love, procrastinating, or any number of other passive-aggressive techniques, your anger will last much longer. One quick outburst is worth several backbiting comments to release your anger. The ability to use the energy in your anger for constructive change and self-assertiveness is related to how much you are aware of your own feelings and how directly you deal with them. The more passive you are with your anger the slower your movement away from the past.

## Admitting Anger: Your First Step Toward Breaking Away

I have talked with a number of ex-intimates who admit that they became consciously aware of their anger toward their ex-mate or their old lifestyle but attempted to rationalize it away or deny it because they did not want to break the emotional ties with their ex-love. They knew when they finally acknowledged that anger, if only to themselves, their past love would no longer be quite so treasured in their minds. As one lady shared:

> For the first four or five months of our separation I felt absolutely wretched. John had left me for another woman. My pride was hurt. I felt betrayed, alone, and disconnected from everyone. Nothing mattered any more. I cried myself to sleep every night, dragged through the day, then returned to an empty apartment. I rarely went out. I stayed by the telephone—just in case John called. He didn't, of course. Sometimes I called him, and even though his stance was cold disinterest (mine varied from "clever and cute" to "warm and serious"), I felt better when I heard his voice. I refused to believe that I couldn't get him back; I'd change, I decided—"fix" the parts of me he didn't like. Then, when he was through with his new girlfriend, I'd be ready. As near as I could see, my options were to stay alone and be miserable the rest of my life, wait for John to change his mind—or kill myself. I remember telling myself that I *could* just forget him and start over again, but that idea was less appealing than the others. John was the only man I ever really loved and spending my life with someone else seemed flat. I could never love anyone again—it was John or no one!
>
> I'm not sure when it happened, but gradually I began, first thinking, then feeling, that our "love" hadn't been all roses anyway. He was a man who "took" and I "gave." At first I shoved those thoughts and feelings aside. I remember tell-

ing myself: "If you really begin feeling like that, you won't want John, even if he does come back." It wasn't very long after that, when I began feeling angry about some of the "garbage" John dumped on me and I took—not to mention what I was doing to myself, I gave up waiting for John and began living again.

Although many may not be so well-informed about the purpose of their anger, most discover after they finally allow themselves to feel this reaction, that they are not quite so forlorn about saying good-bye. The sadness will no doubt return, but each time it does, it will be a little less intense and last for shorter periods of time. If you do some constructive things with your anger—like use the energy to help yourself feel better as a "single-againer," your optimism about the future will grow and the grief from the good-bye will diminish.

## How To Gain Control Over Your Anger

Many people fear their anger because they hold so much of it inside themselves that it only escapes in destructive eruptions. Each little frustration they encounter in daily life is kept inside until suddenly, sometimes over a trivial event, they spew like Mt. Vesuvius. Then the process of swallowing frustrations begins all over again. Ex-intimates often swallow large disappointments, fears, and hurt feelings during the ending process for fear of making things worse or contributing to an ugly divorce and then, when it's finally over, find that they are overwhelmed with their feelings of anger, bitterness, and/or depression. This section is designed to help you learn how to keep anger from overwhelming you or turning into self-destructiveness.

1. *Do acknowledge that it exists.* The greater your awareness of your anger, the better chance you have of controlling it. No one lives "anger-free"; many people say that they do, but they are only fooling themselves. Disowned anger turns into depression, high blood pressure, headaches, colitis, self-sabotage (accident

proneness), mistrust, a sense of feeling "numb," forgetfulness, being "supersweet," sadism, overworking, oversexing, "don't worry about me" stances, gossip, sick and dying fantasies to "get even," violent explosions, and sometimes, in psychiatric patients, a complete divorce from reality. Obviously, admitting the fact that you do experience anger will give you a choice about what you want to do with that emotion. If you deny that you feel it, the anger will continue to exist, but you will have little voice in deciding how to release it.

2. *Don't be afraid of your anger.* Most people who say they are afraid of their anger, really mean that they are afraid if they express how they feel they will no longer appear to be "neutral." But the reality is that we do express how we feel; maybe not directly, but indirectly, the message gets across. If you get angry at your boss because you feel he has treated you unfairly, you will either express that sentiment to him openly or you will begin making mistakes at the office, coming in late, forgetting appointments, etc.. Either way, the anger is shown. When it's direct, it can be openly discussed and resolved. Indirectly expressed anger leaves the issue unsettled and builds up some new ones. There are a few people who should be afraid of their anger but aren't. These people usually have a history of violent outbursts and aggressive and/or assaultive acts. They are individuals who resort to primitive techniques to gain control over their environment. Ironically, most of these people are not afraid of their anger, nor, do they feel any concern when they explode. In general, if you have enough concern to be afraid of your anger, you will not be destructive with it. Ask yourself what you're afraid you will do. If the answer is, in fact, a lethal or destructive action, then you should seek assistance from a mental health professional. Otherwise, do *not* be afraid of your anger.

3. *Don't just talk about it, feel it.* Talking about how angry you are—or could be—is of little value. It does not release any energy or get you in touch with your feelings. Feeling it does. If you have

trouble really feeling this emotion, try the suggestions outlined in Chapter 10. Remember that sometimes just expressing your feelings repeatedly out loud will often help you begin to experience them. Once you've felt your anger, you *know* it's there and can then begin doing something with it. Thinking it exists only motivates you to think about how you might deal with it.

4. *Don't reinforce anger.* Often people blow their anger out of proportion by reinforcement or exaggeration of their own hurt, frustrations, or fears. Purposely setting yourself up for additional anger-provoking scenes may overload your ability to control that emotion. Any time you direct your life into situations where you have minimal control over what happens, or the chances of success are poor, you are setting yourself up for further frustration. Expecting more from yourself or others than your own common sense tells you is realistic will heighten frustration. Ruminating over all the past injustices in your life, from early childhood on, will give you more anger than you can resolve all at once. You do not need to overwhelm your ability to deal with anger by pulling in extras.

5. *Don't hold it inside.* Many people become overwhelmed with their anger just by storing it up. Each time someone hurts their feelings or they are disappointed, they push back their healthy urge to release their anger by rationalizing that "this isn't a good time" or "so and so probably didn't mean it." How many times have you, yourself, trapped your anger inside by wondering if you had the "right" to feel hurt or upset? Each time you swallow a frustration, you are building up your reservoir of anger. Internalized anger turns into depression, self-hate, guilt, self-destructive behavior, and, often, periodic outbursts of rage. The only way to protect yourself from building a "rage reservoir" is to acknowledge your anger and deal with it directly each time you feel it. That way you no longer collect extra anger—to carry around.

6. *Do release your anger through physical activity.* People who have a large reservoir of anger from years of swallowing frustrations find it helpful to work off some of the extra energy from

their anger. Any activity that involves physical exertion will do. Women often talk about how they give their house "Hell" by scrubbing everything in sight when they're angry. Men more typically push the lawn mower around the yard or wax the car. Both men and women use recreational sports, such as tennis, handball, badminton, bowling, or golf, to release their tensions. In therapy, I often have patients beat on a pillow or punch a punching bag to help them release excess anger. You can try the same things at home with a pillow or by making your own punching bag. Incidentally, this is not only a good way to release your rage reservoir but an exellent technique to help you develop constructive insight about the causal factors for your own anger. If you put yourself on a schedule which includes doing physical exercises (taking a brisk walk in the morning, doing some sort of physical activity during your lunch hour or after work, and exercising or punching a pillow just before you get ready for bed) you will be surprised at how much healthier you feel—physically *and* emotionally.

7. *Do learn how to scream.* Expressing your pain, fears, and frustrations through screaming can help you get them out in the open where you can see them and deal with them more directly. Dr. Daniel Casriel, in his book, *A Scream Away From Happiness,* suggests that learning how to scream out your feelings can help release inner tensions, break up your "frozen" emotions and begin the process of becoming a psychologically "open" and healthier being again. If you question the validity of screaming as a therapeutic technique, watch the rooters' section at a football game versus the crowd sitting next to them. The screamers are not only able to openly shout their displeasure about their team's mishaps, but also spontaneously show their happiness and warmth when the team does well. Whatever happens, those who go away exhausted from screaming rarely pick a fight or are disgruntled after the game; the fans who sat on their feelings often are.

8. *Do be prepared for events that frustrate you.* Although we

don't always know what scenes are going to cause additional frustration, most of us know *some* situations that are almost guaranteed to make us angry. I know, for example, that I will start off my day mildly upset if I get up late and rush unprepared to my office, losing my parking space in the process. This is a mild source of anger, but, since I know it exists, I can handle it by making sure I set two alarm clocks or, if I forget to do that, a mild expression of anger before I get in my car releases the tension I could very easily carry into my first appointment. If you take the time to figure out what situations usually make you feel frustrated or angry, you will discover that there are some you can totally avoid and others you will be able to handle quite well because you were prepared ahead of time for your anger. It is even possible to predict situations that you have not already experienced but suspect will be "anger-provoking," like your ex-love coming back to pick up half of the property, your ex-spouse visiting the children with a new love, or meeting with the lawyers (or paying the fees). Since you know that all of these situations can be anger-provoking, prepare yourself to deal with your anger in a healthy manner.

Gaining control over our anger is something that we can all learn how to do. Those who lose control of their anger or express it in destructive ways do so because they were taught that anger is wrong and can not be expressed constructively. This could not be farther from the truth.

## Dealing Directly With What Causes Your Anger

After you have released your anger, take time for introspection. Ask yourself the following questions:

    1. What was I fighting for?
    2. Is there any way I can obtain it?

3. How?
4. Is that something I'm willing to do?
5. If my goal is unreachable, how can I alter it to something that is realistic?

Answering these questions for yourself can give you a great deal of insight about the causal factors of your own anger, plus additional information about how to resolve some of your conflict. Let's look at each question specifically.
1. *What was I fighting for?* People fight for a number of things: respect, approval, appreciation, sympathy, support, never to be caught "off guard," self-confidence, love, agreement from others, a sense of safety, a feeling of importance, and admiration from others. Sometimes it can be won through anger, sometimes it can't.
2. *Is there any way I can obtain it?* If you are fighting for something that is possible to win, your answer will probably be "yes." But sometimes people fight for the impossible and continue to fight because they don't know that or refuse to admit it to themselves. In my opinion, it is impossible to win the following: everything always going exactly the way I would like; all people liking me or giving me their approval/respect; feeling totally "safe" and "secure" in all situations; and never making a mistake again. Somehow knowing that these goals are impossible helps me give up fighting those battles. Sometimes a goal is impossible to win because you are fighting in the wrong battlefield. For example, you canot win self-approval, self-respect, or self-acceptance by demanding it from others. Those are goals that only *you* have the power to give yourself.
3. *How?* If you answered "yes" to the above question, this is the time to figure out how you can obtain your goal. If your goal was to gain approval from your boss, for example, figure out what you would have to do to earn it. Be as specific as you can. If it's worth fighting for, it should be worth your energy to do some problem-solving now. If you *still* come up with a blank, ask the person directly.

4. *Is that something I'm willing to do?* Once you have figured out what you would have to do to obtain your goal, ask yourself whether it's something you're willing to do. How much effort will it take to earn your boss's approval, for example. If the goal is reasonable and you are willing to earn his/her approval, then you can use your energy to *work* for it rather then *fight* for it through the expression of direct anger.

5. *If my goal is unreachable, how can I alter it to something that is realistic?* If you answered question 2 with "no," this is your chance to begin looking at how you can give yourself permission to give up some of your battles that can't be won and replace them with goals that you can attain. Many people discover that their anger comes from fighting themselves; fighting to be different than they are—smarter, kinder, warmer, wiser, stronger, braver, etc.. Whatever the fight, the best way to win is to start by accepting yourself as you are now. Sometimes this is difficult for ex-intimates because they feel that they are currently alone because there is something "wrong" with them, and, therefore, they do not want to accept themselves as they are; they want to change. But change will only begin *after* you have accepted where you are now. If you answered "yes" to question 2 and figured out, for example, that you were fighting for your boss's approval but, upon further examination, discovered that you would have to literally sell your soul or give up expressing your opinions, you may decide that it is impossible for you to ever gain that person's approval and still keep your own self-respect. If this is the case, you will need to decide what you are willing to settle for. Is just keeping your boss off your back enough? Or how about learning to accept that all authority figures aren't gods nor is their approval always worth having?

To practice answering these questions for yourself, go back in your memory to the last time you felt angry. See if you can recall the scene; then try to discover what you were fighting for. If the scene was a battle over what seemed like trivia, look beneath that and see what emotions or issues the trivia symbolized for you at the time.

Use a piece of paper to answer these questions for yourself.
1. What was I fighting for?
2. Is there any way I can obtain it?
3. How?
4. Is that something I'm willing to do?
5. If my goal is unreachable, how can I alter it to something that is realistic?

## Using Your Anger Constructively

Every time you hear someone say, "When I finally get 'fed up,' I do something," you are listening to someone who converts anger into ambition or drive. "I'm too stubborn to quit now" is another phrase often used to express determination to complete a task or reach a goal. One of my friends uses her anger to help her lose weight: "I never go on a diet until I get angry at myself for being fat—then, I *know* I'll stick to it!" I'm sure if you look at your own life, you'll discover many scenes where you called upon your anger to help—most of us do.

Healthy, constructive anger is an especially valuable resource to help ex-intimates grow through a life crisis which offers even the most courageous several opportunities to throw in the towel. To help you become more aware of the different ways you can use your anger constructively, let us look at how other ex-intimates have used their anger productively.

1. *Fighting depression with anger.* Turning your anger away from you and directing it outward can change your mood from sad and lethargic to brighter and active. As one of my clients told me:

> "When I used to come home every evening from work, as soon as I walked through my doorway, I would suddenly feel tired. I knew it was depression and that it depressed me to come home to an empty apartment, but thinking about it

really didn't help. What *did* help was hard work. Forcing myself to clean up the apartment, rearrange the furniture, redecorate a room, wash my car, work on a hobby—there are all kinds of things I can do. Sometimes it still amazes me that I have so much energy, once I get going. I end up feeling better afterwards. In fact, some days I even look forward to coming home and doing something constructive."

A lady talked about how she fought the physical part of her depression by forcing herself to exercise:

"Not only do I feel better after I start moving again, but I've lost 10 pounds in the process—a real ego booster."

2. *Turning anger into ambition, motivation, or drive.* Keeping your anger under healthy control can give you the extra strength that you need to keep yourself working toward a new goal.

I have to thank my ex-husband for giving me the motivation to learn how to drive. If it wasn't for his negative attitude about me being helpless and my decision that I'll show him, I think I'd still be hiding at home, waiting for someone to take me shopping. My next goal is to get a job—that should be a real challenge!

One man gave up drinking after his divorce:

"I'm not sure about all of the fancy psychological reasons, but I do know that I used my anger toward my ex-wife to help me stop drinking. Each time I wanted a drink, I'd remind myself that that's what Harriet would expect me to do. That's all I needed to put down the glass."

A lady told us:

"I'd been married 25 years when we finally divorced and I didn't have very much to show for it. I spent a few months feeling sorry for myself, then decided, "Now's the time to do something, you aren't getting any younger, old girl!" I ended up becoming a teacher and I love it. Looking back now, I can see how I used my anger to help me get where I am now."

3. *Using anger to be creative.* Ex-intimates often develop their hidden talents and perfect them through the use of their constructive anger from the good-bye. One man learned to make totem poles after his divorce, first as a hobby and now as a profession.

"I love it. Used to be in the "rat race." And all I ever got for work was a thin paycheck and hassles with the customers. I used to carve wood as a hobby—a way to release tension, I guess, and keep me from feeling bored. After my divorce, I couldn't afford to do much of anything extra, so, I just kept on carving. One day I saw a picture of an Alaskan totem pole in a magazine and thought "Hell—I can do that!" And, sure enough, here I am five years later making a darn good living at something I like. My new wife admires my talent, too."

4. *Changing anger into self-assertion.* According to Dr. Theodore I. Rubin, author of *The Angry Book,* self-assertion springs from self-esteem, "the spontaneous ability to make a choice and do something on one's behalf without a desire to hurt someone." If you're angry enough to fight for your self-esteem, you have the ability to turn that energy into self-assertion.

"You should have seen the expression on my husband's face when I told him in person, and very matter-of-factly, that he would just *have* to find a way to pay child support—it was his responsibility and, although I did not want to make it hard for him, neither was I going to let him off the hook. Child support has been a fight for the last nine months and I've vacillated between letting it slide and feeling sorry for myself to shrieking like a banshee about the money he owed us. This time it was different and, I might add, much more effective. He heard me standing up for myself (without putting him down) and so did I. I really felt good about it."

## Learning To Let Go Of Part Of Your Anger By Replacing Losses

If you are fighting for something or someone you don't have any more and are frustrated because you feel empty or lost, one good way to win your battle permanently is to replace some of those losses. In fact, many ex-intimates discover that their anger (or depression) subsides quite naturally as they begin refilling some of their emptiness or replacing their old goals with new ones.

It isn't easy to do. In fact, it's very hard to give up an old lifestyle, goals, and familiar faces and replace them with new, not-yet-known ones. But it is possible, and often the substitutes for your past are mentally healthier and much more rewarding than anything or anyone from the "good old days." But you have to go out and get them—or meet someone new.

### Experiments and Exercises

Role playing is a method in psychological practice (primarily Gestalt) which allows you to **act out** your problems. This can be a problem you have with yourself (conflicting feelings) or with another person. The simplest method, created by Fritz Perls, is to set two chairs facing each other. One chair for the **actor** and the other for the person the actor takes issue with—or in the case of conflicting inner feelings, the opposing feelings. (Sometimes a third chair is used as the "decision-making" position—that is, if the conflict appears to need a neutral, decision-making position after both sides have been verbalized, the **actor** will use this third chair to assess the other two positions and come up with a decision or logical resolution of the conflict.)

Try the two-chair role-playing technique to express your anger. Stand on a sturdy chair, looking down at the person you are angry at. Tell that person what you are angry about and why. Make sure you express your feelings to the degree you feel them; don't "soft pedal" your position. Say all the things you've always wanted to say and never dared. Switch to the other chair and allow the person you are talking with to respond as you think he or she would. When you feel "finished," draw the scene to a conclusion.

After this exercise take some time to reflect and ask yourself the following:

- What did I learn from this?
- Is there any way I can prevent this same thing from happening again?
- Is there any other way to get what I was fighting for?
- What do I need to do now?

# 13

# HOW TO CONQUER YOUR SELF-PITY

Don't be embarrassed to admit that you sometimes engage in self-pity. We *all* feel sorry for ourselves occasionally. It's a normal human emotion and a natural part of saying good-bye to an old love affair—especially if your fears of the future overwhelm you.

A little self-pity is healthy. It can be a way of nurturing your wounded pride when you feel all alone—a gift of sympathy to someone you care about whose feelings are hurt.

The problems develop when you wrap yourself in self-pity and use it as your excuse for giving up on your life. "Nothing good ever happens to me anyway, there's no use in trying" can be the arrow that pierces your hope. Such an attitude blocks your normal desire to do something constructive about your unhappiness.

Often people get trapped by their self-pity because they don't understand that they *can* gain control over it. They don't realize which of their personality traits make them susceptible to additional pain and mistakenly pour salt in their wounds with their misguided idealism.

If ending an intimate relationship has undermined your self-confidence to the point that you only have enough energy to feel sorry for yourself, this chapter will show you how to change that. You will learn what it is that you do to reinforce your self-pity and how you can conquer your natural impulse to give up on ever feeling better.

## People Prone To Self-Pity

The ending of an intimate relationship produces a number of circumstances which may trigger your self-pity—especially if you are prone to such feelings anyway. When you can understand why you feel sorry for yourself or how your own personal traits reinforce your sorrow, you can use that insight to reduce your self-pity.

Individuals who have low self-esteem "give in" constantly to others, or do too much to preserve a relationship are prone to self-pity. They end up feeling "used" and may not believe they deserve any better treatment. The following comments were expressed by members in my group who are prone to self-pity.

- "I gave him the best years of my life . . ."
- "My wife used me—She never really cared about me."
- "I always did everything for him—and now look."
- "My wife never understood me."
- "I loved him more than he loved me."
- "I loved my job, and I gave it up for him—"
- "I knew this would happen—I knew she'd leave me."
- "I tried harder than she did."
- "I always knew I'd end up alone."
- "Even after his infidelity I trusted him."
- "I could never figure out what she wanted from me; I bent over backwards."

1. "Bending over backwards" to please someone or save a relationship is a sure way to end up feeling used when it's

over—and a "natural" for self-pity. Ironically, ex-intimates who uphold the idea of "giving more than you get" have a greater chance of feeling sorry for themselves. The one you bend over backwards for rarely appreciates your sacrifices and, in fact, may gradually come to expect you to always do more than you should. In addition, that person sometimes resents your sacrificing because he/she looks "bad" in comparison. Ironically, sometimes this dynamic becomes the underlying reason for the dissolution of the relationship.

> One lady I know always felt "used" because she put everyone else's needs before her own. If a friend called and asked her for a favor, she would drop whatever she was doing to help. Her friends rarely appreciated her efforts, but the lady kept on "doing" for others because she did not believe her friends would like her if she didn't. When *she* needed a favor, her friends seemed to vanish. Usually she ended up taking care of her own problems and feeling sorry for herself in the process. Through therapy, she learned how to feel confident in her own worth so that she didn't have to "sacrifice" in order to be deemed a worthy friend to others. Once she practiced giving only what seemed "fair" to her, much of her self-pity lessened.

2.  Some people are prone to self-pity because they confuse sadness with tragedy. The ending of an intimate relationship with all its painful fallout is not a disaster—it is sad. If you accept your pain and fear as unpleasant and sad rather than tragic, you can learn to heal your wounds and plan for the future. If you treat the death of a love affair as a tragic event that is the irrevocable end to your happiness or the absolute failure of all your relationships, you can only feel sorry for yourself and wallow in pain.

> Laurie was recently rejected by her boyfriend, John. When she first came to my office, she was overwhelmed with

depression. She felt like a loser and feared that she could not go on living without John. "No one will ever love me—I'll never get over John—There's nothing left in my life!" The longer she talked, the more evident it became that Laurie equated rejection with disaster. Once I explained this to her and helped her accept that her boyfriend's rejection was sad but not a tragedy, she was able to let go of her self-pity and look at more constructive ways to deal with her depression.

People like Laurie who overdramatize their painful and scary feelings have a tendency to overwhelm themselves, "give up" trying and stay stuck in unhappiness much longer than others who deal with their feelings more realistically. Friends don't know how to comfort someone who not only feels tragic but actually refuses comforting from anyone who even hints that his or her wounds will heal. "Nobody knows the pain that I feel" is often the lonely theme song for this brand of self-pitier.

3. Another group of people prone to self-pity and closely linked to the "overdramatizers" are those who decide that life is *unbearable* when they don't get exactly what they want. Most healthy adults learn to adjust to their disappointments and replace their losses with viable alternatives. A few people, however, refuse to accept that they cannot always have their own way and, with the ending of an intimate relationship, may run into unchangeable disappointments for the first time in their lives.

Polly was immobilized with self-pity after she divorced her husband of 21 years. As a child, Polly had been spoiled by her parents. When she married, Tom took over the role of a pampering parent. Polly didn't get everything she wanted, of course, but when she wanted something badly enough, Tom would usually get it for her—nice clothes, a pretty house, her own car, and "good" schools for the children. In spite of this "spoiling" Polly didn't feel satisfied. She decided that if she divorced Tom, she could get what she wanted—a sense of freedom. Unfortunately for Polly, the divorce split Tom's income and it was impossible for her to keep all of her "things" and still have her freedom. But she didn't want Tom back nor could she see any way to give up her "home." Polly began to sink into a well of self-pity and was finally brought to the mental health clinic by a friend. In therapy it was discovered that Polly had become overwhelmed with self-pity because she didn't know any other way to deal with her disappointment. She believed that she should get anything she really wanted and when she learned she could not, she gave up. Gradually, she was able to accept her disappointment and learn how to adjust in a healthier manner.

Not every ex-intimate who has trouble adjusting to disappointment is pampered like Polly, but most refuse to believe that they have to accept something different from what they really want.
4. Sometimes people fall into self-pity because they confuse what they want with what they actually need. We need food, shelter, and clothing to physically survive. To be emotionally healthy we need understanding, acceptance, and love from ourselves and other people. We may want that love, acceptance, and understanding from specific individuals, but it is not really necessary for our emotional health that we get it from any one person specifically. Many ex-intimates get trapped in self-pity because they confuse their need for human love and understanding with their desire to gain it from a specific person (usually someone who is no longer available). As long as their confusion with wants and needs continue, self-pity will prevail when they cannot obtain what they want.
5. Some people who are prone to self-pity add to their problems by taking normal failure and rejection *personally*. These

people are overly self-critical and, therefore, overly dependent on others for approval. They belittle themselves and try to avoid situations when they aren't assured of success.

- "I could *never* do that, I might fail!"
- "I can't stand to be criticized, it crushes me!"
- "I'm too sensitive to risk rejection again!"

The possibility of normal failure and rejection in daily living is extensive. If you have recently said good-bye to an old love affair, you will find that, in order to be successful in replacing your losses or building your self-confidence, you will *have* to risk failing at times. Be aware of your over sensitivity so that daily disappointments don't drain you to the point where you have just enough energy left to bemoan your fate.

6. People who decide that they cannot trust anyone with their feelings are prone to self-pity. We all need someone to care for, listen to, understand, and be concerned about us—especially when we're feeling hurt. But when ex-intimates decide (for their own reasons) that no one cares about their feelings as much as they do, *or* that their feelings would not be accepted by anyone, they are stuck with self-pity. Any time you find yourself saying that you wish you could talk with someone but no one cares how you feel anyway, you are engaging in self-pity. When you have what you judge as a "wrong" feeling or experience hurt over some situation that you are ashamed of or embarrassed to talk about, you will end up feeling sorry for yourself. And, the more you use yourself as your sole source of sympathy, the sadder you'll feel, the less objective advice you will gain, and the farther down in the hole of self-pity you'll sink.

## Traps That Reinforce Self-Pity

It isn't easy to pull out of self-pity—especially if you perpetuate that emotion with an exaggerated sense of responsibility and "fairness." Many ex-intimates get caught in self-pity because they are individuals who either attempt to make up for their lack of self-confidence by overachieving or are firmly convinced that if they are "good" they will get what they feel is "fair." But the ending of an intimate relationship with all its painful and often "unfair" fallout is difficult to control, and most of these ex-intimates reinforce their self-pity by falling into the following traps.

1. *Trying to take care of your hurt feelings by yourself.* Getting trapped in self-pity because you don't want to "bother" anyone else with your sorrow is an easy pitfall for some to slide into. Some ex-intimates immediately isolate themselves and refuse invitations from their friends because they "don't feel up to entertaining and would only be a drag." Others initially reach out to other people for emotional comfort, support, and human contact, but after the first few visits decide that their friends have had enough of their sorrow (even though the ex-intimate hasn't) and the "best" thing to do is discontinue visiting with their friends until they feel better. In both cases the ex-intimates do not decide to give up feeling blue, they merely decide to handle their pain by withdrawal from supportive contact with friends. Thus, their self-pity is reinforced by deliberate isolation from others. Obviously the way to get out of this trap is to encourage yourself and others not to let you withdraw. Naturally there will be times when you'd rather stay by yourself, but don't allow yourself to always decline invitations—pretty soon, you will cease getting them. When friends invite you to join them—accept. If you're really worried about being a "drag," *force* yourself to give up the blues for one evening.

2. *Feeling sorry for yourself because your ex-mate or others can't see their "unfairness."* There are a lot of "unfair" things that happen in the dissolution of a relationship—some are self-imposed, others happen by circumstance or are caused by other people. Self-imposed injustices are caused by exaggerated amounts of guilt or making harsh judgments on yourself. Circumstances like the high cost of living on a presently smaller

income, having to give up your home and/or children, or the inequities in divorce courts create "unfair" hardships on ex-intimates. And, finally, other people, (friends, family, and, perhaps, your ex-love) may judge you unfairly or treat you with malice just because a relationship with one other individual has died. Obviously, that's not "fair"—but don't expect everyone else to see the "unfairness"; you'll be disappointed if you do. As a matter of fact, many ex-intimates increase their self-pity by expecting their ex-mates and others to be "fair" when they are not. One lady was drowning in self-pity because of her unwillingness to accept the fact that her ex-mate did not care whether he was "fair" or not. He had deliberately moved to another state to avoid child support payments. "Doesn't he know we need the child support money? I just can't understand how he expects us to live. We'll have to go on welfare and that's not fair to the children. I know he's making good money, what'll I do?" Although she was normally a very reasonable adult, self-pity had blocked her ability to solve problems because her ex-mate could not see his "unfairness." One man got himself into a similar predicament by trying to get his ex-wife to be equitable about splitting the community property. She fought him every step of the way and he made his life more miserable by feeling sorry for himself because his ex-wife wouldn't see that she was being "unfair." Most of us know that we cannot stop others from being unfair but we have trouble actually accepting that fact. Once you accept it, you can give up your self-pity and spend your energy learning to deal with life's inequities rather than becoming overwhelmed by them.

3. *Feeling sorry for yourself because you can't be mother and father to your children.* This is a hard trap to avoid because most parents carry a certain amount of guilt for splitting up the family and often try to make up for the missing parent to absolve their guilt. Sooner or later, all single parents recognize that it is impossible to completely fill both parental roles. But, in the process, many ex-intimates cannot forgive themselves when they fail.

"The first three months I saw Edna, she was almost always in crisis. She and her husband had agreed to divorce in a reasonably "adult" manner—but their 7-year-old son, Danny, reacted like a child. One day he'd be sullen and quiet, the next, he'd rage like a madman—fighting in school and screaming at home. Edna accurately assessed that Danny was reacting to his parents' divorce and the absence of his father, but inaccurately concluded that she could salve Danny's pain and protect him from sadness by filling in for his father. First, she tried to take over the role of a father in addition to her other responsibilities, spending total weekends with her son and playing with him after work each night. For a brief period of time this seemed to quiet Danny, but after a couple of weeks, he once again began missing his father and reacting with sporadic upsets. Edna handled her son's behavior and her failure to be both mother and father by feeling sorry for herself and sinking into a depression. Gradually, both Danny and Edna were able to accept his father's absence and learn to adjust in a healthier manner."

Any situation which gives you an invitation to feel hurt or disappointed but which you feel helpless to change or accept, may reinforce your self-pity. To get out of any of these pitfalls you must decide that you genuinely want to quit feeling sorry for yourself and get on with the business of living. No one can force you to adjust to life's inequities without feeling victimized.

## Admit Your Self-Pity Without Judging Yourself

If you want control over your self-pity, you must first accept the fact that you *do* feel sorry for yourself. A lot of people have trouble accepting their identification as self-pitiers. "Yes, but— you don't understand" is often an automatic response. Immediately they begin to defend themselves when confronted with the reality that they are immobilizing themselves with self-pity. (Some people don't even comment at all—they just feel more "put down" and sorry for themselves.) However, you don't *have* to feel attacked or condemned if someone suggests that you are trapped in self-pity. Of course you have the right to feel sorry for yourself; everyone does! But the fact is that self-pity can often be a trap which keeps its owner feeling sad. And, whether an individual prone to self-pity admits those emotions or not—they still exist.

So, if you have decided that sometimes you *do* feel sorry for yourself at the expense of your growth, avoid self-condemnation. If you have the courage to admit your self-pity, you have enough strength to "grow" on with your life.

## Take Back the Power You Give To Others

Your self-pity will go away when you realize that *you have primary control over how you react* to disappointment or pain. That means you will have to give up viewing yourself as a victim of other people's unkindnesses. Whatever they have done to you (or continue to do) is miniscule compared to what you're doing to yourself now! Long after the wounds have been inflicted, you can keep them open with self-pity and make your life miserable.

Time does *not* heal all wounds! One lady I met was still wallowing in self-pity and bitterness 6 years after her ex-mate had left her for another woman. All she could think about was how unfairly she had been treated in the past, and this kept her from doing something constructive in her present.

When you admit that *you* are the one who decides what you will do about your present unhappiness, it means that "they" no longer have as much power over you. Sitting at home night after night waiting for the phone to ring is far more damaging than the fact that your ex-mate doesn't call. Your ex-mate's abusiveness causes you more pain when you use it as a reason to never love again. Many adults hold on to their hurts from their childhood and keep themselves miserable because of it. Most of them refuse to accept that whatever happened cannot be changed, and they can only make themselves feel worse by bemoaning their past abuses.

The sooner you take back the power you give to others who "control" you, the quicker you can conquer your self-pity. Somehow, the telephone *not* ringing becomes less important when you're enjoying those hours with someone else.

## Give Up the "Doormat" Syndrome

A doormat is something people wipe their muddy feet on when they come into a house. Doormats are useful but they are *not* respected or treated with kindness because they are things without feelings. When they get frayed and worn, most people toss them aside for new ones.

A lot of people put themselves in "doormat" positions. And those who wipe their feet on human doormats think no more about them than do the rest of us when we use regular doormats. Human doormats are natural self-pitiers, and the only way they can get out of feeling sorry for themselves is to get out of that position. As long as they lie there, someone will walk all over them.

Most doormats have trouble standing up—they feel (for various neurotic reasons) that they are destined to stay where they are. Consequently, they are automatically stuck with self-pity and resentment—at the price of respect and kindness. Those who decide to stand up have some trouble at first, but, with practice, they gain respect and kindness from themselves and others while losing their self-pity and resentment about being used.

If you decide you're a human doormat but want to give up that position, let me suggest the following:

## How To Conquer Your Self-Pity 227

1. *Learn to say "no."* Many people have trouble saying "no." It makes no difference whether they want to say "no" or not, the word just gets stuck in their throats—if they don't feel they have a "good" reason to refuse. Practicing to assert yourself is the only cure. At first, you may have trouble with this. Lots of people shout "no" at everyone when they first begin trying. Sometimes, people get scared (or feel guilty) when they come on so strong and immediately give up trying to assert themselves any more. But, if you recognize that you're learning a new skill which will take time to perfect, your clumsiness won't scare you, and with practice you will be able to say "no" without putting other people down in the process. Don't be afraid that others will no longer like you. If they care, they'll adjust to the "new" you, just as you are adjusting to an acceptance of your real feelings. In fact, you might find others far more comfortable with you now that you don't hide what is really going on inside you.

2. *Don't sacrifice for others or do more than you think is fair.* If someone asks you to do something which you feel would cause you a personal hardship or is more than you are genuinely willing to do, don't do it. If you tend to be a doormat anyway, it may be hard for you to even recognize that doing the favor is a sacrifice until after you've already said "yes". If that is the case, may I suggest that you stall on your automatic compliance until you've had time to think it over. Tell your friend, "I'm not sure whether I want/can do that, let me call you back." If your friend is not a "feet wiper," your tactful stall won't be offensive. Practice it. If you decide that the favor is something you want to do and it is not an unfair request, go ahead. If, however, you decide that you would end up feeling used and resentful if you do it, politely decline the invitation to be a martyr. Being a doormat really doesn't help a healthy relationship, anyway.

3. *Never offer to do something which you really don't want to do—or if there are strings attached.* A lot of human doormats wave flags with "Let Me Do More!" painted on them, then resent everyone who accepts. These people can always be found

at the end of a party, muttering to themselves and cleaning up after the guests have gone, or, weighed down with most of the hors d'oeuvres, sputtering how everyone else is selfish for not offering to bring as much as they did. They make life uncomfortable for themselves and everyone else. If someone tells them *not* to do so much, their feelings are hurt. And if other people play along with the doormat's game, they are resented unless they accept one of the strings of the game, which is usually to praise the doormat for sacrificing so much, or agree to sacrifice too. If you have a tendency to *always* offer to do more in a relationship (or at a party) than others do and/or there are strings attached to your kindness, stop! Hold back on your automatic offers to sacrifice. Whatever your historical reasons for starting this game, remember that you are not perpetuating a mutually satisfying relationship by continuing to play. Instead, you are only perpetuating your feelings of self-pity.

4. *Admit the reality that some sacrifices that you make for others are really for your own needs.* Many human doormats insist on being used because of their own needs rather than for the good of others. Sometimes understanding those needs helps doormats decide to stand up or at least give up their feelings of being used. For example, some people sacrifice to avoid feeling guilty. A friend of mine *always* offered to help other people to avoid feeling like a feet-wiper herself. One of my clients sacrificed any time there was an opportunity—to make up for using people when he was a teenager on drugs. Some people do good so that others will like them. But, usually, others are wary of the compulsive do-gooder. Others sacrifice because of their distorted image of giving or kindness. One lady sacrificed for her ex-husband during their marriage because she thought that a good wife was always supposed to give and give in. She really felt sorry for herself when he left! But sacrificing doesn't mean you love someone—it means you're a martyr! If you are prone to take on the martyr role, spend a little energy looking at what needs it meets for *you.* Maybe you can find other ways to build

up your self-confidence or salve your guilt feelings. Being a doormat isn't usually very effective.

5. *Do things for yourself.* A lot of doormats end up feeling used because they do little things for others but *never* anything for themselves. If you're this type of person, spend the extra time and money on *you.* If you are really convinced that you can buy friendship, buy your own. It's emotionally healthy to treat yourself as well as you do your best friend. And you can give much more graciously to others when it's out of an honest desire to do so—not some neurotic need.

## Other Ways To Give Up Self-Pity

If you have a tendency to overreact to your disappointments and catastrophize your negative feelings and fears, you can lessen self-pity by taking the responsibility to both ask and answer the following questions:

1. Just because I'm feeling this way now, does that mean I will *always* feel like this?

2. Haven't there been times in the past when I've felt equally desperate, but resolved it somehow?

3. Am I being totally honest when I judge myself so critically, or is it possible that this is merely what I'm feeling right now?

4. Could I learn something constructive from this experience?

5. How would I look at this if I weren't feeling sorry for myself?

Most of us recognize when we answer these questions that despite sad and fearful disappointments, we are not totally helpless. "When I look more realistically at what I'm reacting to, it isn't nearly so overwhelming—but it does still hurt." There is no doubt about the fact that pain—in any form—hurts. But intensifying that pain by catastrophizing will only lower your self-esteem and immobilize you in self-pity.

## Get Involved In Interests Outside Of Yourself

With self-pity, most problems center on the fact that your primary interest and focal point of attention is yourself. *Your* problems are the worst in the world, *your* feelings the most intense, *your* sadness the most tragic. No one anywhere has ever suffered as greatly or lost so dramatically. A self-pitier has a narrow point of view. Like the ancient astrologers who believed that the sun and galaxies revolved around the earth, when you feel sorry for yourself you will believe that the world revolves around you.

When you feel self-pity and lose interest in other people and events you will find it most effective to force yourself to notice the rest of the world. Keep reading the newspaper or watching the newscasts on television. Stay interested in your career, your friends, and your family. Develop new interests outside of yourself. Many people find it very healthful to help others when they are feeling sorry for themselves. "Helping other people with their problems helps me forget mine or reminds me that I'm not the only one in the world who has troubles" are common statements to hear from people who were formerly wrapped in self-pity.

As with everything, use some common sense when you encourage your own interest in the rest of the world: totally avoiding your painful feelings can be just as unhealthy as wrapping yourself in self-pity. Most people discover that within a short period of time they are actually letting go of their self-pity as they begin to rebuild their self-esteem and nurture other interests.

## Experiments and Exercises

The following is a list of self-pity reinforcers. Go through it and check whether you are likely or unlikely to use any item on the list. Make sure that you answer honestly—the first step in solving a problem is to recognize you have it.

|  | L | U |
|---|---|---|
| 1. Try to take care of "everything" alone. | ___ | ___ |
| 2. "Turn the other cheek" when someone hurts your feelings. | ___ | ___ |
| 3. Feel sorry for yourself because others can't see their unfairness. | ___ | ___ |
| 4. "Give in" consistently to others. | ___ | ___ |
| 5. Give more than you want to. | ___ | ___ |
| 6. Keep an unwritten ledger of what others owe you. | ___ | ___ |
| 7. Take it personally when someone doesn't automatically offer to help. | ___ | ___ |
| 8. "Bend over backwards" to save a relationship. | ___ | ___ |
| 9. View the loss of your love as a tragedy. | ___ | ___ |
| 10. Feel helpless to change your fate. | ___ | ___ |
| 11. Blame others for your problems. | ___ | ___ |
| 12. View rejection as a tragedy. | ___ | ___ |
| 13. Feel that life is unbearable when you don't get what you want. | ___ | ___ |
| 14. Confuse your wants with your needs. | ___ | ___ |
| 15. Get upset when you are frustrated. | ___ | ___ |
| 16. View yourself as more "sensitive" than others. | ___ | ___ |
| 17. Secretly view yourself as an abandoned child. | ___ | ___ |
| 18. Often feel that you were "born to lose." | ___ | ___ |
| 19. Secretly feel that no one has it as "bad" as you do. | ___ | ___ |
| 20. Secretly feel that no one really cares about you. | ___ | ___ |

Now go back through this list and study those you are likely to use.

- How would you honestly rate your degree of self-pity now?
- Is there a pattern you can see—or a "life theme"?
  Make a statement about yourself from this insight:
  "I have always seen myself as _____."
- How would you like to change the above?
- Specifically, what would you have to do differently in your *everyday* interactions with others?
- When will you begin to change that? Be specific.

Now pick one reinforcer you would like to give up. Using the two-chair role-playing technique, go back through your memory and visualize the *last* time you remember doing or feeling this. Remember who was there and what was going on. Allow one chair to be the "abused" part of you and the other to be the rational problem-solving part. Now give the abused part of you permission to feel sad. Give in to all the sympathy you feel for yourself. Express those feelings out loud—including your resentment. When you feel you are finished, move into the problem-solving chair. From this position, look at the abused part of you and acknowledge your sympathy as a friend. Tell the abused part, "You have a right to feel sorry (and resentful)," *but* add your suggestions on how to change this behavior or attitude and feel better. Come up with some sort of conclusion which includes plans on how to change.

When you are finished with this exercise, take some time to reflect on your experience.
- Make a commitment to yourself to follow through on what you have learned for the next week.
- After a week's period of time, re-evaluate how you are doing and add any new ideas you've discovered.
- Continue this pattern until you feel self-pity is no longer a problem.

# 14

# OVERCOMING YOUR LONELINESS

Writing about lonelines is like writing about love; it's a difficult concept to understand or even define. We all seem to have our own definition of loneliness and what it entails. Anthropologist Margaret Mead calls it being alone when you don't want to be; author Ira Tanner defines it as the fear of loving in his book, *Loneliness;* Freud felt that loneliness had something to do with the fear of death; Dr. David Rubin says its related to nostalgia and a sense of longing; and my 5-year-old neighbor, Timmy, told me he was lonely because everyone on the block is too old to play with. However, there is general agreement that feeling lonely is sad, that everyone experiences it occasionally and not one of us likes it. You can be lonely in a crowd or by yourself; at age 3 or 103; whether you're wealthy or poor; man or woman; single or married; black, white, yellow, red, or brown. And, although we may curse our need for others when we're lonely, we revel in feeling "together" with someone.

Telling you that loneliness is part of saying good-bye to an old love affair is probably not very innovative. If you're a sensitive person who acknowledges your needs for warmth and caring from others, you already know that—perhaps, all too keenly. Helping you learn how to lessen your loneliness and offering advice which others have found helpful may be something new.

It is possible for all of us to chisel our loneliness down in size and frequency—but impossible to ever completely erase it. One thing I've discovered for myself and from others—that there are all kinds of ways to handle our loneliness but only a few which are actually effective overall. You can wallow in self-pity because you feel lonely, get depressed or angry, fill up your stomach with alcohol or "pop" pills to avoid it, gorge yourself with food, pretend that you don't need anyone else and you aren't lonely anyway, or constantly keep busy with "strangers." Those are the ineffective ways to grapple with loneliness.

Dealing with your loneliness effectively requires taking the responsibility for how you react to that feeling, developing constructive insight about your loneliness at the time, learning how to be "company" to yourself when you're alone and risking intimacy and close friendships with others.

People who fear inadequacy or intimacy are more prone to loneliness than others, and during times of change, stress, or loss, the feeling is stronger. Sometimes ex-intimates find that they are actually less lonely being single than they were when they were "married." And often married couples seek counseling because of their loneliness and lack of intimacy. In a way, ex-intimates are lucky. When you're alone, you *expect* to feel lonely and, often, armed with that knowledge, expect yourself to learn how to handle it. People who do not end an intimate relationship for fear of loneliness will experience a mild form of emptiness and dissatisfaction all of their lives, but avoid learning how to lessen it in emotionally healthy ways because they can often deny it exists—or place the responsibility for their feelings on their mates.

## On The Fear Of Being Alone

Almost everyone is afraid of being alone, and only those who have chosen it or have effectively learned how to cope with aloneness feel comfortable on their own. "I'd get a divorce, but I'm afraid of living alone" is a frequent statement to hear. Countless unhealthy marriages are held together by two unhappy people who fear being by themselves more than they fear staying miserable. Together and miserable they're used to—alone and ? is unknown.

> *1st person:* What kinds of things do you have to face when you live alone?
> *2nd person:* Two things primarily—taking the responsibility for myself and learning to accept that I'm inadequate at times.

Taking responsibility for yourself and your own reactions means that no one else can be blamed. If the house is a mess and you want it cleaner—you must either clean it yourself or take the initiative to get someone to do it. If you're bored on Wednesday evening or Saturday afternoon, you can't blame someone else for your reactions—you're the one that's bored and you're the one that will either have to do something about it or keep feeling bored. If you're used to depending on someone else to make you feel good or keep you entertained, you will quickly learn the job is yours by default. Many people who begin living alone discover that their panic comes from suddenly discovering that they are overly dependent and, in fact, used their ex-mates to take their own responsibilities, then blamed them when things didn't go well. One man I know discovered that he used his ex-wife to build his self-esteem and blamed her when he felt inferior. When he began living alone, he learned that *he* was ultimately the one who had control over how he felt about himself and no scapegoat was necessary. In fact, it was easier—

and much more rewarding to take control than to dump it on someone else who couldn't be effective anyway.

Learning to accept that you're inadequate at times comes from taking the responsibility for decisions and sometimes goofing in your choices. Remember the times that you slipped out of admitting your mistakes by blaming your ex-mate? "It's your fault we live like we do" or "I didn't want to go to this movie, you're the one that dragged us here!" are both statements of irresponsibility. Even if your ex-mate was the one who finally verbalized the decision, it does not excuse your responsibility in agreeing to it—or worse yet, waiting for someone else to make the choice so that you could sit back and be critical. Being alone means *you* take the credit for your choices that turn out well and the blame for the ones that go poorly.

One of my clients, who has a lot of insight, identified what Freud felt was the core issue in our fear of being alone.

> "The main thing I learned from living alone was that no one could protect me from death. I'm not even sure why I thought of it, but one of my first weekends alone, I got very depressed and suddenly discovered that I was afraid of dying and no one can save me from it. My panic didn't last very long. I remember feeling grief for a short period of time, then thinking: "Even if I wasn't alone, I am still going to die." For some reason that made living more important to me and being alone much less scary."

There is no way of knowing how many people actually get in touch with their unconscious fears of dying and the childlike solution that if you have someone holding your hand, you will stay with that person rather than die. But, if you are fortunate enough to become aware of that fear and resolve it constructively, living alone will no longer be so frightening—nor will living together again with someone new.

The positive part of living alone is that you have the opportunity to learn how to become a mature, independent adult on your own. The negative part is periodically failing to attain that goal and having to accept that failure. And, that's where the fear enters—the fear that you cannot survive without someone taking care of you. Feeling lonely when you're alone is not unusual but feeling lonely and being alone are *not* the same things, nor do they necessarily go together.

## Understanding Your Own Loneliness

Loneliness comes from feeling unloved/unlovable and/or experiencing a loss. Obviously, with all the fallout of dissolution, ex-intimates will experience some loneliness. If you cared at all about your old love or had any sort of emotional commitment to the relationship, you will feel lonely when it's over. The intensity or duration of that feeling depends on a number of factors:

- Your own self-esteem before, during and after the "marriage"
- The degree of investment still commited to the relationship when it ended
- Your own fears of being lovable or loving again
- How much of your own identity, friends, family, and surroundings you've lost by saying good-bye
- Your ability to adjust constructively to change

If you've always felt insecure and basically unlovable, you will feel lonelier than someone who trusts in his/her desirability and capacity to love again. People prone to depression or self-pity will stay immobilized in loneliness longer than others, and those who primarily react with anger or bitterness may feel empty for a longer time. Learning to love again (one of the "cures" for loneliness) will take you as long as it does to work through the grief process. However, you will not necessarily feel lonely all the time nor will the intensity remain the same.

"I feel loneliest during the evenings, right after I get home from work."

"Mornings are the worst for me—when I wake up and no one's next to me in bed."

"During the first few weeks I thought I would die from loneliness. After that, it was only at certain times—like after a party when I went home by myself."

"Holidays are the loneliest—that's when I miss my family the most."

"I get the loneliest when things are going really well for me—or really awful. That's when I miss sharing with someone 'special'."

The times and events that remind you of your loneliness will vary. The longer you treasure your old love the longer your loneliness will linger. If you romanticize your ex-mate, you could be sentencing yourself to a lifetime of emptiness. It's natural to miss your old love for awhile and on occasion become nostalgic, but in so doing, your loneliness will linger.

On a piece of paper, jot down the times when you are aware of feeling lonely.

Understanding the reasons for your own loneliness means that *you* will have to take the responsibility to look at both your feelings (or fears) and your immediate surroundings at the time you are feeling lonely. Probably you will find that your loneliness is a combination of your own internal hurt and fear of loving, plus some external scene or upcoming event which has triggered it. For example, you may discover that you have *always* been afraid to risk loving someone, and, now that you're dating again, that fear has been triggered by the fact that you are just not "turned on" to your current date. It's natural not to fall in love again quickly (although there are exceptions), and some people discover that their loneliness becomes more intense when they try to *make* themselves love someone new. Or, you may find that when you get your feelings hurt by someone (a friend or a stranger), your loneliness becomes stronger. There are all kinds of situations which activate loneliness and whatever the scene that triggers that feeling, the first step toward feeling better is to recognize what set it off.

Internal barriers that stop people from loving and therefore, according to Ira Tanner in *Loneliness: The Fear Of Loving*, lock them in loneliness are:

1. "I don't deserve to be loved and I'll prove it."
2. "I don't trust people who want to give love and I'll prove it."
3. "I've given up trying to give love and receive it."

Whenever you find yourself in any of these psychological stances (a normal protective reaction when you've been hurt), you will be hesitant to replace your loneliness with sharing. And this apparent self-protection, in combination with hurtful or scary scenes, will make your loneliness stronger.

To develop an understanding of your own loneliness is the beginning of its demise. As one of my clients shared:

"Once I started looking at why I'm lonely, my attitude about ever feeling "safe" or "together" with someone new changed. It was like I was taking charge of my feelings— deciding that I could work out the ones that were scary. My loneliness no longer spooked me. It wasn't some mysterious blight that could control me no matter what any more. It was a normal feeling that I could lessen if I choose to."

Anything that is "unknown" can be frightening and feel unsolvable. Once you begin to understand why you feel lonely, some of the fear of your own pain will vanish, and then you can begin to develop constructive solutions toward filling up that emptiness.

## How To Combat Loneliness By Yourself

Most experts will tell you that loneliness can be lessened by

sharing with someone else—a close friend, someone you love, or a relative, for example. And while it is true that loneliness can be eased in that manner, there are also things you can do to combat loneliness by yourself. You will find it most effective to use a combination of both. Many people who live alone are not lonely because they have developed the ability to conquer their fears of being alone and have learned how to be good company to themselves. The following hints come from their experiences:
1. *Make your house or apartment a setting you enjoy.* There's nothing more depressing then coming home to a dreary apartment. Most people spend a great deal of time in their homes and how you feel has a lot to do with the setting you live in. If your home looks empty and bleak and you think of it as just a place to sleep, it's quite easy to "catch" that feeling and attitude from your surroundings. A room filled with sunshine, a few plants and a couple of your favorite treasures is much more enjoyable for you to be in than a dark, drab space. Even if you never paid much attention to what your home looked like when you were living together, now that you're living alone, your environment will be much more important to your psychological state and worth the effort of fixing up. If you're afraid of living alone, make sure that all of the doors have good locks and safety latches. Put sticks or window locks in all of the windows and sliding glass doors—that way you know that you're "safe" to enjoy your home.
2. *Save some alone times to do "fun" or creative things by yourself.* Most people do a number of things with someone else that they could also enjoy by themselves: going to art galleries, dining out and going to a movie, going window shopping, taking a hobby class. going swimming, bowling, golfing, bicycle riding, visiting a park or zoo, painting and redecorating a room, going for a ride in the country, visiting a boat show or an antique auction. Look at some of *your* favorite activities and see if you can come up with a few that you could enjoy by yourself as well as with others; then plan to do them.
3. *Avoid dwelling on your loneliness or scaring yourself with "what ifs."* Most people who enjoy living alone do not spend

large amounts of time ruminating about their feelings of loneliness or scaring themselves with "what ifs": "what if I'm always going to be alone?"; "what if I get sick or injured?"; "what if the refrigerator breaks down?"; "what if I don't get an invitation for Thanksgiving dinner?"; etc.. The healthiest and most effective way to enjoy your life is one day at a time—especially if you have a tendency to be pessimistic and "what if" your pleasure away.
4. *Avoid sinking into self-pity.* The quickest way to increase your loneliness (by yourself or in the company of others) is to sink into self-pity. Avoid falling into that trap as much as you can. If you have a tendency to feel sorry for yourself, follow the advice in Chapter 13.
5. *Do things to build up your self-esteem.* Take the effort to keep up your physical appearance and complete projects that will help you feel better about yourself. Avoid constantly criticizing each piece of your behavior, and give yourself extra "pats on the back" when you do something well.
6. *Develop new hobbies and build on old ones.* Most hobbies give their creators the opportunity to build their skills, talents, and sense of accomplishment with the extra bonus of an end-product that can be useful or aesthetic. Hobbies almost always have to be done alone and give you the opportunity to direct your interest to something outside yourself. People who live alone enjoy themselves much more readily (and so do others) when they have interests outside of themselves and their work.
7. *Change your leisure routine.* If you always spent Sunday mornings lying in bed and reading the newspapers with your old love, continuing that routine when you live alone will increase your loneliness. Changing those "special" leisure routines is an effective way to combat some of your loneliness. Use Sunday mornings to enjoy a new hobby or go on an "outing" you'd like by yourself. The trick is to replace one activity with another that you feel could be equally pleasant and satisfying. Don't replace your old "fun" schedule with drudgeries or tasks that are chores.
8. *Turn on the television or a radio for company.* Many people find that quietness in a lifestyle that was once filled with noise

deepens their loneliness. A radio or television turned on, even softly, can temporarily fill up some of the emptimess that's felt internally. Statements like: "It doesn't make any difference whether I'm even in the same room or not, having the TV on is company for me at times," or "I often have my stereo on when I'm at home," are common to hear from people who live alone but are not necessarily lonely.

9. *Getting a pet may be helpful.* A dog, cat, bird, or even goldfish can be a great companion for someone who lives alone. These animals should not act as substitutes for relationships with others, but can be a warm, supportive addition to any household.

10. *Positive attitude about living alone.* All those I have talked with who lived alone but did not feel lonely had an attitude of confidence about themselves. Even the ones who would prefer living again with someone they loved took the stance that: "This is what I'm doing now, so, it's worth learning how to enjoy." No one can tell you specifically how to develop this attitude for yourself. It's a matter of making the decision to enjoy your life, and then genuinely doing whatever it takes to make sure you attain that goal. Remember: everyone who has ever conquered loneliness started out feeling empty inside.

## Fighting Loneliness With Environmental Change

Some people discover that their loneliness seems to linger and deepen when they continue to live somewhere that brings back painful memories every day. Curling up in the same bed alone, living in the house where the two of you remodeled the garage—all of these scenes and a hundred more can remind you that you no longer share an intimate relationship with your old love. Nostalgic longing for someone or a lifestyle that is no longer available can scrape on your wounds and make it more difficult to begin learning to love someone new. And staying in the same environment makes it almost impossible not to remember those "good times"—especially for those who were not the first to initiate the goodbye.

One of the fortunate things about divorce is the fact that most ex-intimates are forced to sell their homes, and this results in both partners physically moving. As awful as that might seem at the time, many people discover that being forced to move out of their old environment is a blessing in disguise.

> When Paul and Marie divorced after ten years of marriage, Marie and the two children stayed in their home for six months until it was finally sold. Marie moved into a duplex reluctantly, but shortly thereafter discovered that she felt much better. "I don't try to make my duplex look like our home. I tried that with the house and it was always painfully impossible. It's funny, but I don't feel as lonely in the duplex. It's not our bedroom—it's mine. The garage doesn't look bare without Paul's tools cluttering it up—this garage never sheltered them. I think moving really did help me lessen my loneliness.

As therapeutic as being forced to change your physical environment is, making that move voluntarily is ten times more helpful because it requires a deliberate decision on your part to move on.

## Fighting Loneliness With the Aid Of Others

The best way to fight loneliness is to risk intimacy and friendship with others. This is a difficult thing to do sometimes—especially when you're feeling vulnerable, abused, or unlovable—but it is still the "cure" for getting rid of your loneliness. Nothing thaws loneliness quicker than understanding, which is best gained by sharing your feelings with others.

Risking should go in stages. Many people refuse to risk closeness and understanding because they have an exaggerated expectation that risking entails baring your soul to someone without any defenses to protect you from hurt. "I freeze when someone says that he wants to get to know me better. I feel like I should tell everything I've ever done or felt that I'm ashamed of. I know that's silly, but I still feel like I'm not totally honest unless I do." It is natural to share *small* amounts of yourself at a time. Trust is built slowly by gradual acceptance, *not* in one gigantic step. And the fear of taking one gigantic "soul-baring" step can immobilize even the most courageous—not to mention how overwhelming your "here's all my secrets" speech will be to a stranger. To effectively build closeness with others, it is important to mutually risk a little at a time.

Most of us enjoy different levels of friendship with other people. We share parts of ourselves with acquaintances, a little more with friends we have known for a short time or only at specific settings like work or school, and close, lasting friendships with only a few "special" people whom we feel we "know" and trust the most. Reaching out to these friends and acquaintances during the times when you feel lonely will automatically fill up some of that emptiness.

> "Sometimes when I'm lonely, I just call a friend and, hearing his voice—knowing that someone still cares about me and understands, reassures me that I'm not alone in the world."

> "I've become more friendly now that I'm alone—my loneliness forces me to meet people. I even know my neighbors now—they're very nice people. I never knew them when I was married. It was easier to hide in my shell."

> "Since our divorce I've made an effort to get closer to my family. For the first time in my life I feel they love me. I know now that I've always needed them."

> "I used to be afraid that I was a 'cold' person, but now I know I need other people and I let them know that too. I'm less lonely now than I've ever been."

## Pitfalls To Avoid In Loneliness

Throughout this book I have mentioned pitfalls that ex-intimates fall into which increase their depression, self-pity, or anger, while keeping them stuck in the grief process longer than is necessary or healthy. All of these traps may heighten loneliness as well, for often these feelings are caused by loneliness even though many people are unable to recognize that themselves. The irony about the following pitfalls is that most ex-intimates who fall into them purposely do so to lessen their loneliness, and, when they discover that they are even lonelier, usually stick to their favorite trap more insistently. The misconception here is that if they only stay longer, their sense of abandonment and emptiness will lessen—like the man who keeps searching in the same dresser drawer for a missing cuff link. The idea that "this *should* work" is difficult to erase—especially if you desperately want *something* to work. Unfortunately these traps will not lessen your loneliness and, in fact, may do the opposite, so, don't try to "con" yourself—recognize what you're doing.
1. *Risking with the "wrong" people.* Telling you to be careful and avoid risking your feelings with the "wrong" people may sound absurd, but many ex-intimates literally jump from the romantic frying pan into the fire in a effort to fill up their emptiness.

> Sharon went from one emotionally destructive relationship into another—with a married man. After six weeks, her new love affair fizzled, leaving her even more lonely than before. "When I met Bob I knew he was married. As a matter of fact that's what attracted me to him. It seemed 'safe.' I didn't have to worry about making a commitment to him—or falling in love again. Bob could just be someone to be with so I wouldn't be lonely. I certainly didn't expect to feel worse! I guess I started caring about him and then, when he decided to end our relationship, I felt lonely again *and* ashamed."

Sharon is not unusual—many of us make emotionally unhealthy choices when we decide to risk caring again. And, although it is impossible to know for *sure* whether your new love is "right" for you, it doesn't make sense to risk loving someone whom you know at the beginning will probably be "wrong." If your last love was an alcoholic and that didn't work out, don't set yourself up to fall in love with another one. If you have a tendency to be a martyr and your last relationship died because you felt "used," don't risk loving someone new who seems like more of a "feet wiper" than your last love. And don't risk your feelings with an ex-mate who's already rejected you. Let your own common sense be your guide and listen to your instincts for growth when you begin risking with someone new.

2. *Frantically searching for someone to love you.* "If only I can find someone to love me, I wouldn't be lonely," is a typical "faulty" solution to the problem of loneliness. The 'faulty" part lies in the phrase "to love *me*"—implying that you need not risk loving again, you need only find someone to prove that you are lovable. But loneliness has at its root *two* fears: being unlovable *and* being afraid to love. A solution that touches only half of the problem never works, and, in fact, usually increases the loneliness and frustration. For example, if a man succeeds in finding someone to love him, his own doubts about himself as a warm, caring person worth loving are heightened. "She loves me and I don't love her" increases self-doubt, guilt, bitterness, and resentment—all of which add to frozen emotions and isolation. There are a number of people who marry someone they don't love with the hope that, in time, they will learn to love that person. Usually this results in a mutually self-destructive relationship which ends with both partners seriously questioning their ability to love and be lovable. (If you've been in this kind of relationship, you know how painful it is.)

To frantically search for someone to love you rarely works out. Everyone senses your panic and emptiness, including you, and the "success" rate for those so desperately searching is minimal.

Making yourself available to meet someone new and encouraging that person to see you as lovable is one thing. Rushing out every night after work searching for your savior from loneliness is quite a different matter. Love grows slowly and risking takes time, both of which are necessary in order to truly develop an understanding, intimate relationship. Ex-intimates who decide they don't want to risk loving again but do want someone to love them will stay lonely for a long time—"in" or "out" of a relationship.

3. *Deciding to "kill" your need for love so you'll never be hurt again.* Most experts agree that the loneliest people are those who have decided to stop loving entirely. Yet many ex-intimates mistakenly decide that if they disavow their normal needs and feelings, no one will ever be able to hurt them again and they'll never be lonely. Someone who chooses this alternative connects emptiness with the loss of a specific person. And while it is true that the loss of a specific person triggered their loneliness, it is *not* the cause of loneliness. Each of us has control over how we deal with out emotional needs; we do *not* have control over whether we have them or not. When someone decides to handle the normal need for love by pretending that it doesn't exist, that person has chosen to feel empty or dead inside.

4. *Substituting physical closeness for emotional intimacy.* Prostituting yourself for physical closeness rarely decreases loneliness, yet many ex-intimates go through a phase of attempting to fill up their emotional needs in this way. "Maybe I'm not capable of loving or being loved but I am a good bed partner" has a very hollow ring to it. Sexual intimacy can be the ultimate expression of emotional closeness and caring, but it can also be used in emotionally unhealthy ways—to "get back" at the opposite sex, to increase feelings of self-doubt and guilt, or mistakenly to try to *prove* that you're sexually adequate. The trouble with this trap is that it's difficult to get out of. One of my divorced friends is in his fifth year of prostituting his emotional needs for one-night stands and he's still just as lonely as he was at the beginning. Evenings, weekends, and holidays are still very empty, and plan-

ning a vacation with someone "special" six months from now is, of course, out of the question, because his faith in anyone's ability to be honest, caring, or faithful (including his own), is quite badly shaken. If you're in this kind of trap, give yourself a time limit on how long you're going to stay in it—then climb out of it when your time is up. That's the only way you'll ever replace going to bed with everyone for making love to someone "special."

Loneliness is not owned exclusively by ex-intimates; the world is full of people "married" and single who are emotionally isolated. Nor is it a mysterious aura that controls how you feel. Loneliness comes from building walls rather than bridges.

**Experiments and Exercises**

List how you currently deal with your loneliness.

Now reflect on your list.

- After reading this chapter and evaluating them from your own experience, would you rate them as "healthy" or "unhealthy" techniques?
- Which ones should be changed or altered to be more effective?
- Are there some that should be dropped altogether?

In this chapter, several suggestions on combating loneliness were offered. List one or two "new" ones you are willing to try during the next week.

Next, plan what you will have to do in order to try one of these.

Now, follow through on your plans.

At the end of two or three days, evaluate your progress and add any alterations you may have discovered.

Keep practicing this exercise until you have chiseled away some of your loneliness.

**Transition Exercise**

Making the transition from your old lifestyle and relationship to enjoying single status can be a painful and bumpy process at times. Especially when you get lost in your hurt feelings and fears. The following exercise will help you gain a clearer, more objective, understanding of your past relationship as well as your plans for the future. Do it when you are feeling strong, not "down" and will have *at least* 30 minutes of uninterrupted time for yourself. Choose a setting that is physically and emotionally comfortable. Read the exercise aloud into a tape recorder. Then, play it back while you do it. Practice as often as you need: it may take several rehearsals before you actually "experience" it.

Close your eyes and take a few minutes to relax. Practice taking deep, slow, rhythmic breaths. Once you feel your body relax, imagine that you are in a movie theater.

Tonight you will see one movie plus the preview of "coming events." In the movie *you* were the writer, director, producer, and star. Tonight you are the audience. The movie is about your old relationship. The preview will be your plans for the future: you are the writer, director, producer, star, and audience.

*The movie:*
1. The title goes on the screen. What is it?
2. What kind of theme does it have?
   (a) melodrama (e) tragedy
   (b) soap opera (f) mystery
   (c) fairy tale (g) adventure
   (d) comedy (h) ?
3. Is the movie in color or black and white?
4. What kind of background music does it have?
5. Are you viewing certain scenes or do you see the whole picture?
6. What does the dialogue sound like?
   Who talks and who listens?
   What is talked about? What issues are hidden?
7. Is there a "hero" or a "heavy"?

8. As the viewer how do you feel about your old role in the movie? How were you dressed? Did you stand straight or slump?
9. As the viewer how do you feel about the theme of the movie?
10. What feelings are aroused as you view it?

When you are ready, draw your movie to its conclusion. Then, take some time to reflect.

When you are ready to move on, sit back and view the "preview." Include anything you would like to place in your future.

1. This time, what is the title?
2. What is the theme?
   - (a) melodrama
   - (b) soap opera
   - (c) fairy tale
   - (d) comedy
   - (e) tragedy
   - (f) mystery
   - (g) adventure
   - (h) ?
3. Are the "coming events" in color or black and white?
4. How is the background music?
5. Are you viewing certain scenes or do you see parts of the total picture?
6. What does the dialogue sound like?
   How is it different from/same as the movie?
7. As the "star," what is your role?
   How are you dressed?
   Do you stand straight or slump?
8. Do you have one co-star or several?
   Does it change as the "previews" progress?
   What's your supporting cast like?
9. What feelings are aroused as you view the "previews"?

Conclude the "previews" when you feel the viewer would want to return for the total showing.

Now take some time to reflect:

1. Where are you in the production of your new movie?
2. What steps will you need to take to enjoy single status again?

# 15

## STARTING ALL OVER AGAIN

Starting all over again could be an entire book rather than the concluding chapter in a book on good-bye. The time between your last love affair and the next one can be one of the most creative and enjoyable periods in your life, or it can be empty and desolate—depending on how you deal with the grief process, your attitude about beginning again, and your ability to enjoy being alive. The majority of single-agains, just like their counterparts who are still "married," have both "good" and "bad" days; times when they feel on top of the world and moments when they feel crushed underneath it. When you're feeling "on top," you'll wonder why you ever felt badly about saying good-bye; and when you're crushed, nothing in the present or future will seem half as bright as the dreariest days in your past—and you will blame being single for all of your sadness regardless of whether that's true or not. Gradually you will discover that your "up" days are far more frequent and lasting than those that are down. Especially if you genuinely want to feel good and it's worth your effort to make life enjoyable.

## Viewing Yourself As a Single Adult

> "I know it's silly, but I still feel 'married' to Paul even though we've been separated for months."

It's natural for ex-intimates to still feel "tied" to their last love, even when that person has long ago vanished. But, being emotionally tied to a "ghost"—whether it's a person, an idea ("being single again means I'm a failure") or a fear ("I can't make it by myself. I'm too fragile")—can stop you from truly enjoying your single status. As a matter of fact, the unconscious psychological purpose of feeling tied to a ghost is to keep you from feeling alive and self-confident enough to risk enjoying your new life. Like an emotional governor allowing you to progress past your grief period but regulating your desires and actions to join in on the fun parts of being single again, the ghost appears just as you begin planning or right after you have taken action on an exciting plan.

> "I started to plan a vacation to Hawaii by myself and thought 'What's with you, you'll never have fun by yourself?' At first I had trouble shaking that fear—but thank God I did. I went and had a fantastic time. I can hardly wait for another vacation. It doesn't even have to be so exotic. I know now that I can go on vacations by myself and enjoy them."

> "I told myself I would never join a singles' club—it didn't seem right. Probably I'd just meet a bunch of weirdos there. But I finally shook the idea that there's something wrong

with people who go to those places, and joined in. I'm glad I did—I've made a lot of new friends there."

"After I came home from my first date, I felt like I was cheating on my ex. It was the strangest feeling. I had a good time but felt guilty. 'I shouldn't enjoy someone else's company so soon.' I'm glad I got over *that* feeling!"

To enjoy the fun parts of being single again—dating, going on vacations, being self-indulgent at times, or trying whatever you'd like to try—you will need to risk having fun in spite of your self-doubts. Unhooking from the ghosts that stifle your enjoyment requires:
1. Recognizing which ghosts you own.
2. Admitting to yourself that you are putting a damper on your life by carrying them with you always.
3. Forcing yourself to give up the ghosts.
4. Taking action to enjoy your new plans in spite of your fears.

Naturally, the more self-confident you are, the easier it will be for you to let go of your fears and fantasies. And nothing builds confidence more quickly than successful experience.

## New and Exciting Vacations

Ex-intimates often dread their first vacation because they've decided that they cannot possibly enjoy it alone. But nothing could be farther from the truth! As a matter of fact, many single-agains discover that vacations can truly be fun—sometimes for the first time in their lives because the choices about where to go and what to do are totally their own and not a middle-of-the-road compromise that no one enjoys. There are literally hundreds of travel clubs and tours set up exclusively for singles, and thousands of resorts all over the world cater primarily to single adults. You can find everything from dude ranches in the mid-west, rafting down a river, skiing in the Swiss Alps, and sailing on the Caribbean, to roughing it in a hut in North Africa. A vacation can be short and cheap or long and expensive.

When you decide on a vacation, make sure that your first one is something you would really like to do. Don't settle for filling your time up with something you feel you *should* do—like staying at home and working on the yard, or going to visit relatives you've never been close to anyway. If you feel awkward going by yourself for the first time, go on a planned tour or to a resort for singles only. If you're a bit braver, you might try a tour that is not exclusively designed for singles or couples. (Incidentally, according to a travel agent friend of mine, around 50% of all tours or resorts are filled with singles—I guess married couples stay home and remodel their garages!) If the great outdoors "turns you on," but camping alone is less than appealing, ask some of your single friends to join you. One lady I know loved to go camping but couldn't find any friends to go with her, so she put an ad in the paper inviting strangers who were interested to contact her. Eleven of them joined her for a pot-luck dinner on a Saturday night, and six of them went camping together for a week in the mountains. If art shows, antiques, historical landmarks, or beach bumming is your forte, gather together some new friends who enjoy the same interests and organize your own tour. You'll be pleasantly surprised at how many fun-loving people are just waiting around for a leader like you to organize a different and exciting vacation.

## Fun Ideas For Around Town

You don't have to wait for vacation time to enjoy life or fill part of your leisure with exciting or creative pastimes. In fact, planning to enjoy the people, activities, and sights in your own home town is just as easy as planning a vacation—maybe even easier. You have everything that is already established and available in addition to whatever your own imagination and creative abilities can develop.

## Starting All Over Again

One woman I know has made it a practice to plan a mini-weekend vacation once each month. At first she had all the normal doubts about choosing a "spot" and indecision about where and what to do. But, after the first couple of times, her fears and doubts were happily replaced by enthusiasm and a sense of adventure. Her guideline is to visit some place within a hundred-mile radius of her home. There's a map in her study with a red circle outlining the perimeter of her mini-vacationland with stars showing the areas she's visited so far. Before she chooses a town, she writes to the local chamber of commerce for information and reads up on the different areas. Then, after deciding "where," loads up her camera, film, notebook, and weekend wardrobe and is off on vacation again. Over the past year, she has gathered together enough material to write feature articles for the local newspaper—a profitable hobby that pays for her monthly vacations.

If you have less pioneer spirit, but enjoy physical recreation and outdoor activities, contact your local parks and recreation district office. During the summer and springtime, especially, the planned activities are usually in full swing—and, contrary to popular opinion, local recreational activities are *not* just for children. Most good city park systems have organized adult activities ranging from dances, tennis matches, and softball games to open swimming classes. If your system doesn't have one yet, you might want to help your community get one organized.

Many people have fun helping others. Volunteer work is available in every area—from convalescent homes to day-care centers; the USO to the Peace and Freedom Party. You can volunteer for as few or as many hours as you want and, happily for those who have trouble committing themselves, you can quit anytime you wish. Being a volunteer can help everyone, including the volunteer, feel a little more compassionate about people in general. So, check with a volunteer bureau in your community and spend some of your leisure time giving enjoyment and kindness to others. You'll discover how quickly your warmth is returned.

## Other Singles and Where To Find Them

With the frequency of dissolution, no one who is single again needs to feel alone or embarrassed about being single. But, in spite of that fact, many ex-intimates begin their single-again status hovering in a corner feeling as if they are the only ones who have ever ended a love affair. "Everywhere I look, there are couples—I feel like I'm the only person in the world without a partner" is a familiar lament amongst single-agains.

The best way to prove to yourself that you are not alone in the world is to meet other people who are in the same spot. For ex-intimates this usually means attending singles' clubs, groups, or organizations designed specifically for them. Although this may seem like a simple solution for a complex problem, most ex-intimates are extremely reluctant to join *anything* specifically for them.

> "I'd feel funny going to a group like that."
> "What would everyone say?"
> "I wouldn't know what to do."
> "What if I met somebody awful?"
> "I'm not *that* desperate!"
> "No thanks, I'll wait until I meet someone through a friend."

All of these hesitations are natural, but do need to be overcome—for unless you are one of the fortunate few who already know a number of single adults, your social life will consist of being alone or tagging along with couples. And, enjoying single life again *has* to include socializing with other single adults.

Because of the rising divorce rate *and* the current popularity of choosing single status as a lifestyle, there are literally thousands of singles' clubs, groups, bars, resorts, apartments, and every other type of organization you can think of for single adults. Almost every town of moderate size has at least one singles' club—and in many cities it is possible to live in a singles' apartment, socialize at singles' clubs exclusively, and attend a church with a special group for its single members on Sunday.

Many papers have a weekly column announcing singles' club dances, dinners, and meetings. Churches often have singles' clubs connected to their parishes, and several groups, such as the Sierra Club in the West, have special events for single members only. Community colleges and universities are beginning to conduct classes for living alone effectively, and recently some of the YMCA groups have started rap sessions for singles.

Attending one of these organized activities can broaden your ability to enjoy single status by helping you meet new people and increasing your self-confidence. Although at first it may seem scary, it is important to *force* yourself to attend at least three or four singles' events alone. Once you're there, it won't be so frightening, and it is much easier to maintain flexibility when you don't feel that you have to worry about whether your friend is having a good time. Best of all, you will be giving yourself another opportunity to prove that you do not have to depend on someone else in order to attend and enjoy social functions.

One of my clients recounted her progress in learning to assert herself and meet new friends by attending a singles' club dance:

> "I had to *make* myself go to a singles' dance alone. The idea seemed easy—but doing it was hard. I almost backed out, but kept telling myself that I had to do this—to prove to me that I could. The first time I stayed for about an hour, talked to one other woman, then faded into the woodwork and out the door. The following week I went again. That time I stayed much longer, met several more people, and actually forgot how scared I was at times. It boosted my ego to go there by myself and not fall apart. I've gone several times since then and really enjoy it. As a matter of fact, I've made

several good friends (everyone's not as awful there as I feared) *plus* I've discovered I can go anywhere by myself and have a good time. I used to just stay at home until a friend suggested we do something together. Now, if I hear about something special or get an impulse to go somewhere, I go—whether I can find someone to join me or not."

Once you've increased your self-confidence again, you might want to organize your own singles' group—a lot of innovative people do. For example, one lady I know has a Wednesday night bridge club for singles only at her home. She runs an ad in the local paper, asking bridge players to contact her for reservations. In that way she can pre-screen her guests. The club is growing in popularity and often, I'm told, she has to turn down interested bridge players because all the reservations are filled. Then, there's the man in the San Francisco area who organized a group of taxpayers to lobby for decreased income tax for single adults—at last count he had over two hundred men and women joining together with him to help lower taxes *and* get to know each other.

Regardless of what your favorite pastime or own "special" cause is, it is possible to continue with it while developing new friendships with other single adults by inviting them to join in the fun. Just remember that there are hundreds of other singles in your community who share your interests and are just waiting to get things organized. Contrary to popular myth, it is not necessary to go bar-hopping to meet other single-agains, but it is necessary to keep your mind open for new ideas and use your courage to assert yourself.

## Dating Again

For most ex-intimates, dating again produces anxiety—a kind of renewed adolescence filled with excitement and fraught with self-doubt. The mother of four teenagers getting ready for her first date with a new beau may feel excited and just a bit foolish while upstairs putting the final touches on her make-up. And downstairs, her middle-aged date may be awkwardly squirming while the children inspect their mom's boyfriend. It's a tense time for everyone. And this type of scene, or others which are just as emotionally charged, will happen repeatedly during the time that you're single again. Gradually, the self-doubt and nervousness lessen and the pleasure of dating again grows stronger. But it takes time—and using the constructive insight you've gained through the grief process.

How quickly you are able to adjust in an emotionally healthy manner to the dating scene and enjoy the pleasure of others varies with your own self-image, the insight you've gained through ending, and the length of your last relationship. Ex-intimates normally begin dating again before all of their wounds from their last love affair have totally healed, and, as a matter of fact, dating is the *only* way you can really know that you are still attractive to the opposite sex and have the ability to love someone new. Since most ex-intimates still feel vulnerable, there are several issues and problems that come up with dating again—along with the pleasures.

The major issues that come up usually revolve around:
1. Trust of intimacy (emotional and sexual)
2. Feelings of self-doubt
3. Unresolved conflicts from dissolution
4. Fears of vulnerability

These four issues can come in the form of self-questioning:
1. Will I always be alone?
2. What's wrong with me that I can't "make it" with anyone?

Unconscious decisions:
1. I'm too vulnerable to risk loving again.
2. I don't have the ability to love.
3. No one who knows me could really love me.
4. I'll never love or trust anyone again.

Or actions:
1. Dating several people at the same time
2. Dating one person at a time—but briefly
3. Dating someone you know will be a "dead end"

It is natural to ask all of these questions, periodically decide not to risk loving again, and practice these unconscious solutions by dating with emotional distance. Gradually as these issues become less overwhelming (through the pleasures of dating), your need to protect yourself from hurt and disappointment will lessen and your ability to risk intimacy will strengthen. Most ex-intimates fluctuate between actively dating again and doing things by themselves or in the company of friends.

One of my friends who has been divorced for 3 years recounted his dating experience to me in the following manner:

"The first four months I did nothing—oh, I went to parties at friends' houses, but for the most part, I just stayed at home and felt sorry for myself. Then, I started going out with some of the other men at work—barhopping and picking up one-night stands. I did that off and on for a few months, then quit. In between, I dated a couple of women that I really developed friendships with. For the most part my dating the first couple of years was casual and pretty sporadic—always, in the back of my mind, I was hoping it would work out with my ex-wife. Oh, yes, there was a brief period during the first year when I fell passionately in love with someone. But it only lasted for a couple of months. It's funny, after that bombed out, I went into a "blue funk" for about three days and then snapped out of it. But then, all my love went back to my "ex" again. It's only been in the last six months (really, since I've decided that I *could* live alone for the rest of my life if I had to) that I've found someone I think I could marry—I'm not sure yet where that will go—but, it's a great feeling".

Obviously my friend does *not* speak for the whole singles' group—or even the male part of it—but, he does recount a fairly typical pattern of dating again. All men and women will need to deal with the issues of trusting intimacy, self-doubt, unresolved conflicts, and fears of vulnerability while dating again. The problems that evolve and sporadic withdrawals from dating are attempts to deal with these four basic issues. The pleasures of dating come from occasional resolution and the melting away of these fears.

There is also another layer of issues that dating often reveals:
1. *Confusion in sexual self-image. Both* men and women suffer blows to their sexual identity when they end an intimate relationship. And dating quickly uncovers those hang-ups. Women are perhaps the most vocal with their frustrations and confusions, but men, too, when they're honest, acknowledge these fears. For both, the issue is how they see themselves now that they are sexually experienced but no longer in a "permanent" relationship—and how others may view them. "I know that I'm not a blushing or rowdy teenager any more, but does that mean I'm damaged goods or someone else's reject?" is an underlying question many will need to resolve. The obvious answer is "No, you are not 'damaged goods' or sexually inadequate." But you must discover that answer for yourself. It is natural to fear your sexuality and ability to enjoy sexual happiness if your last relationship was sexually destructive or unsatisfying, *but,* happily, most ex-intimates discover their ability to enjoy sexual relationships directly connects with their ability to risk loving and expressing that warmth through touching. Avoid judging yourself harshly when dating again—and go with your feelings, *not* your fears. Most ex-intimates discover that they automatically choose dates who reconfirm their own sexual self-image and as they begin feeling better about themselves and their own bodies, they date people who see them as sexually attractive and potent.
2. *Ambivalent feelings about sexual intimacy.* It doesn't take more than a few dates for most ex-intimates to discover that they

may have very strong feelings about sexual intimacy. Men sometimes feel they are *supposed* to ask their dates to go to bed with them, at least after the third or fourth date, and women often *assume* that "men are only after one thing." In fact, the assumption goes, if you don't go to bed after the second or third date, then the relationship won't progress. I suppose there is some validity in these assumptions—but only among the emotionally immature. Nonetheless, the fear that these notions are true for every potential new love accounts for a great many "short" dating patterns.

> "I dread the scene at my front door. I know as soon as I tell my date "no"—I'll never see him again—plus, he's liable to be nasty in the process. So, usually I date a man a couple of times—then make excuses about why I can't see him again."
>
> "Women *expect* you to proposition them. If you don't, they think you're weird. Well, maybe I am weird but I feel guilty about going to bed with someone just because she wants me to—or, it's the thing to do at the end of a date. Furthermore, I've tried that and if I don't feel like making love, I just can't do it. So, I end up dating a lot of different women—but, not for very long."

Both of these comments were made by sexually normal, responsive adults whose fears of sexual intimacy—and others' expectations—kept them from learning to develop caring relationships with their dates. Those who find themselves in this type of "short" dating pattern need to be honest with themselves and their dates about their feelings. Usually, this honesty relieves a great deal of tension and anxiety and opens the door for the development of a closer relationship in addition to helping each individual gain a little more constructive insight in the process.

In spite of the widely publicized liberal views on sexual intimacy, the majority of adults over 25 *still* have traditional values.

Those who remain married can objectively view our culture's changing attitudes toward sexual freedom. Those who are single again quickly find they can no longer take a detached viewpoint. As soon as you begin dating again, you'll discover that traditional morals about sexual intimacy have been replaced by a more liberal and open attitude, one which values sexual freedom for its own sake and not necessarily as a way to show love to a spouse. If you were "married" for more than six or seven years or came from a sexually conservative heritage, you will discover that your value systems are in conflict. If you add individual fears about sexuality, of being "used," and of not being valued as a total person or connect emotional nakedness with sexual intimacy, you can easily see why all ex-intimates will have to constructively examine and probably alter their own sexual morality.

Whether *and* how you decide to alter your views on sexual intimacy is a personal choice. But I believe it is safe to say that you will have a very difficult time finding another spouse *if* you refuse to share sexual intimacy while dating again. If you believe that your views on sexuality are too conservative (even for you) but you don't feel "comfortable" about changing them, examine them carefully. If it is intellectually "okay," act on that acceptance, then deal with your feelings afterward in a supportive, constructive manner. Most people discover if they wait around until they feel perfectly "comfortable," they never change anything. On the other hand, if you decide, after close examination, that even intellectually, you cannot accept altering your values— better hold off for awhile and stay with the old ones.

3. *Unrealistic expectations of dating again.* Many ex-intimates create extra problems for themselves and hamper their pleasure in dating by *expecting too much or too little* from their dates. Those who expect too much view each new date as a prospective life-time partner. A date is not enjoyed just for the evening, but is seen as the first step toward a life-time commitment. It is easy to understand why you might proceed so cautiously or place such extraordinary importance on dating again—especially if you are feeling vulnerable and believe that you need to quickly find a

replacement for your ex-mate. Unfortunately, such unrealistic expectations usually place too much tension and anxiety on a casual date and doom it to failure from the beginning. Moreover, the "type" of man or woman you are willing to date is thereby automatically restricted, erasing your chances of learning to enjoy different people. Many ex-intimates repeatedly fall "in love" and then "out again" with the same type of mate because they repeat their first choices in dating and commit themselves to one of the first two or three people they date. If you have a tendency to expect too much from each new date, try to remember that *one drink is not a life-time commitment!* Enjoy the drink and your date's conversation and avoid daydreaming about what it will be like ten years from now.

Expecting too little from dating again can rob you of the pleasure of dating just as quickly as expecting too much. Those who expect too little, date for a "free" meal, or to avoid eating alone. Usually these people have very low opinions of themselves, are quick to judge harshly, prone to self-pity and bitterness, and carry equally low opinions of anyone who would date them. You or your date may not be Prince Charming or Cinderella, but if you think in terms of "frog" and "scullery maid," you will rob yourself of another opportunity to enjoy the fun in dating.

4. *Confusion and/or acting out unresolved conflicts from past relationships.* Some of the more destructive problems in dating again evolve when a misguided ex-intimate attempts to work through unresolved conflicts with a past love by confusing current dates or *all* members of the opposite sex with an old love. So-called man- or woman-haters fall into this category. Women who literally lash out at their dates for no apparent reason, or passively demean them and scoff at their offers of friendship and kindness, are obviously confusing the current men in their lives with someone who is no longer present. Men who literally "screw" every woman they date, then proudly announce their opinion that *all* women are sluts are perhaps the most obvious. Others, who are a little more sophisticated, show their anger less

openly, but their dates still know they've been put down. These misguided ex-intimates are emotionally damaging to themselves and whomever they date—for no one can genuinely experience the pleasures of dating while getting even with a ghost. Most emotionally healthy ex-intimates attempt to avoid these types of games if at all possible because they understand that they are counterproductive for their own emotional growth and happiness. Unfortunately, many people continue the games through ignorance. If you find yourself making statements like "men (women) can't be trusted" or "no man (woman) will ever hurt me again"—*while* you are dating, you may be robbing yourself and your current date of the fun in dating because of some "unfinished business" for which you still hold your past love accountable.

As you resolve some of the problems in dating again, you can start looking around and experiencing pleasure with other people for its own sake and not out of internal anxieties or anger. For most ex-intimates, this is a sporadic process. One moment you'll notice that you're actually listening, talking, and laughing with your date and the internal "push" has magically disappeared—only to return an hour later. But gradually the pressure will lessen, and soon (within a few weeks) you will find that most of the time when you're with someone you are actually *with* that person and not far into what the future might hold or mucking over some pain from the past. You can quicken this process of learning to enjoy the pleasure in the present by deliberately focusing your attention on the here and now and your current feelings—rather than what you might feel later or did feel before.

## Assessing New Loves

Some dates will last no longer than one or two evenings, and either you or your "date" will decide (for any number of reasons) that you do not enjoy each other's company well enough to continue. Other "dates" will turn into platonic friendships and, perhaps, one or two will develop into intimate, caring relationships that last for several months. With each of the "endings" you may experience a certain amount of grief but gradually, as you begin feeling more secure about yourself as a separate person, you will be able to understand that every "rejection" is not a rejection of you (or your new love) as an individual—but, rather, normal personality differences which are not compatible.

In dating again it is important to develop the freedom and self-confidence to enjoy different types of dates, but equally important to evaluate more serious relationships and reject those which appear to be emotionally destructive for you. This flexibility to accept or reject new "loves" based on your own emotional health and needs can increase your enjoyment of dating—for it gives you the freedom and internal security to risk caring for others without the fear of being emotionally crushed if you pick someone who just isn't right for you.

As a result of the self-awareness gained during the grief process, most ex-intimates have a better idea of what it will take to make them happy than they did before. Use your insight to assess each new "love." The important thing is to look at what you really need or want to be happy—not what you'd like to want or what someone else suggests you need.

## Look Before You Leap Again

Mel Krantzler, author of *Creative Divorce*, suggests that divorced men and women, especially after a long marriage, need a period of experimentation with a variety of different people and relationships before they commit themselves to another marriage. It doesn't make any sense to go through all the pain of the grief process (or even part of it) and commit yourself to another relationship immediately. It can be a great temptation, especially during the first few months when you may feel overwhelmed with sadness. But avoid jumping into another "marriage" out of desperation or loneliness.

As I commented in the beginning of this book, many intimate relationships end because the lovers failed to realistically assess their relationship at its beginning—before they made a commitment to each other. Use your common sense and the insight you've gained from saying good-bye to your past love before you commit yourself again to someone new.

Being single again does not mean just going through the grief process or learning how to deal with your pain in emotionally constructive ways. It means enjoyment—and laughter—and excitement—and all sorts of warm pleasantries that help you feel better about *you* as a separate person, your world, and the people you share it with. Take the time to enjoy your single status by yourself—with friends—and new "lovers."

Those who have grown through the grief process and learned that they can enjoy themselves as separate people rarely trade in their freedom for anything less than a happy, emotionally healthy commitment the next time around. Many will even tell you that they feel *good* about having struggled through the grief process—even though there were times when they felt like dying.

> "It was like having an operation to remove a ruptured appendix. It hurt like hell! And the recovery period was agonizing at times. But thank God I did it—and didn't give up salving my hurt."

**Experiments and Exercises**

Use a separate sheet of paper to complete these exercises. Come back and do them again in three months and compare your answers.

List five things you currently enjoy about being single again.

List five more you would like to begin trying (use your imagination and suggestions from the book).

- What will you need to do to try these?
- Pick one and make a commitment to begin working on it immediately.

Now list five things you value most in life.

Ask yourself:
- How do my values relate to my life now?
- Does the way I am living my life now reflect what I say I value?
- What are my goals for the future?
- What potentials do I have in attaining those goals?
- What are the barriers?
- What am I going to do about the potentials and barriers?

The following exercise was at the end of Chapter 1. Jot down the first words that come into your thoughts as you read the sentences. After you have completed it compare your responses. Pat yourself on the back for the growth you have made. Encourage yourself to continue growing in the areas that could still be improved.

1. If I were to use three words to describe myself, they would be _____, _____, and _____.

2. If I were to use three words to describe my ex-mate, they would be _____, _____, and _____.

3. When I look at my past, the word that comes to mind is _____.

4. When I look at my present, the word that comes to mind is _____.

5. When I look to the future, the word that comes to mind is _____.

6. My three greatest fears are _____, _____, and _____.

7. My three greatest strengths are _____, _____, and _____.

8. The one quality I would like to develop in me is _____.

9. Right now I feel I can look forward to _____.

# BIBLIOGRAPHY

Beck, A. T. (1972), *Depression: Causes and Treatment.* Philadelphia: University of Pennsylvania Press.

Beck, A. T. (1967), *The Diagnosis and Management of Depression.* Philadelphia: University of Pennsylvania Press.

Casriel, D. (1972), *A Scream Away from Happiness.* New York: Grosset & Dunlap, Inc.

Krantzler, M. (1973), *Creative Divorce.* New York: M. Evans & Company, Inc.

Mead, M. (1970), Anomalies in American Post Divorce Relationships, *Divorce and After,* ed. Bohannon, P.. Garden City, N.Y.: Doubleday, p. 97-112.

Mead, M., and Metraux, R. (1970), Double-talk about Divorce, *A Way of Seeing.* New York: McCall Publishing Co., p. 197-206.

Mead, M. (1968), *Male and Female: A Study of the Sexes in a Changing World.* New York: Dell.

Miller, A (1970), Reactions of Friends to Divorces, *Divorce and After,* ed. Bohannon, P.. Garden City, N.Y.: Doubleday, p. 56-77.

Perls. F. (1969), *Ego, Hunger and Aggression.* New York: Vintage Books.

Perls, F., Hefferline, R., and Goodman, P. (1951), *Gestalt Therapy.* New York: Dell Books.

Perls, F. (1973), *The Gestalt Approach.* Palo Alto, Ca.: Science & Behavior Books.

Rueben, D. R. (1971), *Any Woman Can! Love and Sexual Fulfillment for the Single, Widowed, Divorced and Married.* New York: David McKay Co..

Rubin, T. I. (1969), *The Angry Book.* New York: Macmillian.

Scheresky, N. and Mannes, M. (1972), *Uncoupling: The Art of Coming Apart.* New York: Viking Press.

Tanner, I. (1973), *Loneliness: The Fear of Love.* New York: Harper and Row.

# READER QUERY

This book was written with the idea of helping people grow through the grief process after the ending of an intimate relationship and build a better life.

Your comments about AFTER YOU'VE SAID GOOD-BYE are important to me and I welcome your feedback. Answers to the following questions will help make this and related books continually more helpful to others. Please complete this questionaire and send it to me in care of:

                        BROOKS PUBLISHING CO.
                        P. O. Box 6099
                        Bakersfield, Calif. 93301

1. Below is a list of major topics in GOOD-BYE. Please mark an "x" beside areas that had the *most* meaning to you and a check (✓) beside the items that you found *least* helpful.

    _____ Healthy reasons for ending
    _____ Fall-out from dissolution
    _____ How to build your own backbone
    _____ Gaining strength outside yourself
    _____ Separation pitfalls and how to avoid them
    _____ For the one who was left behind
    _____ Healthy ways to mourn the loss of a love
    _____ Depression and what to do about it
    _____ Anger and how to use it constructively
    _____ How to conquer self-pity
    _____ Overcoming loneliness
    _____ Starting all over again on your own

2. What additional topics and information would you like to see included in this book or its sequel?

   _____ More about children
   _____ More about dating again
   _____ More about finding community resources (singles clubs, etc.)
   _____ More about jobs/careers
   _____ More about solving financial problems
   _____ More about legal matters
   _____ More about underlying problems with itimacy and how to resolve them
   _____ More about learning to love again
   _____ Other, please specify _____

3. If you were to give one piece of advice to someone recently separated, what would you tell them to *definitely* do?
_____
_____

What would you *warn* them against doing? _____
_____
_____


Optional information about yourself: (answer any or all)

_____ female    _____ male

\_\_\_ under 20 \_\_\_ 20-30 \_\_\_ 31-40 \_\_\_ 41-50 \_\_\_ 51-60 \_\_\_ 61+

Occupation _____    Level of education _____

Name _____

Address _____

_____

_____ I would like to be placed on your mailing list for future books on this and related topics.

_____ Please send a brochure and order form on AFTER YOU'VE SAID GOOD-BYE to my friends:

_____

_____

_____

_____

_____